ASANG

ASANG

Adaptations to

Culture Contact in a Miskito Community

MARY W. HELMS

1971

UNIVERSITY of FLORIDA PRESS

GAINESVILLE

A University of Florida Press Book

The type for the text of this
book is ten-point Caledonia.
The display is Ludlow Garamond Bold.

DESIGNED BY STANLEY D. HARRIS

*Library of Congress
Catalog Card No. 70-630257
ISBN 0-8130-0298-2*

PRINTED BY STORTER PRINTING COMPANY, INC.
GAINESVILLE, FLORIDA

Acknowledgments

As is usual in an undertaking of this sort, successful completion of this study would have been impossible without the many acts of kindness, hospitality, encouragement, and general assistance offered by numerous individuals at all stages of the investigation. To all those who in so many diverse ways contributed their patience, time, and skills go my humble and heartfelt thanks.

I am particularly indebted, however, to the following persons who often went well beyond the usual limits in offering their help: Dr. E. A. Wallace, Director, Gray Memorial Hospital, Puerto Cabezas, Nicaragua, who, with his family and hospital staff, provided services far too numerous to be listed here; Miss Alice Hooker, who found the time in her busy schedule to teach me the rudiments of the Miskito language and whose support and encouragement in the field can never be fully repaid; Rev. and Mrs. Joseph Grey, who gave invaluable information from their own wide experience among the Miskito and also made available to me otherwise unobtainable manuscripts written by various Moravian missionaries, all in addition to unfailing hospitality; Rev. and Mrs. Rinkart Watson, whose home and warm hospitality provided a welcomed haven on many occasions; Srs. Bayardo Watson and Harvey Watson and family, who provided much assistance as well as friendship; Dr. and Mrs. Howard Stortz, who voluntarily assumed much responsibility for my well-being; Fr. Germain Langweld and Fr. Gregory Smutko, O.F.M. Cap., who have shown constant interest and offered much encouragement both during field work and in the subsequent preparation of the report; Rev. and Mrs. Santos Cleban, with whom I lived during my stay in Asang.

My sincere thanks also to the Pan American Union, which provided financial assistance for the study; to the Rev. Vernon Nelson, Archivist, for making available to me records of the Archives of the Moravian Church in Bethlehem, Pennsylvania; and to Leslie V. Lippany for his aid in translations.

Finally, I wish to acknowledge my deep gratitude to my husband, James W. VanStone, who offered invaluable assistance and advice and constant encouragement during the preparation of the manuscript.

Contents

Introduction

WITHIN the framework of Latin American studies, Central America, with the exception of Guatemala, has been badly neglected. Only a handful of studies of unequal quality exist. Yet this small, geographically diverse expanse of land supports a wide variety of cultures. The study presented here attempts to describe and explain certain aspects of the way of life of one of these heretofore little-known Central American societies—the Miskito, who live along the coast and rivers of eastern Nicaragua and Honduras.

Two major sources of information have been combined within this report. An historical context and ethnohistorical data have been provided by scattered travelers, traders, and missionary reports spanning three centuries of contact with the Western world. This background material provides a framework within which to interpret the data obtained during nine months residence—November, 1964, through July, 1965—in the village of Asang, a Miskito community located on the Río Coco in northeast Nicaragua.

In the study of Asang and discussions of Miskito culture in general an effort has been made to emphasize primarily those areas of social, economic, political, and religious life which have been most influenced by contact with various agents of the Western world. Additional information on Miskito culture may be most readily found in Eduard Conzemius' monograph, *Ethnographical Survey of the Miskito and Sumu Indians of Honduras and Nicaragua* (1932).

The information contained in the following pages reflects not only the quality of the historical literature, but also the avenues of approach used by the ethnographer in the field and the general attitude of the villagers toward her. It will be obvious to the reader that in this account the work and influence of the Moravian church

1

is greatly emphasized. Although not the only mission church on the Miskito Coast at the present time, the Moravians are and have been the most strongly entrenched and the most influential missionary group both on the Coast in general and in Asang in particular. Therefore, it is only proper that they should receive due emphasis. However, the amount of attention given to them in this report is also predicated on the fact that many of my contacts on the Coast are Moravian missionaries or active church workers; that my entrance to Asang was smoothed and in a sense underwritten by some of these Moravian friends who have close and influential ties with the village; and that while a resident in Asang I lived with the family of the Moravian lay pastor, a Miskito, and took an active part in Moravian church affairs rather than in the activities of the smaller Church of God congregation also resident there.

On the other hand, I do not feel that this leaning distorts unduly my interpretation of village activities since almost all the inhabitants of Asang also include the Moravian church in their world view. It should be noted, however, that Asang is known to be more committed to Moravian influence than are some other villages which may lean more strongly towards the Roman Catholic faith and/or the Church of God. Since Moravian impact is closely related to the nature of the home church a short summary of Moravian history, beliefs, and practices is provided in an appendix to the monograph.

The nature of my interaction with the people of Asang was also greatly conditioned by the fact that at the time of the study I was unmarried. Consequently, I automatically was placed by the Miskito within the category of *tiara*, single woman. Although a *tiara* has definite responsibilities and fills an important position in family and community life, nonetheless, in some ways she is not considered to be a full adult regardless of her age or abilities and, consequently, is not expected to be as concerned with the full range of home and village matters. I found this social role somewhat handicapping, particularly when it came to investigating some of the work of adult men.

Finally, I found my activities were influenced by the fact that I am an American. Americans, or more accurately, English-speaking foreigners, are greatly respected by the Miskito, who feel that their own way of life is inferior in some respects. No American, therefore, no matter how friendly or willing should be subjected to the indignities of working in the fields, fishing in the lagoon, or eating at an "improperly" set table. For an American, especially a woman, to insist on doing these things even occasionally is upsetting to the Miskito because the special position assigned to her is underwritten by an overall world view. Out of deference to this situation and because it threatened on occasion to affect general rapport, I did not push the issue when the conflict became too strong.

Generally speaking, however, I found the people of Asang to be very warm, friendly, and cooperative. It was the mutual realization and appreciation of the fact that both I and they were quite human that permitted me to establish workable rapport.

All information was obtained in the Miskito language without the aid of an interpreter. Therefore, what is presented here is my interpretation of the local situation as I perceived it through the double filter of my state of fluency with the Miskito language and a limited period of participant-observation in Asang. Except for historical data concerning the founders of Asang, first names of villagers mentioned in the study have been changed. An effort has been made, however, to maintain the style and flavor conveyed by the informants' real names.

Although the major orientation of the study is descriptive, an effort also has been made to place this material within a wider theoretical framework. Two mainstreams of anthropological interest seemed relevant at first. On the one hand, the Miskito could perhaps be viewed as acculturated natives, indigenous peoples who have gradually effected some sort of adjustment between their own traditions and influences from the outside world of Western civilization. Thus, the Miskito might be placed in the category of "Tribal Indian" or possibly "Modern Indian" as defined by Wagley and Harris (1955). Similarly, John Gillin's proposed "Republican Native" or "Recent Indian" classification might be a possibility (1949: 166).

In spite of the many significant guidelines which these typologies offer, there is one point where use of such categories fails to emphasize one of the most significant features of Miskito society; namely, Miskito culture did not exist as such before European contact. To utilize typologies of the type noted above risks forcing the Miskito into analytic frameworks which carry with them, either implicitly or explicitly, the notion of an aboriginal, precontact identity for any given society. In contrast to societies with aboriginal bases, Miskito culture originated as a direct response to European colonialism. To be sure, many specific culture traits are based in the precontact scene, but the overall structure and function of Miskito society is oriented towards and adapted to successful interaction with the wider world. Although it is not entirely inaccurate to view contemporary Miskito society as illustrative of a particular stage in the acculturation of once aboriginal peoples, to do so could be very misleading without careful reading of the fine print.

The other theoretical framework which seemed to offer possibilities was the body of knowledge that has developed from the analysis of peasant societies. Here the starting point does include a more complex and more powerful society, a state, with which the local society or community interacts. The question which now arises, however, concerns the nature of the state and the type of interaction by means of which the local community or society is involved with it. In other words, what do we mean by the term "peasantry"? A widely used approach which has underlain most substantive and theoretical work in this area labels as peasantry rural cultivators who carry on agriculture as a traditional way of life, rather than for profit in the capitalistic sense, and part of whose production is tapped by the state in order to support its own structure and activities (cf. Redfield 1956:18; Wolf 1966:2–4). When this definition is applied to the Miskito, the fit is poor.

First, the villagers of Asang have always been rural and have never entered the capitalistic world of investment for profit. However, agriculture has not always provided the basis for subsistence, although it predominates today. Hunting and fishing, gathering of natural resources for barter and sale, and wage labor have all been equally important to the Miskito economy since its origins in the seventeenth century. Indeed, the present emphasis on cultivation can be viewed somewhat as historical accident, as one of several possibilities that might be open to the Miskito as a means of livelihood. The overall structure of society is not geared specifically to agriculture alone, but rather is oriented toward a variety of economic activities. To be sure, recent refinements in the definition of peasantry have widened the occupational base to include nonagricultural activities—fishing or craft production, for example (Foster 1967b:6–7). Nevertheless, most anthropologists still consider peasants primarily as agriculturalists (cf. Foster 1967a:4 ff.).

Second, and most significant, is the matter of interaction with the state, a criteria which is emerging as the most important aspect of the study of peasantry because it focuses attention on relational and structural ties, regardless of the nature of the occupational base (cf. Foster 1967a). Here also, the consideration of Miskito society as a type of peasantry runs into difficulty. Only if we consider as peasantry all noncapitalistic rural peoples involved with a state can the Miskito unquestionably qualify. This is, of course, one possibility, yet it is a position I find unsatisfactory because it would place into a single sociocultural category both those local societies which interact with industrial states and those involved with nonindustrial states, and, as a further consequence, quite possibly fail to differentiate adequately between the different types of ties by which local societies may be involved with the various categories of state (cf. Wolf 1966:3–4; Halpern and Brode 1967:52–53).

The other possibility, which seems more useful heuristically, is to restrict the application of the term peasantry to a narrower range of societies. This generally has been done by defining peasantry as rural societies structured primarily for interaction with "agrarian" or "preindustrial" or "old" civilizations (Redfield 1956:20; Wolf 1966:12; Foster 1967a:7). The ties which link peasants in this sense with the nonindustrial state are, to be sure, multidimensional, but the most characteristic feature of this relationship is that all aspects of peasant life must somehow take account of the state's superior political power and organization. By virtue of the demands of this political network, the peasant household must be geared to provide labor, produce, or money from its own resources at the express demand of the state in order to support the state's bureaucracy and activities (cf. Wolf 1966:10–11; Foster 1967a:6).

In the case of the Miskito, it is difficult to claim that their activities have ever contributed much to the support of a nonindustrial state. Although officially resident within the republics of Nicaragua and Honduras, the Miskito have never paid significant taxes, either in produce or cash, have never been drafted for conscript labor or served in the armed forces, and have not engaged in extensive trade and commerce with representatives of these states. In all areas of potential influence, the states' activities have always been of a de jure rather than de facto nature in the isolated regions where the Miskito live.

On the other hand, the Miskito have actively engaged in barter and wage labor with representatives of Great Britain and, later, the United States for approximately three hundred years. From the point of view of England and the United States this economic activity involved the acquisition of Coastal resources as part of their respective efforts to develop not as agrarian, but as industrial states. In order to obtain the lumber, rubber, and other Coastal resources which they desired for growing industries at home, local residents were encouraged to participate in trade and/or wage systems in which Western manufactured goods were exchanged for local resources or labor.

From the point of view of the Miskito, the motivation to participate in such activities was not based on inescapable demands by state officials for a share in their energies and production, as is the case with peasant-agrarian state relations. Instead, it centered on a growing desire for the foreign material goods which quickly became cultural necessities for them over the years, a situation that Kroeber has termed "voluntary acculturation" (1948:sec. 179). Although the introduction of these goods came originally from the outside world, it was the increasing dependence on such items as manufactured cloth, iron tools, sewing machines, and rum that provided the impetus for continued Miskito involvement with the West.

To be sure, peasantry also is heavily involved in trade and commerce with the state, but the important point is that peasantry also is subject to superior state power holders who demand the payment of additional rents. In contrast, the Miskito have escaped such one-sided political holds in their involvement with state organizations, and have operated instead solely on the more symmetrical level of economic exchange.

The definitive area of articulation of Miskito culture with more complex societies seems to me to be significantly distinct from that characteristic of peasantry. To view the nature of Miskito culture and its adaptations within the framework of peasant studies appears to be insufficient and potentially misleading. Instead, the possibility must be considered that the Miskito and others like them have developed structural and functional adaptations to the outside world of a different sort than have peasants.

In order to emphasize the nonaboriginal, nonpeasant nature of Miskito society, and because I believe that numerous other societies could be seen in a similar light, I propose the delineation of a new sociocultural category, here termed the "purchase society," within which the nature of Miskito culture may be more profitably considered (cf. Helms 1969c). The definitive characteristic of any purchase society is the articulation of local society with the wider complex world through economic channels of trade and wage labor, while political autonomy and a stable social organization are maintained. The term "purchase society" is suggested because it emphasizes both the economic referent in general, and the specific aspect of that referent which appears most important from the point of view of the local society, and towards which local adaptations will be directed, i.e., the need to obtain, to "purchase," through one means or another, foreign manufactured goods which have acquired the status of cultural necessities. To be sure, something must be exchanged or sold in order to acquire these goods, but to the local population, that which is sold is merely a means to the all important end of purchasing. Miskito society, as evidenced through ethnohistorical material and the field study of Asang, will be viewed in this monograph in terms of the specific adaptations that have been made to the conditions of trade and labor that have occurred on the Coast and to this need for the wherewithall to purchase.

It should be emphasized that the definitive characteristic of the purchase society as a sociocultural type is structural, i.e., the interaction through symmetrical economic ties with more complex society(ies) together with the maintenance of political autonomy and a social organization directed towards these aims. I do not wish to imply that to qualify as a purchase society a group must also exhibit a cultural identity or ethnic origins that have been formulated primarily after contact, as in the case of the Miskito. From a theoretical standpoint, the particulars of Miskito culture history are important primarily in that they focus the problem more sharply. It may well be that as a whole, Miskito adaptations are more extensive or more readily observable than ordinarily would be the case for a society with precontact identity. What is required of any purchase society, however, is a positive adaptation to state contact of the type outlined above.

Relatively little work, particularly in a theoretical vein, appears to have been done along these lines by other investigators, although regions and cultures with comparable contact experiences can readily be found. The well-known paper by Murphy and Steward (1956) comparing the adaptations to contact made by the Mundurucú of interior Brazil with those adopted by the Montagnais of eastern Canada contains pertinent data, although these societies are viewed theoretically as acculturating natives. Eleanore Leacock, however, warns that contemporary Montagnais society should not be viewed simply as a native society with a veneer of foreign traits, but that "one must work from an understanding that fundamental socioeconomic changes have been taking place in some parts of their area for over 300 years . . ." (1954:43). Unfortunately, Leacock stops short of suggesting a more precise theoretical framework within which her material may be viewed.

Edward Spicer's proposal of a "fur trade" community as one of several types of "contact communities" that have evolved among American Indians in response to European pressures is directly pertinent to our problem. As with the purchase society, the fur trade community is characterized by "a purely market linkage, non-coercive roles, and structural stability" (1961:526). However, as the Miskito material will indicate, the fur trade was not the only type of contact experience leading to this form of adaptation. Thus, Spicer's category can be seen as one example of a wider phenomenon.[1]

In his study of the Chin of southeast Asia, Frederick Lehman also depicts a situation very similar to that found among the Miskito. He emphasizes the position of the Chin in this way: "Chin society traditionally found itself in the most marginal of peasant situations: a fundamental economic adaptation to a civilization without inclusion in that civilization's institutional network and without permanent formal structure to its interaction with the Burman population. This is a limiting case between peasantry and tribal society" (1963:223). Lehman goes on to propose the term "subnuclear society" for such societies as the Chin and a whole series of mountain-dwelling peoples across all of mainland Southeast Asia and into the tribal area of southwest China. These peoples hereto-

1. Carleton Coon emphasizes the importance of trade as a major variable in his scheme of six "levels of complexity" to be discerned among "contemporary and historically documented societies, which have existed without the benefit of gunpowder, coal, and steam engines" (1948:612). Coon's interest is in the "amount of consumer goods obtained by trade," and the correlation of this factor with specialization of individuals, number of institutions to which an individual may belong, and complexity of institutions (1948:612). However, Coon is not concerned with acculturation situations between the state (level six) and nonstate societies, nor with the nature and adaptations of institutions which result from this impact. Hence none of his levels are applicable in the present context.

fore have been pushed into the primitive world as "tribes" (cf. Sahlins 1968:47), or seen as "hill peasants" (Izikowitz 1951). By "subnuclear" Lehman means: ". . . groups of cultures and societies that
abut on a civilization . . . but are distinct from that nuclear culture
and its society. They are not civilized, but neither are they primitive. The subnuclear society's adaptation to civilization is so complete that it is necessary to propose a categorical relationship between the two" (1963:225).

Lehman's subnuclear society, Spicer's fur trade community, and
my proposed purchase society are clearly concerned with the same
phenomenon, although widely separated regions are involved and
different labels are attached. In my opinion, the connotation of
"purchase" as I have outlined it above provides a more specific description of the characteristics of the sociocultural category with
which we are all concerned than does either subnuclear or fur trade
community. The important point, of course, is not what label is attached, but the underlying problem itself.

1

The Setting

ASANG is a community of Miskito Indians located approximately 200 miles up the Río Coco or Wangks River in the heart of the Miskito (Mosquito) Coast, the name given to the eastern or Caribbean region of Nicaragua and Honduras (see Figure 1).[1] Although this territory falls officially within the boundaries of these Central American republics, the way of life found here is thoroughly unlike that usually associated with Latin American countries. Throughout its history the Coast has remained outside significant Hispanic cultural influences. Instead, it has formed part of the rim of sparsely settled, non-Hispanic territories which characterize the east coast of Central America from British Honduras through Panama.

In Space

Within this region hostile natives, lack of readily available precious metals, a difficult climate, and encroaching British interests combined to discourage and hinder initial Spanish colonial efforts. Hispanic settlements were formed instead in the environs of the more salubrious Pacific coast, but even here Central American colonists were faced with difficult problems of supplies, transportation, and communication with the distant Spanish capitals in Guatemala

1. Although a considerable portion of the Miskito Coast is located in eastern Honduras, as Figure 1 indicates, most of the material in this monograph applies to Nicaragua alone. Most of the historical documents consulted dealt mainly with the Nicaraguan sector, and my own travels were restricted to Nicaragua. This was due in no small measure to the fact that travel in eastern Honduras is much more difficult than in eastern Nicaragua, a situation which reflects the fact that this region has generally been more isolated from the world than has eastern Nicaragua. The Miskito resident in Honduras are considered backward by their Nicaraguan counterparts, and in fact have had fewer contacts with Western influences.

and Mexico, as well as with rivalries and disputes among themselves, which further blocked successful exploration and settlement of the eastern regions.

Into the void left by the Spanish stepped Britain and, later, the United States, and the influence of these colonial powers is readily discernible. On the Miskito Coast today English and Miskito are spoken much more than is Spanish, while Protestant missions rather than Catholic predominate. Large numbers of Negroes, termed Creoles locally, have come to the Coast over the centuries,

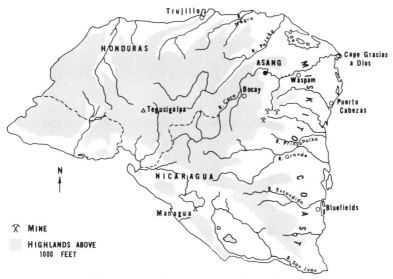

Fig. 1. Map of Nicaragua and Honduras.

some with early English woodcutters and planters, others from the West Indies seeking jobs as laborers with twentieth-century commercial enterprises, particularly on banana plantations. These Creoles, together with Miskito Indians, North Americans, and a few Chinese, comprise the bulk of the population.

Thus, for all practical purposes, the Miskito Coast is not and never has been part of the effective national territory of Nicaragua and Honduras. It has looked east, instead, to the Caribbean Sea, the United States, and northern Europe, rather than west across the core of central highlands to the Pacific centers of Nicaraguan and Honduranean life. So isolated has this region remained from Hispanic Central America that, in the words of one twentieth-century traveler: "Until the establishment of regular airline service from Managua [the capital of Nicaragua] to Bluefields, Puerto Cabezas and the gold camps, it was easier to reach the Miskito Shore from New Orleans than from the interior capitals . . ." (Parsons 1955b: 63).

Coastal topography is flat for the most part, and rarely exceeds 600 feet in altitude. In spite of extremely heavy rainfall, at least 100 inches annually, most of which falls from about May through December, the predominant vegetation is not the evergreen tropical rain forest that generally characterizes much of the Central American Caribbean, but extensive pine savannah with only occasional stands of hardwoods. This savannah gradually gives way to secondary forest and regrowth towards the west. Beyond this lies mature rain forest and the central highlands (Conzemius 1932; Parsons 1955; Taylor 1959).

The savannah is crossed by numerous rivers which begin as torrential streams in the highlands and then become deep and meandering as they cross the wide coastal plain. The largest of these is the Río Coco on the Nicaraguan-Honduranean border. Along the banks of these numerous rivers and their tributaries are strips of fertile alluvial soils which are either cultivated or support secondary forest.

Finally, in contrast to both the pine savannah and the twisting rivers which cross it is the seacoast itself, a narrow strip bordering the Caribbean and composed of beaches and sandhills backed by an intricate system of lagoons interlaced with mangrove swamps. Coral reefs and numerous cays are found offshore.

From the point of view of the wider world, the Miskito Coast culturally is a fringe territory; a frontier. Yet there are several types of frontier (cf. Forbes 1968), and it is necessary to identify the situation found on the Coast more carefully. For example, one very common category which the term "frontier" immediately brings to mind has been termed the "Pioneer Fringe" (Bowman 1931). Here territory marginal to major settlements of a country or region is exploited by a wave of settlers advancing from the central region. These pioneers are agriculturalists or livestock keepers looking for land. They carry with them their distinctive social, political, and religious patterns as they optimistically seek a new and better life for themselves and their children, while, at the same time, maintaining communications with the developed center (cf. Forbes' "unilinear expansive" frontier category, 1968).

The type of frontier exemplified by the Miskito Coast is different. In this case individual settler families from the immediately adjacent Hispanic west, staking permanent claims to farm land, are not found. Rather, European and, later, North American entrepreneurs concerned with commercial exploitation of natural resources periodically have moved into the area, far from their home contacts. Such men, with or without their families, are apt to stay for several years at the most, and then make way for others. To the extent that permanent settlements have developed, they have been peopled primarily by laborers such as West Indian Creoles who sought jobs in commercial enterprises rather than in agriculture. Thus, while geographically close to the Hispanic world, the Coast in effect has become an economic frontier for distant industrializing nations, Britain and the United States in particular.

The commercial undertakings developed on such frontiers are often centered on barter and/or unstable boom-and-bust cycles rather than on steady long-term operations which would lay a foundation for permanent economic development. Such has been the case on the Miskito Coast. While lumbering, banana plantations, rubber tapping, or mining were profitable enterprises, towns grew, laborers immigrated, and companies flourished. In each case, however, when the world market collapsed or resources were exhausted, the company left, and with it went the managers and many of the laborers, leaving deserted saw mills, ghost towns, and increasingly useless transportation facilities. At such times the atmosphere becomes one of apathy, of living in a has-been region, in the backwoods.[2]

Pioneer fringe and commercial frontiers have important differential effects on indigenous native or rural populations in the area (cf. Fried 1952). As our study of Asang documents, the requirements of commercial enterprises can be made to dovetail rather smoothly

2. This is not to say that there is no pioneer fringe in Nicaragua. As with the other Central American countries, population is increasing at a phenomenal rate, and although most population movement is directed towards the large cities, there is some eastward spill-over from the west. This movement is relatively recent, however, and has not yet made itself felt on the Miskito Coast (Zelinsky 1966). Relatively few Nicaraguans from the settled west are interested in the frontier east, and those who are stationed there as teachers or militiamen are only too glad to leave as soon as their tour of duty is completed.

with local culture patterns. Agricultural pioneering, on the other hand, places more extreme pressures on native populations, mainly through land loss. The development and continued existence of the Miskito as a population with a culture pattern uniquely its own, and our conceptualization of this culture pattern as exemplifying a purchase society, is due in large part to the fact that they inhabit a commercial, rather than a pioneer, frontier.

In Time

While the Miskito Coast may be quite divorced from life in the more cosmopolitan regions of the country, nonetheless it has a colorful history in its own right. It is important to note a few of the major developments as further background, both to our theoretical considerations and to discussion of life in Asang, since the customs and attitudes of the villagers reflect this past in a number of ways.

It is generally accepted that the aboriginal culture of the Miskito Coast, along with that of all the Central American Caribbean littoral as far north as the Bay Islands of Honduras, can best be understood in terms of affiliations with the lowland tropical forest tribes of South America rather than with the Mesoamerican cultures of Mexican and Mayan affinity to the north.[3] Actually it is singularly difficult to describe the precontact culture of the Coast. The first accounts were written in the late seventeenth and early eighteenth centuries by English buccaneers whose very presence quickly initiated change, and whose eyewitness reports of native life are far from complete. These pirates found that the intricate lagoons and winding rivers of the Coast provided ideal hideouts from whence to prey on wealth-laden Spanish ships and especially Spanish fron-

3. This position is based on a variety of South American culture traits that characterized the area: a basically hunting and fishing economy with relatively little emphasis on agriculture; manioc rather than maize as principle cultigen; emphasis on canoe travel; excessive intoxication on ceremonial occasions; conical headdresses and fringed costumes for funeral ceremonials; use of low wooden seats and hammocks; manufacture of bark cloth (Lehmann 1910:692; Spinden 1925:543; Kidder 1940; von Hagen 1940:253; Adams 1956:897; Chapman 1958:5, 162; Stone 1962; Kroeber 1963:110). Linguistically there has been controversy over whether Miskito, along with Sumu and Matagalpan, the so-called Misumalpan or Misulua languages, is related to or can be lumped with the larger Chibchan stock of northern South America, or should be given independent status. The tendency today seems to be to place it with Chibchan (Greenberg 1960; Swadesh 1962; Stone 1966:210). For general discussion of this problem see Lehmann (1920:461–62), McQuown (1955), Mason (1962:75–76), and Helms (1969b).

tier towns. Eventually small settlements sprang up on the mainland at Bluefields and at Cape Gracias a Dios, the latter in particular becoming a home base for pirate activities (Floyd 1967:chap. 3).

The buccaneer accounts thus apply mostly to the Río Coco, Cape Gracias, and the immediately adjacent coast. They describe the native population as living in small scattered groups, each composed of several families, camping more or less seminomadically along the seashore and rivers. Open-sided thatched huts provided shelter. Land and sea mammals, fish and turtles, various wild fruits and small plantings of bananas, plantains, maize, and sugarcane provided subsistence.[4] Social equality and the lack of any kind of specifically political structure were noted. Several dialects were differentiated, and those who spoke the same dialect apparently considered themselves as a unit against all others. There may have been as many as ten or more such groups throughout the Coast (Fig. 2a). Periodic warfare seems to have obtained among them (Dampier 1703:31–37; M.W. 1732; Esquemeling 1893:chap. 8; de Lussan 1930:280–88; cf. Helms 1969b).

Relations between Cape Gracias natives and buccaneers were friendly and apparently mutually satisfying. For a knife or an old axe or hatchet a pirate could obtain the services of an Indian woman who carried out all the duties of a wife for him for the duration of his stay. For their part, the pirates were free to come and go as they pleased, but were careful not to arouse the hostility of the natives. Indians, presumably men, also accompanied the pirates to sea, sometimes for periods of several years, to provision the buccaneers with tortoise, manatee, and fish (Esquemeling 1893:chap. 8; Conzemius 1932:85, 86; Wafer 1934:xviii).

One of the most important items acquired by the Cape Gracias natives through their partnership with the buccaneers was a supply of guns. One gentleman of fortune recounts how the "Mosqueto," as the pirates termed their friends, then invaded the upper reaches of the Río Coco to attack unarmed peoples resident there— a pattern the Miskito were to develop further in succeeding decades (M.W. 1732).[5]

4. Sugarcane and bananas were introduced to the New World by the Spanish.

5. Various spellings of "Miskito," the term preferred in this study, occur in the earliest literature, specifically with reference to the natives of Cape Gracias directly contacted by foreigners. These include forms such as Mosqueto, Mosquito, Moskito, Mosco, Moustique, Musketo, and Musquito (cf. Conzemius

There is also mention of mulattoes residing with Indians of this area. A number of sources report a slave ship wrecked on the Miskito Cays slightly south of Cape Gracias about 1640 or 1650. Those Negroes who reached the mainland were captured by the Indians, and soon adopted their language and customs. They were allowed to intermarry, and their children were fully accepted by the indigenous population (Conzemius 1932:17–18). In addition to shipwrecked slaves, Negroes escaping servitude on West Indian plantations and in the Spanish mines in interior Honduras probably sought refuge on the isolated Coast. Negro slaves were also brought by seventeenth-century English planters, and small settlements of Indians and Negroes grew up, especially at Bluefields and Cape Gracias (Squier 1858:633; Helbig 1959:179; Floyd 1967:21). According to one source it was mulattoes rather than indigenous natives who assisted the buccaneers (de Lussan 1930:286–87).

Negro admixture, guns, and aboriginal dialect groups with some semblance of unity are significant elements in the problem of the origin of the Miskito as an identifiable ethnic group. These factors also played a part in the emergence of the Sumu, the second most significant native population living on the Coast today. In the general anthropological literature the Miskito and Sumu are assumed to be separate aboriginal cultures.[6] At present there is no doubt that definite linguistic, cultural, and even biological distinctions can be

---

1938:929; Lehmann 1920:465). Although there is no evidence that the name existed aboriginally, some authors imply that the term was of precontact origin (e.g., Costa Rica 1913:443; Ireland 1941:170). On the other hand, Heath suggests that origins may lie in the Spanish phrase *Indios mixtos*, referring to the fact of early biological admixture between natives and Negroes (Heath 1913: 51). Professor Charles Gibson, in a personal communication, has suggested that the term may be derived from the idea of "musket" since the population in question was distinguished from its neighbors as a literally musket-bearing group. This idea seems highly plausible since the spellings used in the earliest accounts of the coast employ forms (Mosqueto, Mosquito, Musketo, Mustique) which compare closely with contemporary Spanish, English, and French spellings for musket: mosquete, musket, mousquet, respectively. The association between Miskito, a people, and mosquito, a species of insect, is generally discarded by all serious writers.

  6. In the widely cited *Handbook of South American Indians*, Julian Steward considers the Miskito and Sumu to be deculturated peoples, broken down under the pressures of conquest and colonization from stratified societies to their present nonstratified condition (Steward 1948:1–2, 26–27, 30). The ethnohistorical literature does not support Steward's position. There is no evidence of a precontact stratified society (cf. Chapman 1958). Moreover, neither Miskito nor Sumu existed as such until after contact. Miskito culture in particular is best seen as a *positive* response to culture contact.

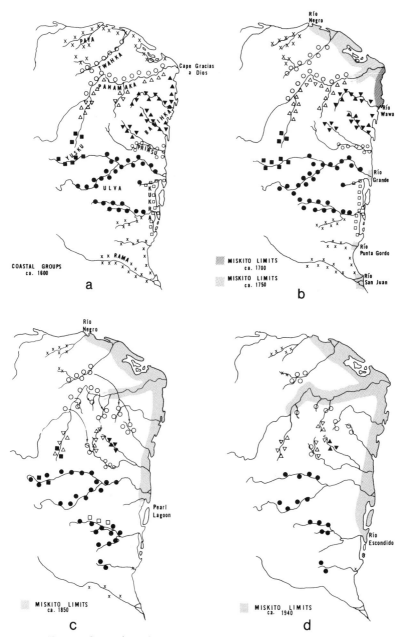

Fig. 2. a,b, Origins of the Miskito. c,d, Expansion of the Miskito.

made between the Miskito, found living today along the coast proper, and the Sumu, located for the most part in extreme isolation at tributary headwaters of the main rivers. This does not mean, however, that the same distinctions existed aboriginally.

Biologically it seems that the Miskito are a mixed group which developed *after contact* through the admixture of an indigenous population with Negroes and buccaneers. Intermarriage of Miskito women with non-Miskito men has continued to this day. The Sumu, on the other hand, did not encourage intermarriage with foreigners, and do not do so now (Squier 1858:633, 659; Heath 1913:50; Conzemius 1932:12–13, 14, 17; von Hagan 1940:252–54).[7]

Culturally it appears that the Miskito were originally a small group living near Cape Gracias, perhaps members of the Bawihka linguistic group (see Figure 2a,b),[8] which gained political suzerainty over their neighbors, who gradually retreated from the coast to protect themselves from the more powerful Miskito. These interior peoples, found today living along the Bocay and Waspuk tributaries of the Río Coco, along the Patuca River in Honduras, and near the headwaters of the Río Wawa, Río Prinsapolka, Río Grande, and Río Escondido in Nicaragua, have been identified since the 1860's by the collective term "Sumu."[9] They can be thought of as scattered refugees with a traditional culture pattern that is gradually dying out, along with the population itself (Roberts 1827:115; Conzemius 1932:17; Helms 1969b).[10] The Miskito, in contrast, ex-

7. The theory of biological admixture among Miskito versus genetic "purity" among Sumu has received limited support from a study done in 1960 which analyzed blood antigens from 150 Miskito and 103 Sumu, all from the Río Coco area (Matson and Swanson 1963). The ABO distribution showed 100 per cent O among Sumu; and 90 per cent O, 8 per cent A_1, 0.67 per cent A_2, 1.33 per cent B, and 0 per cent AB for Miskito. Adopting the premise that unmixed Indians in Central and South America will show type O blood, the Sumu tested showed no evidence of foreign admixture, whereas the Miskito did show evidence of racial crossing. The MN determinations also suggest a high degree of inbreeding and genetic drift among Sumus, while the Rh and B frequencies show foreign admixture for Miskito.

8. Figures 2a,b,c,d are based on information from Edwards 1819; Costa Rica 1913, Conzemius 1938, and Hodgson 1965. The maps are not entirely drawn to scale. They do not indicate the coastal regions inhabited by English-speaking Creoles of mainly West Indian origins.

9. Prior to mid-nineteenth century the peoples now comprising the category of Sumu were identified by their various tribal names, e.g., Ulva, Kukra, Yusku, Prinsu, Bawihka, Panamaka, and Twahka (cf. Fig. 2a).

10. Further dislocations in the late nineteenth century were brought about by gold prospectors and rubber tappers who penetrated this area seeking exploitable resources (Conzemius 1938).

tended their territory during succeeding decades until they were in control of virtually the entire littoral from Río Negro in Honduras to Río Escondido in southern Nicaragua, as well as much of the Río Coco basin (Fig. 2b,c,d). Along with territorial expansion went cultural adaptation, so that in contrast to the Sumu, the Miskito were able to adjust in a positive sense to the Western contact they were continually to encounter from then on. In fact, territorial expansion itself seems to have been a response to contact and a form of adaptation to its demands.[11]

Miskito dominance was achieved through ownership of a new weapon, the gun, which, as we have seen, was obtained as a direct result of contact with Europeans. Armed with this noisy and smoking device, the Cape Gracias natives conducted a series of expansionist raids, not only on the coast and its rivers, but also farther afield. North to Honduras and even to Yucatan, south to Costa Rica and Panama, and west to Nicaraguan border settlements went an-

11. There is also linguistic evidence for the comparatively recent, postcontact spread of Miskito culture in that the dialect variations of the Miskito language are comparatively insignificant even though they are distributed over a fairly large territory. Three major linguistic divisions are recognized by the Miskito: Coastal (including two divisions which are sometimes listed in the literature as separate dialects—Kabo and Baldam), found along the Nicaraguan coast from Pearl Lagoon to just south of Cape Gracias; Wangki, spoken along the Río Coco (Wanks); and Honduranean or Mam. These three are mutually intelligible although there are some differences in vocabulary and pronunciation (Heath 1927 and 1950; Conzemius 1929:59). Conversely, the various Sumu dialects are, in Conzemius' words, "*almost* mutually intelligible" (1932: 14; my italics). Miskito and Sumu dialects are also quite distinct, though structurally quite similar and, according to Lehmann, closely related (1910:714). However, it would seem that there is more linguistic commonality between the various subdivisions of present day Miskito than between the various Sumu dialects or between the latter and Miskito (Conzemius 1929:67). This supports the idea of a single, relatively recent origin for the Miskito, while suggesting that the Sumu are a composite group, composed of more fragmented, although related, units.

Miskito vocabulary also includes a number of foreign words, Spanish and English especially, which to the best of my knowledge are not as numerous among Sumu dialects (Conzemius 1932:16, 17). In addition, African influence has also been noted (Heath 1913:51; Lehmann 1910:714). This suggests that the Miskito language may differ from Sumu at least in part because of the greater amount of culture contact experienced by the Miskito. It was necessary for them to maintain effective communication with such diverse groups as buccaneers, refugee African slaves, and American and Jamaican traders. It is not at all unlikely that this contact led to various changes in the original language spoken by the Cape Gracias natives, which changes have produced the present form of Miskito speech. For further discussion of this problem see Helms (1969b).

nual Miskito raiding parties, destroying property and capturing men, women, and children, some of whom were then sold to the English who shipped them to the West Indies.[12]

These raids, which lasted throughout the eighteenth century, were often encouraged by the British who were interested in obtaining a foothold on the Coast for reasons of their own. Officially the Miskito Coast belonged to Spain during these years, but in the absence of actual Spanish settlements, Britain was encouraged to use this area as one means of effecting contact with Hispanic America. However, in order to make her activities appear legal in the eyes of other European powers, she maneuvered to effect a paper protectorate over the Coast by officially designating a Miskito leader as "king of Mosquitia," and claiming that it was at his request that English interests were on the Coast. In actuality, at no time did the native culture of the Coast include a centralized political organization. Village headmen and respected elders directed village affairs, and there was no organization of villages or groups into permanent larger units. The king himself was merely a figurehead and seems to have had little or no influence either with respect to British actions or to the management of day-to-day Miskito life. The concept of king, however, was useful to the Miskito in foreign affairs, in that it provided a rationale for raids, which were conducted "in the name of the king." British authorities also had little political control over the Miskito. Rather, English interests were economic and were oriented toward obtaining coastal resources and conducting contraband trade with the Spanish frontier (for more detailed discussions see Floyd 1967 and Helms 1969a).[13]

The goods captured by the Miskito in their expansions and

12. In addition to the Miskito and Sumu, the "native" populations of the Coast include the Rama and the Paya. In reaction to Miskito raids, the Rama, thought to have lived aboriginally between the Río San Juan and what is now Bluefields (Fig. 2), retreated offshore to the Rama Cays where approximately 200 live at the present time (Bell 1862:259; Conzemius 1938:934). Similarly, the Paya of Honduras were driven from their former coastal position into the interior of the country. They are thought to occupy a few villages along the Wampu and Paulaya rivers and along the Río Platano (Helbig 1959:map 6).

13. Although Englishmen were beginning to settle on the Miskito Coast from mid-seventeenth century on, "official" British influence began approximately in 1687 when the first Miskito "king" was appointed by British authorities in Jamaica. From 1740 to 1763 forts were established and settlers continued colonizing projects. Black River, Cape Gracias, and Bluefields were the most important settlements. Through the terms of the Treaty of Paris (1763) forts were destroyed, although settlers remained. From 1786 to 1848 all official

forays not only provided one source of income for the British, but also served the Miskito as a means of obtaining European goods through the exchange of loot with the British, and it was primarily for this reason that the raids took place. During this period and into the nineteenth century European goods also became available at a series of trading depots which were established along the coast proper, maintained by trading agents for the British who collected such items as dyewoods, tortoise shell, sarsaparilla, cacao, skins, and India rubber from the local populace, and gave in exchange cloth, machetes, guns, ammunition, rum, and beads.[14]

The Miskito seem to have quickly adapted to this trade; indeed, they became dependent on it to provide, either directly or indirectly, basic economic needs.[15] By mid-nineteenth century Miskito villages were scattered all along the coast itself, with the greatest concentration near the Cape Gracias area. Some Miskito settlements were found farther up the rivers, but this territory was inhabited mainly by Sumu peoples driven, as was indicated previously, from shore locations to areas along the higher reaches of the

---

British contacts, including settlers, were removed, although contraband trade continued and links remained with Belize to the north (British Honduras). The interest in a trans-Isthmian canal in mid-nineteenth century occasioned a renewed claim by Britain in 1848 which lasted until 1859 and 1860 when the territory was officially ceded to the republics of Honduras and Nicaragua, respectively.

14. Many of these trading agents were Jamaican Negroes, although a few North Americans are also noted (Roberts 1827:52, 108–9, 131, 286).

15. It appears that Coast peoples may have been involved to some extent in regional trade even prior to contact. There is evidence of a small Nahua colony, probably commercial, located at the mouth of the Río San Juan (Lothrop 1926:9). Quite possibly a branch of the far-flung Mayan trade network ran along the coast as far south as Panama (Roys 1943:56). The influence of such contacts on local Coastal peoples is undetermined, but judging from the type of material goods associated with the indigenous population it was not extensive. Dependence on European trade goods after contact appears to be of much greater scope, necessitating considerable cultural reorganization and readjustment. It is quite possible, though, that additional information on pre-Columbian conditions would show that trade was of greater significance than it appears so far.

The first contact with Western trade occurred in 1634 when a trading station was set up at Cape Gracias a Dios by English colonists from the island of Providence. Relationships with the natives were friendly, and trade was moderately successful. The venture lasted until the fall of the colony in 1641. It is significant to note that those in charge of the trade were under orders from their superiors not to furnish the natives with guns and ammunition (Newton 1914:144–45, 166, 272–76). Firearms, with the attendant consequences, were not obtained until contact with buccaneers.

rivers (Fig. 2 b,c,d). The coastal, i.e., Miskito, territory provided excellent fishing conditions, but was poor for agriculture, with the exception of manioc which can grow in the sandy coastal soils, and a
few fruit trees; it also lacked forest resources for the local manufacture of numerous household items. Consequently, in order to obtain these products, the Miskito either had to tend plantations located along the river banks some distance upstream from the coast,
obtain the necessary produce from interior tribes through trade, or
obtain comparable European goods from nearby trading posts
(Porta Costas 1908; Roberts 1827:115, 142, 150, 152; Bell 1862: 251;
1899:127, 266–67).[16]

All methods were used. While women and children tended small
plots of land, men and older boys would travel to numerous spots
along the coast, especially to the Miskito Cays near Cape Gracias
and to Tortuguero (Turtle Bogue) on the Costa Rican coast,
where turtling was profitable. In a few months time considerable
amounts of meat and shell could be obtained. Shell was then sold
to the foreign traders in exchange for European goods. These goods
were utilized by the Miskito themselves, and also facilitated trade
between Miskito and the Sumu of the interior, who, sometimes
under pressure, exchanged game, rough-hewn dugouts, gourds and
calabashes, skins, net hammocks, sarsaparilla, or agricultural produce for European items—axes, adzes, beads, mirrors—and local
coastal products such as salt and turtle meat offered by the Miskito.
The Miskito could then obtain additional European goods in exchange for skins and sarsaparilla obtained from the Sumu. In a
word, the Miskito became middlemen in coastal trade, and depended on this trade for foods and materials otherwise unavailable
to them (cf. Helms 1969a).

There were channels other than the insatiable Jamaican traders
open to Miskito who desired Western goods. Foreign settlers at
Bluefields and Pearl Lagoon would hire the services of the Miskito
as hunters and fishermen at a set rate of pay in goods per month.
After 1849, trade items were also available in exchange for India
rubber and agricultural produce at the small shops run by missionaries in order to support their work. In addition, Miskito men found

16. The dependence of coastal peoples on interior areas for various material
items and the use of trade to obtain produce may have roots in aboriginal exchange since a contrast in subsistence patterns between coast and interior presumably existed then, too.

a market for coastal products at Belize, and found employment there as laborers, hunters, or fishermen. Local mahogany cutters hired them as laborers, while India rubber traders employed Miskito as rowers for their buying trips upriver (Roberts 1827:111, 271; Young 1847:28; Moravian Church 1849–1887:vol. 27, p. 34; vol. 31, pp. 195–96; Moravian Church 1881:21; Conzemius 1932:39, 40; Borhek 1949).

Trade and odd jobs were fitted into the ongoing Miskito culture pattern with no outstanding incongruities after the initial development of the Miskito as an identifiable group (Young 1847:159). This adjustment was due, first, to the nature of the division of labor in Miskito society and, second, to the pattern of marital residence. Several nineteenth-century sources mention that men's work centered about hunting and fishing with much leisure time between excursions, while women were responsible for all other duties, including the constant chore of maintaining agricultural plots (Young 1847:28; Cotheal 1848:237–38; Moravian Church 1849–1887:vol. 22, p. 512; vol. 33, p. 166). As a result, men were freer to come and go and to fill their time, if they wished, and as family needs required it, with turtling expeditions, visits to trading stations, even trips to Belize, much as earlier Miskito men traveled with buccaneers or made raiding visits to interior areas without drastically affecting home life as far as we know. Women stayed at home and were responsible for a smoothly operating household on a day-to-day basis.

This division of labor was paralleled and facilitated by matrilocal (uxorilocal) marital residence, i.e., married couples resided either under the same roof as the wife's parents or in a separate dwelling located in the same village as the wife's parents.[17] Matrilocality contains several adaptive features in these circumstances. First, under this arrangement the stable residential core of a Miskito village was composed of groups of related women—mothers, daughters, sisters. The nature of their work was such that these women usually did not have occasion to become directly involved with foreign contacts. Thus, they became the conservative element in Miskito society, maintaining traditional customs and socializing their children

17. Strictly speaking, matrilocality is taken to refer to the overall residence pattern obtained in a village through the individual postnuptial residences established by each couple. Individual residence with or near the wife's parents is described by the term uxorilocality. Both terms will be used throughout this study, and for the nonspecialist may be considered synonymous.

according to these patterns. Consequently, no matter what the nature of their later wanderings, particularly with reference to boys, there was always a solid base of Miskitoness firmly established in the early years of village life.

Second, the core of related women remaining at home also meant that there were functioning households for husband-fathers to return to when adventures farther afield were unavailable or not of interest. Later these same men could leave again, to take advantage of whatever opportunities were available or whatever openings suited their individual fancies. The family unit apparently survived these absences rather well, although the absence of all but old men and boys could limit the immediate availability of the food supply to some extent (Bell 1899:85–86; Conzemius 1932:39).

In both areas, traditional socialization and successful maintenance of a household in the periodic absence of able-bodied adult men, matrilocal residence would seem to be more positively adapted than patrilocality for the type of economic frontier found on the Miskito Coast (cf. Solien de Gonzalez 1961:1272). Patrilocal residence centers around a core of related men whose wives join their husbands' villages or families quite possibly as strangers one to the other. Should the men leave, there is no consanguineal core remaining to stabilize the community. Hence there is a greater probability that traditional customs, particularly those pertaining to generosity, kinship, and cooperation in general, will fall into disuse over time. Without the cohesiveness of consanguineal ties between the women now left as family heads, families are likely to become independent social, as well as economic, entities. Under these conditions the wife is likely to return to her own relatives for cooperation and assistance (Solien de Gonzalez 1961:1272). Traditional forms of intervillage contacts and cohesion may also decline.

Matrilocality, on the other hand, does provide a core of related women whose consanguinity helps to tie separate nuclear families together into larger, more viable units, even if husband-fathers are absent, or, as also frequently happened among the Miskito, if husband-fathers are of non-Miskito background. Furthermore, a basis is provided for the continued local expression of traditional forms of kinship, generosity, and general culture patterns.

Since, by allowing for participation in a wider economy without the loss of ethnic identity and traditional social norms, matrilocality is so admirably suited to the type of contact situation found on the

Coast, it is worthwhile to ask whether, in fact, the demands of trade with Europeans actually may have produced matrilocality in a society that was not so before this contact. The historical literature is frustratingly silent on this matter, particularly for the crucial period of initial contact in the seventeenth century. The earliest direct evidence of matrilocal residence known to me does not appear until 1869, nearly 200 years later, and about the time that missionaries began to encourage the heretofore seminomadic Miskito to settle in more permanent villages for ease in proselytizing (Moravian Church 1849–1887:vol. 20, p. 381; vol. 22, p. 347; vol. 27, pp. 46, 196; vol. 28, p. 197; vol. 29, pp. 53, 281; vol. 31, p. 58; vol. 33, pp. 166, 175; Moravian Church 1890–1956:vol. 5, p. 671; vol. 1, pp. 190, 200; Moravian Church 1903–1954:vol. 9, p. 222). Pim and Seemann (1869:306–7) record that a girl was likely to be betrothed before puberty, her fiancé then taking up residence in her parents' home until she was old enough to marry. After marriage the young couple might start their own household, although generally they resided with the bride's parents. After 1870, what few statements of marital residence rules are found in the literature agree with Pim and Seemann (cf. Helms in press; but see Bell 1899:88).

The only evidence prior to the nineteenth century comes from a seventeenth-century English resident, M.W., who noted a period of "trial marriage" lasting about two years, after which time the couple were married if the girl's parents consented (1732). Trial marriage here may refer to the practice of a new son-in-law residing in his in-laws' home until a growing household leads him to build his own nearby, as Conzemius has suggested (1932:147). However, trial marriage also might simply mean a period of bride service, which could then lead to patrilocal or even neolocal, as well as matrilocal residence. M.W. himself adds a tantalizing note when he records that the composition of a Miskito leader's family included, in addition to the household head, his two wives and three daughters, *a son with his two wives and a concubine,* and numerous others not identified.[18] This, of course, could well be an exception, perhaps

18. As did many before him, Conzemius (1932:149) notes that polygyny was also practiced by a few Miskito in the eighteenth and nineteenth centuries, when matrilocal residence was also preferred. He states in addition that the women involved were often sisters or orphans. In the case of sisters, matrilocality could easily be maintained. When the additional wife was orphaned, postnuptial residence may have meant a change in location for the woman, who may have left her home or village to join that of her husband.

reflecting the leadership qualities exhibited by the head of the family.

Evidence from accounts dealing with the Sumu, who, as we have seen, share a common precontact heritage with the Miskito, is also scanty and inconclusive. Here again nothing is recorded until after the middle of the nineteenth century, when extensive relocations had already occurred among those groups which had so far avoided extinction. Yet it is interesting to note hints of what might be patrilocal residence among Sumu groups. Wickham (1895), for example, records that among Sumu in the vicinity of the Bluefields River the prospective bridegroom resided with his future father-in-law until his fiancée was ready to be taken to his own lodge, although where this home was likely to be located Wickham unfortunately does not say (cf. Bancroft 1883:733).

Some Sumu groups lived in communal longhouses, smaller versions also being used by certain seventeenth-century Miskito (Conzemius 1932:31). On the other hand, the first observers also note that seventeenth-century peoples living along the seacoast proper, the area where the Miskito originated, were more nomadic, with less substantial shelters. Furthermore, whenever a man traveled, his wife and children went with him (Esquemeling 1893:233 ff.; de Lussan 1930:288).

Perhaps it was the case that after residing at his wife's home for several years before and/or after marriage, a coastal man was free to move about with his family as the food quest necessitated, a situation likely to be found among shore dwelling peoples who were predominantly fishermen. It was from just such a coastal group that the Miskito evolved after Western contact, and it seems plausible to suggest that instead of taking his family with him on his moves about the coast, the Miskito man, now going farther afield for trade or raids, simply left them at home, thus developing a pattern of matrilocal residence which became institutionalized.

Although we cannot prove conclusively that matrilocal residence is a postcontact development among the Miskito, we cannot automatically assume that it was aboriginal. But even if it were found in precontact times, matrilocality has proved to be of positive value for the Miskito during the centuries of contact, rather than merely being a nonfunctional survival. On the one hand it assured the continuation of traditional culture in the face of an increasingly heterogeneous world; on the other it provided Miskito men in particular with the necessary individual freedom, not only to hunt and fish as they had always done, but also to take advantage of diverse new activities which would yield European goods, even if these jobs required lengthy absences from home.

In 1894 most of the Miskito territory was officially incorporated into the Republic of Nicaragua as the Department of Zelaya. Although the Miskito were now technically under the law and order of the state, they were, however, exempt from all military service and personal taxes, and were to be permitted to live according to their own customs as long as the national statutes were not compromised (Nicaragua 1895:xviii–xix; Hooker 1945:56–58).

Coastal economics also remained in foreign hands as before. However, there seems to have been an important change in the nature of this exploitation. Simple trade or barter of a wide range of local products gave way in the last half of the nineteenth century to exploitation of a few major natural resources involving private investment of large amounts of foreign capital. These investments tended to be of a speculative nature, which is to say that the chance to make an immediate profit stood foremost. Consequently, interest in a promising new area of exploitation could drain money and labor from a previous attempt, thereby hastening the development of the one and the decline of the other (cf. de Kalb 1893:259).

The speculative nature of these investments, combined with additional factors such as plant disease, exhaustion of resources, government instability, wars, and depressions tended to produce a rather irregular economy characterized by small booms and subsequent busts. In Figure 3 an attempt is made to chart the various enterprises. Roughly speaking, rubber tapping and mahogany cutting provided the first brief booms; gold mining and banana plantations followed; pine lumbering has been the most recent development. The chart is not entirely based on production figures, and therefore its purpose is not to indicate quantitative measures of rate of growth and decline, but merely to illustrate the sequential occurrence of the various enterprises. Periods of national or international disruption are indicated to show the general effects of these outside affairs on the coastal economy.

Several of the ventures, rubber and mahogany, were exploited during preceding centuries. They can be pictured as being in the nature of economic booms either when a foreign company conscientiously expanded production, as in the case of mahogany, or when the foreign market for a product was such that the local population found it advantageous to spend more time gathering that forest resource in particular, as in the case of rubber. The most famous of all these operations concerned large-scale banana production. However, the nature of banana production on the Miskito Coast was less extensive, more fragmented, and less coordinated than that in Central America in general, with the ultimate result that this region was not disrupted by the banana empire nearly as much as were other Central American countries (Kepner 1936; Wilson 1947:chaps. 3 and 4).[19]

The most immediate effect of boom-and-bust economic cycles on Miskito life was to provide a range of job opportunities for Miskito men who, for example, could contract as laborers in the mines or with mahogany gangs, work in the bush tapping rubber, or hire out as boatmen for foreigners traveling the rivers. Wage labor was not a new phenomenon to the Miskito as we have seen. However, it would appear that the decline of simple barter with individual traders along with the increased number of opportunities for wage labor forced a greater degree of dependence upon monetary earnings as the major means to obtain desired foreign goods. Furthermore, as dependence on cash grew, sources of money were increasingly unsteady due to boom-and-bust conditions.

When work was scarce for Miskito men several reactions may have occurred. A religious revival, corresponding with the end of the first rubber boom and the beginning of extensive foreign exploitation of bananas, gold, and mahogany may be one reflection of this instability. Missionary reports also complain that people tended to leave their villages, especially those that had grown up around mis-

19. The Miskito Coast, especially near Bluefields and along the Río Grande, was involved in the early stirrings of the Central American banana boom in the late nineteenth century. Operations were usually in the hands of small companies, particularly Standard Fruit, rather than under the control of the giant of the industry, United Fruit. Less land was involved, and fewer subsidiary operations such as railroads, roads, and ports were built. World War I and the precarious Nicaraguan political situation during the 1920's and 1930's provided another deterrent to extensive banana exploitation, as foreign businessmen hesitated to invest large amounts of capital in so unstable a country. Hurricanes also occasionally ruined plantations, and finally, by 1940, large-scale production had halted altogether as World War II again disrupted world trade and, locally, epidemics of sigatoka and Panama disease wiped out most of the banana holdings. Along the Río Coco local exporters attempted to continue buying fruit from native planters, but by the time of this study even this final effort had ended (Kepner and Soothill 1935; Kepner 1936; von Hagan 1940: 258; Wilson 1947; May and Plaza 1958; Macaulay 1967:chap. 9).

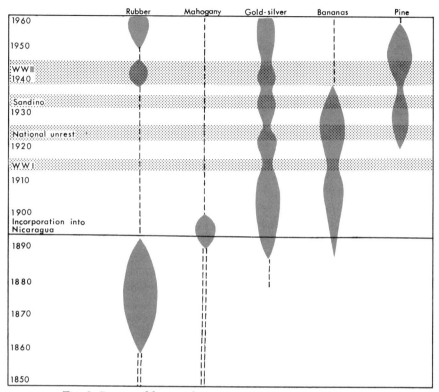

Fig. 3. Boom-and-bust cycles on the Miskito Coast of Nicaragua.

sion stores and churches, and take up a more nomadic way of life, seeking what few work opportunities might still afford some earnings. The return to a seminomadic pattern during times of hardship does not in itself imply breakdown or even great change in Miskito social organization. All descriptions of the Coast from the seventeenth century on have commented upon the wandering nature of these people. These moves might be interpreted, then, as normal, traditional reactions to the problems of living in general.

On the other hand, it would seem significant that changes in kinship terminology of the sort often attributed to dislocation, migration, and unusual mobility occurred soon after the turn of the century.[20] This would strongly suggest that there was, in fact, greater

20. The particular change referred to here is the loss of cross-parallel cousin distinctions to form a generational pattern. In addition to economic pres-

social instability than before. In addition, the search for new areas of employment when there was a decline in job opportunities emphasizes that the guns and ammunition, iron pots, axes, machetes, cloth, and rum bought with labor had become cultural necessities, and all possible avenues of work had to be explored in order to assure a more or less steady supply.[21]

It is important to note that most of the mission stations from which reports are drawn were located along the seacoast. As we mentioned earlier, good agricultural land is hard to find there, and, in addition, hurricanes and floods make agriculture even more undependable. Consequently, lack of employment no doubt meant increased hardship for coastal people who were more dependent on wage labor for provisions, as previously they had depended on trade.

Direct information on the reaction of more fortunate groups living along the rivers, with agricultural land more easily available, is not usually given in the documents. However, one reference notes that many of the men in the San Carlos area of the Río Coco went to Honduras to find work when food was scarce (Moravian Church 1903–1954:vol. 27, p. 96; cf. Moravian Church 1890–1956:vol. 11, pp. 266–67). In general, information for the Río Coco reports hardship and dislocation, but this was due primarily to the Sandino Affair, a series of bloody encounters between United States Marines and Nicaraguan patriots protesting American intervention in na-

---

sures, depopulation due to disease may have been a contributing factor leading to this change. Edwards (1819:210) and Young (1847:73) state that smallpox had caused considerable deaths, and there are occasional references to outbreaks of cholera, measles, and whooping cough in missionary accounts (Moravian Church 1849–1887; Moravian Church 1890–1956:vol. 9, p. 371). The effect of such illnesses on population is hard to determine, however, and there is nothing to indicate *extensive* social disruption, with attendant changes in social organization, as an immediate consequence. Pijoan (1946:38–53) discusses the lack or rarity of many diseases in the history of the Coast with particular reference to the Rio Coco. He does note sporadic epidemics of whooping cough which, however, were localized and declined after the late nineteenth century. Work in gold mines in the interior was responsible for deaths among young men with symptoms of tuberculosis, but Pijoan notes that clinical findings of tuberculosis were rare among Indians in isolated villages at the time of his study. Malaria, intestinal parasites, dysentery, and skin diseases were the salient health problems he encountered (cf. Moravian Church 1903–1954:vol. 11, p. 83). See Dole (1957:chap. 9) for a general discussion of the forces leading to generational kinship nomenclature.

21. See Moravian Church 1903–1954 for numerous reports of the ups and downs of the Coastal economy for this period.

tional politics (Macaulay 1967;chap. 2n2). In 1931–32, clashes occurred on the Río Coco. In fear of attack, or as a consequence of raids, villagers fled their homes and either settled elsewhere or returned when all was quiet again (Moravian Church 1903–1954:vol. 32, p. 50; vol. 33, p. 51). Information from Asang, however, shows that men have tended to return to the village and engage in agricultural activities when economic depression strikes. We can only surmise that this pattern might have been followed by similar riverine Miskito in previous years.

Another potential area of increased frustration lies in what appears to be an intensification of the problem of debt peonage, although just how serious and damaging this system became it is hard to say. It is clear, however, that laborers hired to work in mines or on plantations and men who contracted to work more independently in the bush were victimized to some extent (de Kalb 1893: 264–65; Heath 1916b:172; Nogales 1928:184; Hamilton 1939; Grossman 1940:30–31).

On the other hand, at least one observer reported that the local population simply moved elsewhere when pressure from a trader became stronger than their inclination to work (Mierisch 1893:31). This point is of some importance, not only for Miskito culture history, but also in terms of the legitimacy of recognizing the Miskito and others like them as exemplifying a purchase rather than a peasant society.

In the general literature credit systems are often pictured as harshly controlling and exploitative, and thus would seemingly thrust purchase societies into a coercive system analogous to the state's control of peasantry. The classic case which generally comes to mind in the economic frontiers where purchase societies may be found is that which occurred at the height of the rubber trade in the Amazon basin, where traders often had absolute control over the lives of people within their domains, and where brute force was used if necessary to keep collectors at work (cf. Wagley 1964:93– 95). However, this may prove to have been an extreme case. On the other side of the ledger it is possible to find examples of harried traders forced to cope with the inconsistent demands of their native clients or helpless to collect back debts, or of employers constantly threatened by the natives' tendency to work only long enough to earn what they needed for immediate use (cf. Helm 1965:39–40).

It is also possible that what Western observers see as exploitation is considered desirable from the point of view of the native population. The villagers of Asang, for example, will gladly accept as much credit as the local shopkeeper is willing to extend, and are likely to be considerably put out if he refuses still another request for yet another round of goods and credit (cf. VanStone 1965:23, 24). It may be, then, that at least with respect to economic frontier regions such as that found on the Miskito Coast, the general impression of credit systems as being unfair and undesirable to the local population by definition is an overstatement. This impression is aided perhaps by the tone of potentially biased sources such as missionary reports (which provide most of the information on this matter for the Miskito Coast), which seem to emphasize the immorality of the credit system more than to point to really long-lasting effects.

Additional cross-cultural research on this point may very well indicate considerable leeway for maneuvering on the part of local populations in many credit systems, and show that traders or commissary managers may not always have had their way. This relatively flexible relationship between trader and purchaser is not comparable to the demands of landlords and state officials which are less easily avoided by peasants, who are powerless to combat the authority of the state. Credit systems in general are basically symmetrical arrangements for exchange, even if the purchasing portion occurs prior to payment, whereas the state's exploitation of peasantry is heavily one-sided (cf. Foster 1967a:8, 10).

At present the economic situation on the Miskito Coast is depressed. Pine lumbering, the latest boom, has declined, and the Miskito are once more on their own, as the situation in Asang illustrates in more detail. Some income is obtained by selling agricultural surpluses and fish at the markets in Puerto Cabezas or Bluefields, but since these are frontier towns they, too, tend to lose population when depression hits, and thus there is a smaller market for the Miskito to supply. The limited number of jobs still available at the gold mines are far from adequate to provide work for the numerous applicants who have flocked there seeking employment.

One major result of depression has been to increase the isolation of the region from the rest of the world. Communication with Hispanic Nicaragua has never been satisfactory, even by Latin American standards. It is possible to travel overland from east to west with any amount of convenience at only one point—along a road connecting the Río Escondido, and ultimately Bluefields, with western Nicaraguan cities. It is possible to travel from east to west via the Río Coco, but because of the dangers and hardships involved, this trip, which requires several weeks, remains in the nature of an expedition. Traditionally, most contacts with the outside were made by sea as freighters picked up lumber and other products and discharged necessary supplies, or small craft traveled from settlement to settlement. Now, however, there is very little business for freighters.

While the lumber business prospered, logging roads were maintained in fair condition and served to connect the major settlements in the area between Puerto Cabezas and the Río Coco. (There are no roads south of Puerto Cabezas.) Another road ran from the major Río Coco town of Waspam to Auasbila, a Miskito village near the end of the easily navigable portion of the Río Coco (see Figure 4). However, this road is no longer used, and the other logging roads are gradually falling into disrepair. Consequently, travel time has increased and trips from Río Coco villages to Puerto Cabezas, for example, which used to take at most one day on the road now require as many as three days since one must rely on time-consuming travel on the river with its many meanders, and fewer craft are available to provide transportation. Occasional single engine planes fly from Waspam or Puerto Cabezas to San Carlos or Bocay on the river, but do not serve as means of public transportation. Since in the absence of roads the major communication routes for the bulk of the population around and about the territory are the sea, lagoons, and rivers (which have served this function for centuries), it follows that most settlements are riverine or ocean oriented.

Presently there are two main types of settlements found in the region—commercial-administrative centers and rural villages such as Asang. There are two or possibly three communities which can be classified as commercial and administrative centers: Bluefields, which services the southern portion of the coast; Puerto Cabezas, located farther north, also on the coast; and as a possible third, Waspam, the jumping-off point for most travel up the Río Coco. Daily business in town is handled by people representing a wide variety of cultural backgrounds. Political and administrative affairs are in the hands of Spanish-speaking Nicaraguans, called "Spanish"

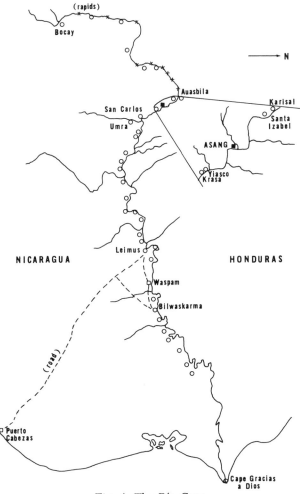

Fig. 4. The Río Coco.

locally; the shops and commissaries, which carry anything from
kerosene to hair ribbons and rice, are owned by Chinese merchants
and their families; a wide range of odd jobs and services are provided by the dark-skinned, English-speaking Creoles. A number
of Americans work at various jobs such as lumber officials, hopeful
gold prospectors, and missionaries.

In the wide spaces separating the few towns are numerous small
villages located for the most part along ocean or lagoon, or on river

banks. The population here is almost entirely Miskito. Although detailed statistics are lacking, it can be safely stated that the rural Miskito, along with remnant populations of related Sumu, form at least half and probably more of the eastern Nicaraguan population. Combining the figures from several sources, a population of approximately 45–50,000 for rural eastern Nicaragua, excluding Bluefields, Puerto Cabezas, and the interior mines might be in order. Of this total, approximately 15,000 persons live on the Río Coco alone. However, it must be emphasized that these are at best tentative figures (Taylor 1959:54; Steinberg 1965:1278).

Coastal residents divide the Miskito population into three subcategories described primarily in terms of geographical location with corresponding dialect differences and possibly minor cultural distinctions. Thus, Miskito peoples are considered as either coastal, referring to ocean- and lagoon-oriented villagers primarily living in Nicaragua; Río Coco or Wangki, indicating Miskito residents along this major river; or Honduranean or Mam, referring, as the name suggests, to Miskito living within Honduranean territory. Since Asang is a Río Coco village, it will be useful to note in more detail the pattern of life found along this river during the time of the study.

2

Introduction to Asang

THE Río Coco or Wangki is one of the longest rivers of Central America, flowing approximately 750 kilometers from sources located near the Pacific coast to the Caribbean shore where it terminates at Cape Gracias a Dios, known locally as The Cape (Tamayo and West 1964:97).[1] Like many tropical rivers, its length is a function of innumerable meanders which make the river resemble a gigantic brown serpent when viewed from the air.

The World of the Río Coco

The lower half of the river, from the Miskito village of Karisal to the Cape, is navigable by small, powered craft, and there is a fairly constant trickle of traffic. Several slow barges serve as floating commissaries; dugout canoes or *dories*, some powered by small outboard motors, others by the traditional poling and paddling technique, are common (Fig. 5); an occasional wooden or bamboo raft can be seen; and one or two speedboats thrust all other traffic to the wooded banks with the swell from their rapid passage.

This part of the river appears rather placid to the observer until a series of whirlpools or the bobbing and thrust of floating debris reveal a strong current beneath the surface. As the river winds through the flat, open savannah its fertile alluvial banks are lined with mangrove, secondary bush growth, or bamboo groves where tall featherlike spears of green lean out from the bank to be reflected in the brown-black water. Sometimes a cleared area can be seen where manioc, maize, rice, beans, bananas, plantains, or even a few watermelon and tomato plants cling to the burned soil.

1. There are many names for this river, Río Coco being perhaps the most common, at least in eastern Nicaragua and Honduras. "Wangks" or "Wangki" is the Miskito name, while "Segovia" is used in the Hispanic West.

Then a curve looms ahead and a village appears, strung along the edge of a high bank overlooking a gravel and sand beach where cattle and a few horses may be standing knee-deep in the water to escape the swarms of mosquitos. On the beach, remains of a Miskito dry season fishing camp may be descried in the few pieces of bamboo and wood which still clutter the stones. A few brightly colored birds or a chain of butterflies suddenly erupt from the bush along the bank, contrasted pleasantly for a moment against the endless green of the vegetation. A woman, kneeling quietly in the bottom

Fig. 5. A loaded dugout is slowly poled upriver.

of her dugout which lies anchored at a sheltered spot along the bank, glances up from her fishing to watch the passage of the motor craft.

As we proceed upstream the land gradually rises, and low mountains form a constant backdrop for the riverine panorama. Near the village of Karisal the character of the river abruptly changes. Instead of sloping mud banks draped with greenery, stretches of lush bush and plantations, quiet beaches, and a subservient river, the landscape alters to show huge black rocks abruptly jutting from the middle of the river which now roars and churns its foamy path between them. More rocks line the bank, making a torturous, twisting path for the narrowing river. Swift boiling rapids take control of the dugout, leaving the motorman and bowman little to do except protect the motor from the stones and attempt to keep the craft from crashing broadside onto the menacing rocks as it bounces from wave to wave in its erratic path against the now rapid current. Some rapids are impassable, and goods and passengers must be landed for portage.

Because of these difficulties, this section of the river is more isolated than the lower half. No commercial barges from downriver pass here. Some merchants reach the upper extremes from the Pacific side, but the difficulties of travel make their goods very expensive. No government speedboat flashes through the rapids either. Except for an occasional missionary, and the Miskito who pole their dugouts and rafts through this region with calculated risk to life and property, there is no traffic.

The best time to attempt a trip on the upper section of the river is during the dry season which is from January until about the end of April. Then the river level slowly drops and safe passage may be found through the now subdued rapids. On the lower river, however, travel can become more difficult during dry season since the falling water level uncovers larger and larger stretches of beach. People hesitate to take trips downriver because trouble is almost assured. Loaded dugouts may become grounded, forcing the occupants to unload the cargo, and pull and pry the heavy boat across the offending bar or beach until an open channel is reached once more. During this period the commercial barges sometimes cannot travel upstream as far as Karisal.

The situation alters when the rains begin in May, and the river quickly changes to become a raging torrent carrying huge trees and mobile dams of debris in its swirling path. But then travel is again dangerous, for one blow from a hurtling log and the dugout or raft can easily be capsized. As the water rises the banks disappear, and low-lying bush areas and plantations are covered with a muddy liquid carpet. Flooding becomes more severe as the river approaches the delta since land lies progressively lower. If the floods are too severe or prolonged, there may be damage to or even complete loss of crops in this lower quarter of the river.

River life depends on the rains, however, because the annual renewal of low-lying fields by flood-carried silt makes agriculture more productive. People also rely on the river for transportation and communication. Travelers, merchandise, and news reach these populations only via the river, discounting for the moment the erratic flights of occasional single-engine planes to San Carlos, and the snatches of world news heard, but not necessarily understood, over transistor radios. Most of this traffic flows in and out of Waspam and Leimus; the former, headquarters for government and some missionary activity, the latter, a lumber ghost town where travelers from Puerto Cabezas often leave for points upriver. Below Waspam and closer to the delta, business is conducted through the Cape. Beyond Karisal, on the upper river, the rapids effectively block most non-Miskito traffic. The heart of river life flows between Waspam and Karisal. Since Asang lies within this area it will concern us most.

Between Waspam and Karisal distance is measured mainly in hours or days of travel time, depending on the status and contacts of the traveler. For the government representative it is a quick thirty minute flight from Waspam to San Carlos. If there is no plane, the official will probably travel by speedboat, making the trip in four or five hours. Missionaries and local merchants will probably travel by motor-powered dugout, which can run from Leimus to San Carlos in eight hours if not loaded too heavily. On the other hand, a heavily loaded craft, or one with a smaller motor, may require two days to go from Waspam to San Carlos. The commissary barges, stopping periodically for business, take about three days to travel the same distance. Finally, the Miskito with his pole and paddle also must count on about three days travel from Leimus to Karisal.

Since there are no provisions for travelers in the way of food or sleeping quarters, each must provide for his own comforts. For those without access to plane or speedboat, the barges offer the next best arrangement if time is no problem. They are roofed and have canvas "curtains" that can be lowered to protect against rain; a comfortable seat may be found on a sack of rice, or, better yet, beans. Dugout travel, on the other hand, is more demanding, although motor-powered dugouts are especially popular if plane or speedboat are unavailable and barges are too slow to suit the traveler. One must be prepared to endure sun and rain while sitting immobile for hours on several sections of bamboo wedged between the narrow sides of the dugout. For hand-poled dugouts, the seasoned passenger has learned to sit cross-legged with each knee resting against the side of the craft. This helps him adjust to the constant roll of the craft as it is poled along.

The majority of river travelers are Miskito who laboriously pole their heavy dugouts upriver or effortlessly drift downstream. The non-Miskito who travel the river can be placed into four main categories—missionaries, merchants, miners and other speculators, and government officials. Missionaries include representatives of three groups—Moravian, Roman Catholic, and Church of God, known locally by its Spanish name, Iglesia de Dios. The Moravians have been in the area the longest, beginning work on the river in 1896 (Heath n.d.). Most Moravian parsons are either Creole or American. However, there are perhaps a half dozen parsons of Miskito ancestry currently working in Nicaragua along with a number of Miskito lay pastors who staff villages without a resident parson.

Catholic organization is similar. The work of the church is divided between padres, who are all, as far as I know, North Americans of the Capuchin Order, and Miskito lay catechists. Catholic efforts on the river have been fruitful only for about the last twenty-five or thirty years. Generally speaking, the Moravian and Roman Catholic mission groups have kept to separate areas of the river.

The third missionary group, the Iglesia de Dios, is the latest to appear on the river and has only a few organized congregations. It appears to be under no direct local control by foreigners although both American and Nicaraguan functionaries occasionally pay fleeting visits to the congregations. In contrast to the more restrained Moravians and Catholics, Iglesia congregations are definitely fundamentalist and concentrate more heavily on Miskito tendencies towards emotionalism.

At the time of the study there were two floating commissaries plying their trade between Waspam and Karisal. One barge was owned and operated by an ancient Chinese and his sons, while the other was under the control of a Creole. These two worked out of Leimus and Waspam, and would make their trips about every ten days, provided the river wasn't too dry. They carried a variety of articles for sale to Miskito villagers, including flour, salt, sugar, kerosene, cloth, thread, canned goods, candy, paper, pencils, tobacco, Vicks Vaporub, chewing gum, shoe polish, diaper pins, and fishing line. On the return trip downriver, they carried agricultural produce, primarily rice and beans from the upriver villages to merchants in coastal towns. Just as important for the life of the river, though, were the letters and passengers brought by the barges. In addition to the floating commissaries there are local Nicaraguan or Creole merchants with commissaries located in principal villages who also sell supplies to the Miskito and sometimes buy produce. These men are the chief owners of motor-powered dugouts.

The medical representative for the Alliance for Progress also travels on the river. This doctor, working alone, is responsible for the entire river area below the rapids. In addition, there is a government clinic at San Carlos which provides outpatient treatment. Most of the medical work of the area, however, is under the control of the Moravian mission which supports the hospital at Bilwaskarma and is building several clinics farther up the river. The Catholic padres also dispense medicine at their stations.

Although the region is far from the political centers of Nicaragua and Honduras, there are nine or ten police stations at various points along the river to maintain order and represent government interests. However, due to its isolation, the Coast is an excellent area for hatching revolutions, and the Río Coco shared in the fruits of one such endeavor—the Sandino Affair of the early 1930's (Macaulay 1967).[2] The terroristic methods of Sandino's guerrilla fighters as they opposed the United States Marines left a strong impression on the local populace. News of similar encounters with "outlaws," frequently involving reports of terroristic practices, stir up the area to this day. There are constant rumors floating from village to village that "bandits" were seen upriver, or that there is a new war involving the United States which will result in bombing or invasion of the river at any time. Attempts to show the distance of Vietnam from the Río Coco, for example, do little to alleviate apprehension.

In one sense, fear of impending war has been shown to be justi-

2. During the Coolidge administration United States Marines were sent to Nicaragua under the pretext of protecting American lives and property in the face of disruptions caused by a military coup which had recently overthrown the Nicaraguan government. In actuality, U.S. intervention was aimed at backing the new government against the possibility of a return takeover by the ousted party. An uneasy peace descended when American military and diplomatic pressures led to a compromise president. Such heavy-handed intervention was bitterly resented, however, and sparked a six-year (1927–33) guerrilla war against the occupying Marines and American property-holders by a young revolutionist, Augusto Sandino, and his companions. This little-known (to Americans) chapter in United States history has been vividly described by Neil Macaulay in a recent book (1967).

fied. In 1960 the World Court ended a long-standing controversy by declaring the Río Coco the official boundary between Nicaragua and Honduras. Unfortunately this decision has raised a certain amount of ill will between the two countries. For a number of reasons the decision also forced the Miskito living on the Honduranean side of the river to move to the Nicaraguan bank. This relocation is known locally as the *traslado*.[3]

The government constructed homes and schools for the relocated villagers, but the Miskito are bitter about the loss of what they consider to be their land in Honduras. Actually, they still have agricultural privileges on Honduranean soil if they obtain a permit, but the Miskito are not used to the idea of needing permits to cultivate their own land and therefore do not apply. Those who attempt to cultivate across the river run the risk of being molested and having their property stolen by Honduranean police, at least in certain areas. This harassment serves to preserve memories of previous troubles during the Sandino era.

The last type of non-Miskito individual found traveling on the river is the representative of a foreign business enterprise. In contemporary Miskito world view, the commercial production of bananas was the foremost determinant of the condition of the river economy since the turn of the century. During the '20's and '30's, operations were primarily under the control of the Standard Fruit Company, which bought thousands of stems of fruit each week from local Miskito growers. Money was readily available, commissaries flourished, and Western merchandise was plentiful. Standard ceased its operations in the early 1940's, and a local company continued to buy bananas, although on a smaller scale. However, in 1961 this company also ceased buying, presumably as a result of the *traslado*. Consequently, the business that at one time spelled unheard of prosperity for the local population now is largely responsible for the economic depression that has reduced a once bustling river to a deserted backwater area (see chap. 1n18).

3. According to those in control, the *traslado* was made for the good of the populace. Their chief argument held that while the frontier was still in dispute, the Miskito living on the Honduranean side had access to the facilities of the Moravian hospital at Bilwaskarma and to commercial activities at Waspam. After the Court's decision, these people technically would become Honduraneans, and Nicaraguan facilities would no longer be readily available to them. Furthermore, there are no comparable towns or services on the immediate Honduranean side.

The decline of the lumber business is also partly to blame for this situation. Although the Nicaraguan pine savannahs were depleted some years ago, there was still plenty of timber available in the disputed territory across the river. The World Court decision put an end to lumbering of what was now Honduranean property by a company located in Nicaragua.

The Court's decision also closed the truck route from Leimus to the Miskito village of Auasbila, which ran along the Honduranean side of the river. Travelers from Auasbila were able to reach Leimus and from there the "big cities" of Waspam and Puerto Cabezas in a matter of hours, which allowed river people to maintain greater contact with the activities and products of the towns. This opportunity is now gone since the road is on Honduranean land, and, due to the Nicaraguan-Honduranean estrangement, arrangements to transport passengers across the river at Leimus have been suspended. Only the silent cable lines still stretch across the river at what had been the ferry, and the local population has been plunged back into an isolation it had not known for decades.

The Miskito share their river not only with various groups of "Westerners," but also, to a limited extent, with the Sumu. Sumu place names are found along most of the river, and only the lower hundred miles show a predominance of Miskito names (Heath n.d.). Today, however, one would only rarely pass Sumus traveling on the river. With one or two exceptions their villages remain located in the most inaccessible areas of the entire river system, most being situated on the headwaters of the upper tributaries of the river, especially along the Bocay River and its tributaries. It is reported that they are most inhospitable to all strangers, and that their villages are reached only by first crossing a body of water.[4]

Among the approximately forty Miskito settlements, which extend from Cape Gracias to at least the village of Bocay, three or perhaps four types of villages can be noted. They are all located high above the flood line of the river on top of a mud and grass bank

4. This holds true for the Sumu village of Umra, a short, half-hour walk from San Carlos. It is located high on the opposite bank of a stream and can be reached only by ferry service. This village is composed of nine houses and a school taught by a Miskito who instructs in Spanish. At least some of the villagers are members of the San Carlos Moravian congregation. Both Miskito and Sumu are spoken by the inhabitants. There are several other Sumu villages located either close to or directly on the main river. However, the vast majority of the Sumu are not found in the Miskito section of the river.

which is climbed by a series of twisting, slippery, narrow paths. One type of settlement cannot really be honored by the title of village, for it consists of only a few houses clustered under trees. Some of these settlements are only temporary quarters used during periods of peak plantation activity, but others are the permanent homes of one or two families. However, it is from just such a grouping of a few isolated huts that larger villages grow.

A second village type has been briefly mentioned previously. These are the half-dozen or so conglomerate or multicentered villages created by the population movements of the *traslado*. Such communities may be composed of several smaller relocated villages. These villages can be identified by their Spanish names, with which the authorities have replaced the Miskito names, although the original names are often used by natives of the region, by the unique "chicken shed" type of house architecture, and by the relative lack of trees and bushes which gives the town a barren and artificial look.[5]

Still another type of village can be identified by the addition of a *guardia* or police station, small shops and commissaries, and perhaps a rice-hulling mill to the basically Miskito community. These few villages acquire a greater proportion of Spanish-speaking peoples and become local trade and information centers. An atmosphere of "being in town" exists due to the presence of commerce, slight though it be. Such villages are considered the regional centers by the government. Consequently, more elaborate schools and communication networks such as radio transmitter-receivers are sometimes maintained.

The last and most numerous category of Miskito village types may be termed single-centered, since these communities are not agglomerations of several villages as are the multicentered type, but, instead, have grown as a unit from a single point of settlement. The population is predominantly Miskito, and lacks the *guardia* and many other non-Miskito elements.[6] However, within this cate-

5. Note, however, that not all villages with Spanish names are new. A map of the river dated 1905 shows a few village names in Spanish at that time (J. Hamilton 1905:728).

6. These villages are Miskito in the cultural rather than ethnic sense. Creoles and occasionally a stray European or American (but only rarely a Spanish-speaking Nicaraguan) may have settled in the village and intermarried with Miskito women. The children are raised as Miskito although their background is remembered.

gory we can also distinguish the savannah-oriented village from the riverine village. This distinction is made strictly on the basis of geographical location, although it is possible that riverine villages show minor cultural differences in greater utilization of river resources. The savannah villages are found below Waspam where the lay of the land is lower and flooding is more severe. It is therefore necessary to live farther inland, away from the river, to escape the annual inundations. On the other hand, the villages upstream from Waspam can be classified as riverine since the land rises sufficiently to permit protection from floods by simply building along the higher river banks. These villages, therefore, face directly onto the river. A riverine, single-centered village will be described and analyzed in detail in the village study of Asang.

In general, villages today range in size from two to about one-hundred houses. Maximum village size apparently has been fairly constant, at least since the general description of the "river Indians" written by Bishop Karl A. Mueller in which he states that the Indians who live on the river courses have scattered settlements of from two to one-hundred families (1932:30). Conzemius (1932:29) notes that "the Miskito of the lower Rio Coco and of certain parts of the Nicaraguan coast have some large villages with from 100 to 500 inhabitants . . .," which would seem to correlate with Mueller's report, since many households contain a single nuclear family. Only a few villages on the river have more than 500 inhabitants today. Comparing these estimates for the twentieth century with data scattered throughout nineteenth-century reports, when settled villages were becoming more prevalent through missionary efforts, it seems that there has been no radical change in average village size although the overall Miskito population has been gradually increasing (Moravian Church 1849–1887; 1890–1956).

The Lay of the Village

Asang[7] is a large community, with a population of 665 at the time of this study. It is located on the most prosperous, or, rather, potentially prosperous part of the river, lying on the Nicaraguan bank below the rapids so that the advantages of school, church, and commerce are available. Yet the village is well above the lower reaches of the river where excess flooding can be detrimental to agriculture.

7. The word *asang* is a Sumu term meaning "hilly land covered with forest" (Heath 1950:21).

Seen from the river, the main avenue of approach, Asang appears
to consist of a single straggling line of houses perched atop a high
(roughly 15 feet) bank, and separated from the river proper by a
small creek which enters the Río Coco in front of the village (see
Figure 6). The red-roofed Moravian church dominates the scene
and can be seen from several miles downriver (Fig. 7). Because of
the creek, a spit of sand and stones covered with trees and bushes
has grown in front of the village. If the river is high enough it is
possible for loaded dugouts and commissary barges to round the
spit and proceed a few hundred yards up the creek to mooring
spots at the foot of the 15–20-foot bank on top of which the village

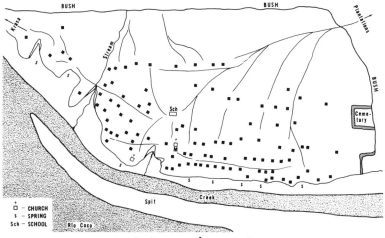

Fig. 6. Asang settlement pattern.

is located. If the river is low, however, dugouts and barges stop at
the far side of the spit, along the main stream of the river. Passengers must walk across the few hundred feet of spit to reach the
stream at the foot of the bank. The stream is crossed via impromptu
bridges of dugouts, lined up bow to stern, making a fairly dry, if
somewhat unstable passage, or a small child may be called to ferry
goods and people across the stream.

Seen from the top of the bank, the village is much larger than it
appeared from the river. It contains ninety inhabited dwelling units
(sleeping quarters and kitchens), in addition to a school, commis-

sary, and two churches, and is roughly divided into three main areas. The oldest section extends from the centrally placed Moravian church and mission house north along the bank for about 400 yards.[8] At the far end of town in this direction is the cemetery, and then the bush. Houses are placed in three more or less parallel rows facing east and looking across the river to Honduras. This street arrangement may be a response to missionary contact (cf. Moravian Church 1890–1956:vol. 10, p. 407). Behind the main rows of dwellings are a handful of scattered newer homes. Because they are so few, they do not yet show as clear-cut a pattern of parallel rows. Asang's single commissary building is located in this oldest section of town, fairly close to the Moravian church.

Fig. 7. The Moravian church. Women and girls wash dishes and laundry at a spring nearby.

Behind the Moravian enclave is the government school, and from this area south to a small creek lies the second part of the village. Here again, homes form roughly parallel rows stretching about 180 yards from the Moravian mission to the creek. Again a few newer homes lie behind this area. The church of the Iglesia de Dios sect is located here, not far from the Moravian mission.

8. Asang is situated on one of the curves of the river which at this point flows south. Consequently, the main axis of the village runs north-south.

The third section of the village lies still farther south, stretching from the creek to the edge of the bush, a distance of about 290 yards. This is the newest and most thinly settled section. It was first cleared about ten years ago, according to informants, by a household head from the second area of the village who wished to have more room for cattle raising. Today, only a few scattered homes are located along a main path. This path continues past the southern boundary of Asang to Krasa, the next village to the southeast, which can be reached in about a half hour on foot in dry season. There is another major path which leads out of town at the northern boundary and eventually ends up at Santa Izabel, the nearest village to the northwest. This is about a three-hour walk.

The village is surrounded on three sides by bush. The fourth side overlooks the creek, the spit, and the river. Except for the extreme southern part of town, the bush has been cleared back to a depth of about 360 yards from the edge of the bank. The front third of this cleared area contains most of the village buildings, while the second third is mainly planted in citrus groves. The back third is open and serves as grazing area for cattle and horses. This empty space is also intended to allow for community expansion.

The village has a pleasant appearance. Except during dry season there is grass between the huts which is kept trimmed by grazing animals. Numerous orange, grapefruit, and lemon trees are scattered throughout the village, providing shade as well as fruit. Coconut palms are not too plentiful, but some are found. There are scattered trees of cashew, Spanish plum, rose-apple, papaya, mango, pejivalle palm, zapote, soursap, and annatto. Calabash are numerous. People also cultivate small gardens of herbs and young trees near their homes. The gardens are fenced with rough wood or bamboo against the inroads of cows and pigs. Garden flowers, grown for ornament only, are common, as are flowering bushes.[9]

Benches have been built along the front bank, overlooking the river. These are merely long pieces of bamboo raised off the ground at convenient sitting height. They provide resting places with a magnificent view of the surrounding country, and are popular spots, especially for young people. Among the most attractive features of Asang are the dozen or more natural springs which flow from the sides of the bank. These provide fresh water for drinking, cooking,

9. The cultivation of flowers was borrowed from Creoles or Spanish-speaking Nicaraguans (Grossman 1940:29).

bathing, and washing clothes and dishes. Without the springs it would be necessary to utilize river water or the impure water of the creeks or stream in front of the village. Creek water is used for washing clothes and dishes, but not for drinking.

Individual homes are built for sleeping and eating. Fifty-two of the ninety inhabited dwellings (58 per cent) are composed of two buildings sometimes connected by a board ramp (Fig. 8). The larger of the two, measuring 18–19 feet by 22–24 feet, is divided by wood or bamboo partitions into sleeping compartments which con-

Fig. 8. Sleeping quarters and separate kitchen. Note window platform used for dish washing.

tain single beds of wood or bamboo raised about 3 feet from the floor. For children, and occasionally women, bedding may be placed directly on the floor. Sheets of bark cloth are used together with purchased cotton cloth for covers. Occasionally pillows and thin mattresses are made, stuffed with silk cotton seed fiber. If at all possible, a mosquito bar made from thin purchased cotton cloth is used. The sleeping unit may also include a main room where a few tables and stools, and perhaps a sewing machine, are kept. There is always a porch along the width of the house with a long, low bench, often carved from one piece of wood, a V-shaped wooden chair, or a hammock of braided fibers for repose. The smaller building, approximately 14 by 19 feet, serves as kitchen and produce center, and usually has a table with stools or a bench, shelves for silverware, cheap enameled dishes and cups, odd cans, boxes and bottles, and the traditional calabashes, and the *kubus* or clay stove or cooking platform. This is an oblong table with raised sides filled with a

Fig. 9. The *kubus* or cooking platform.

local white clay on which the fire or fires are built (Fig. 9).[10] Heavy three-legged iron pots called *dikwas* rest on two parallel iron bars which are supported by endpieces of wood or perhaps old *dikwas* partially buried in the clay. These raise the iron rods, and their load of pots, above the fire. Fishing rods, machetes, knives, cooking spoons, and *wabul* stirrers are hung on the walls or jammed behind upright posts against the wall. (*Wabul* is a staple beverage made by mixing mashed boiled bananas or plantains with water.) A variety

10. Sometimes the clay is molded to form a single or double horseshoe shape. The fire is then built between the arms of the horseshoe. I did not see this type of stove in Asang, but did see it in other villages.

of woven carrying baskets and fishing nets may be stored in corners or on the rafters. One corner is reserved for produce from the bush or cultivated plots. Most kitchens have a small slatted platform extending outward a foot or so from one window for washing dishes and preparing food. There is also a porch extending the width of the kitchen (cf. Conzemius 1932:32–35).

House units, both the sleeping quarters and the kitchen, are raised about 4 feet from the ground on wooden pilings, often of tamarind. This practice, along with that of building a separate structure for cooking purposes, was introduced to the Coast by missionaries and other foreigners and is considered a mark of modern "civilized" living by the people of Asang (Mueller 1932:38; Conzemius 1932:31–36).[11] An elevated structure serves to keep the house drier and cleaner, and discourages livestock from wandering through. Supplies of firewood are stacked under the house along with mortars, and chickens and pigs spend the night there. Buildings are constructed of wood (Santa Maria is commonly used) and/ or split bamboo, and the peaked, sloping roofs are thatched with large palm leaves which have been tied with lianas to bamboo strips. Access is by rickety steps or a single notched log or piece of bamboo. Nine of the main, or sleeping units, have been painted on the outside, and twelve sleeping units, including these nine, are roofed with corrugated iron. Four of the kitchens belonging to this group are also roofed with corrugated iron, but no kitchen is painted.

Thirty-eight dwellings (42 per cent of the total number of inhabited dwellings in the village) combine sleeping quarters and kitchen under one roof. A rough correlation can be found between this practice and the type of materials used in house construction, i.e., it is more likely that a dwelling made of bamboo will contain both units in a single structure than a dwelling made of wood. For example, 64 per cent (sixteen out of twenty-five) of all bamboo

11. According to Conzemius (1932:30–31) the traditional house was a rectangular dwelling generally rounded on the short sides with the fire built directly on the leveled mud floor which was often raised a little to avoid dampness. The hearth was formed by three logs placed so as to form a "Y"; these logs supported the cooking vessels. He then notes that in regions where the Indians had had considerable contact with foreigners they had added side walls and an elevated floor of split bamboo or wood. The fireplace was then transferred to a small adjoining hut. Conzemius also mentions that long communal or multiple family houses were formerly used by both Miskito and Sumu, but at his time only the single family type was found.

homes do not have separate kitchen units, nor do 75 per cent (six out of eight) of those homes constructed of wood and bamboo. In contrast only 28 per cent (sixteen out of fifty-seven) of the wooden homes combine sleeping and kitchen quarters, and none of those homes which have metal roofs combine the two. Beside many homes an elevated wood and bamboo platform is built primarily for drying bunches of rice.

The Miskito home comprises more than just physical structures. It also extends conceptually to include an open yard area in front of the main or sleeping hut. This yard is kept clean and neat, sometimes even to the extent of hoeing up all the grass in order to leave an open area of bare earth. Here certain types of heavy work are done, such as beating bark cloth, crushing sugarcane, or threshing bunches of rice with mortar and pestle. In general the Miskito lives out of doors, working either on the porch of the sleeping hut or in the yard. Homes serve mainly as storage areas, as places to cook, eat, and sleep, and as shelter from the elements.

The most imposing building in the village is the Moravian church with its red corrugated roof which towers above ordinary dwellings. It is one of the largest churches on the river. Both it and the nearby mission house where the lay pastor and his family live were built by the local congregation. In front of the church and the mission house is a large open area known as the churchyard, where religious plays are sometimes performed, children play games, and adults congregate after church and in the evenings. This space forms the center of the village. The Iglesia church is a much smaller structure and is located off to one side, near the village center. The only other non-residential buildings are the school, the commissary, and a medical clinic built after I left the village.

Definitions of Asang

By way of introduction to our analysis of Asang we may note that the community can be identified and described structurally from several points of view. More specifically, we can recognize four spheres of organization, each of which may be called Asang, depending on the circumstances. These are, respectively, Asang as a site, as a political entity, as a social unit, and as a set of religious congregations. This fourfold division is not only a useful heuristic device of the investigator, but corresponds to observable realities.

First, Asang has physical or geographical identity as a cleared area of land which is separated from other communities by stretches of bush and plantation.[12] This is the Asang pointed out by any traveler who passes the settlement on the river. It is a unity based on geographical location alone, i.e., Asang as a site.

Second, the site contains a population involved in communal activities by virtue of common residence. This is Asang in the political sense. It is legitimate to make a distinction between population and place if for no other reason than that the people of Asang see a difference. For example, statements such as "Yes, this is a nice town, but the people are bad (gossips, greedy)" are not uncommon.

Political Asang is composed of all those who have been born in the village, and are still living there, plus those who have married into the community.[13] These affines are village members only in the political sense. In Miskito society, the individual who lives in a community as affine always retains his or her social identity with the kin group in the village of his birth, both in his opinion and in the opinion of others, no matter how long he has lived within his spouse's village. One of the best examples of this position was provided by a family head who, in response to my queries, said his community was not Asang, but San Carlos, several miles downriver. I asked how long he had been staying at Asang. "Twenty-five years," was the reply.

Asang as a political unit is visible at times of community-wide activity such as funeral preparations, periodic village clean-up days, or holidays. All people currently living in Asang, whether by birth or marriage, are expected to participate together in these activities because they involve the good of the entire community. This political unit is also the Asang recognized by the Nicaraguan government. The village, as seen by these outsiders, is defined as all people currently living at that place. Its unity is represented in the per-

12. The term plantation as used here and elsewhere throughout this report is the local English word referring to the small plots of land cleared and cultivated by the Miskito. The Miskito term is *insla*. Plantation here definitely does not have the more familiar connotation of a large, often market-oriented estate.

13. There are in addition to those born in Asang and their spouses, "strangers" such as the four Nicaraguan schoolteachers. These particular foreigners are not considered to be part of the political unit of Asang because, although resident there, they did not participate in community activities. The Miskito also tended to exclude them from their concept of "Asang." The Creole husband of a Miskito woman, on the other hand, is considered part of Asang in the political sense because he took an active part in village affairs.

son of the *wita,* a Miskito resident of Asang, who acts as the official
government representative in the village, as the secular leader and
judge of the community, and as the official contact between Asang
and the national state. His authority extends over all who reside
there, regardless of their origins.

The residents of Asang also conceptualize the village as a unit in
reference to the outside or non-Asang world. This category includes
both other Miskito and all non-Miskito under the general heading
of "strangers." This concept of political unity can reach out, however, to include people on temporary leave—men working at the
mines, or husbands who have deserted their Asang wives. When I
took a village census I was told that my figures were not complete
until I had made allowance for these absentees who were still considered part of the political community. (Such individuals, however, are not in the same category as people born in Asang who now
reside permanently in another village as affines.) In day to day affairs, however, political Asang does not take these absentees into account. It is the population knit together by common activities within
the geographically defined boundaries that is significant for community events and that forms a unit: *"yawon* Asang *uplika nani"*—we,
the people of Asang, facing the non-Asang world.

From the third point of view Asang can be identified as groups
of people related to each other through kinship. In this sense the
village loses a common unity and is seen instead as composed of
many *kiamps*—kinship groups to which an individual belongs by
virtue of having the same family name.[14] Because of the pattern of
marital residence, the *kiamps* tend to occupy separate geographical
locations within the village. Members of one *kiamp* are tied to various members of the other *kiamps* through marriage, the extension
of classificatory kinship terms, and/or ritual kin ties. In addition,
as we shall see, the separate kin groups are crosscut and thereby
connected by common age and sex categories as well as by personal
friendships. In this way Asang does become a social unit.

However, the boundaries of this Asang are hazy since some members of the *kiamp* have taken up residence in other towns as affines.
These permanent absentees, whom we noted were not particularly
important in contributing to the political unity of Asang, are essen-

14. The plural of all Miskito nouns is formed by adding *nani* to the singular; for example, *kiamp nani.* For ease in reading I have anglicized the plural
forms by suffixing *s* to the singular.

tial to its social organization because, along with non-kin-based friendships, they form major ties that link the people of Asang with other Miskito villages. In the same way, affines living in Asang are the local representatives of *kiamps* in their respective villages. Seen in this light Asang becomes one more vital link in the series of connected villages which constitute "Miskitodom." This social definition of Asang is perhaps the most meaningful to the inhabitants of the village, and is least understood by outsiders.

The final area of organization found in Asang is ecclesiastical. There are two missions with representative congregations in the village—the Moravian, which includes almost the entire village, at least nominally, and the Iglesia de Dios, which is composed of four household heads, three wives, and their children who have broken away from the Moravian church. From the Miskito point of view, his membership in one or the other congregation gives him ties with all other congregations of that denomination. Thus, the activities of the Moravians in San Carlos or Santa Izabel or even in distant Puerto Cabezas become of interest to the Asang congregation and vice versa. Likewise, the Iglesia members feel a commonality with Iglesia congregations in other villages. Sometimes the cross-community ties become even stronger as is the case within the Asang Moravian church which formally includes not only people resident in Asang but also some from the neighboring community of Yiasco. In the eyes of foreign missionaries, to mention Asang is to refer to their congregation there, which, as far as the Moravians are concerned, would include people of Yiasco, but exclude the members of Asang who have joined the Church of God.

Thus, there are four ways in which to refer to Asang: as a site on the river, as a political unit, as a group of kin units, and as congregations. The definition being used by any one individual will depend on who he is (Miskito or non-Miskito) and the context of the situation. In actuality, of course, all four Asangs are interwoven to make a functioning whole.

It is worthy of note that none of these definitions is economic. The reason is simple: the economic unit is usually the nuclear family, and in terms of identifying the major units which constitute Asang, the nuclear family becomes part of the larger *kiamp,* to which it is tied by social, rather than strictly economic mechanisms. In terms of individual dealings (mostly with the outside world, but sometimes within the village), economic relations may certainly be primary. There is no meaningful way, however, by which Asang can be defined as a permanent and organized economic unit, or even a set of such units. In economic terms, there is no larger Asang, only an aggregate of unrelated nuclear families.

We can summarize by noting that strangers, both Miskito and non-Miskito, looking at Asang from the outside tend to define the village as a combination of the geographical and the residential political units, and sometimes as religious units. In the same way, Asang residents utilize the geographical-political unity concept when dealing as a group with the non-Asang world. Similarly, when Asang residents leave their village, they speak of being members of Asang, using the word in the geographical-political sense, or sometimes in the congregational sense if they are speaking to other Christians.

Although this unity concept is strongest when directed outside the community, it can be found operating within the village at times of common participation in such events as funerals or holidays. However, this internal unity is revealed only on specific occasions. Everyday life in Asang is centered around the village as a social and religious unit, which, in effect, means seeing Asang not as a unit at all, but rather in terms of households, groups of relatives and friends, or, if church is in session, as congregations or segments of congregations. However, as we shall see in the following chapter, those rules of social organization that operate to blur the social outlines of Asang by creating intervillage ties are weakening. It seems likely, if the trend continues, that Asang will become increasingly self-contained as a social unit with perhaps only religious links to other Miskito communities.

3

The Social Framework

THE VILLAGE of Asang was founded about 1910. The family which was to form the core of the new village had been driven from its original home, Kaharu, by a flood, and had moved to a new location which turned out to be unpleasantly muddy in rainy weather. Consequently, it was decided that Asang's high bank would be a more desirable location. At that time the sandy spit that now fronts the village did not exist, and the river flowed deep and rapidly there. Such dangerous river areas were thought of as homes for evil spirits called *lasas*, who caused canoes to founder and people to drown. Therefore, in order to make the place habitable, it was first necessary for a shaman to exorcise the malevolent spirits. After this was done, patches of bush were cleared, and a few houses built. From a modest beginning of three huts, the village has grown to its present size of ninety households. Similarly, the reputation of the population has changed from that of "the dirtiest and laziest Indians of the Upper Wangks," as the first missionary to the region uncharitably described them (J. Hamilton 1920:19), to a group widely known for its exceptional "Christian" living and strong village pride.

Village Founders

The nucleus of the village formed around five daughters (one of whom was adopted) and two sons of a Miskito man surnamed Bobb (Fig. 10). However, the actual clearing of the site is accredited to the husband of one daughter, Jesús George, who therefore is said to have "created" Asang. *Dama* ("respected elder") George became the most influential Miskito member of the new community, serving as a famed arbiter of disputes and instigating missionary activities a few years later.

57

Jesús George and the Bobb sisters and brothers were Miskito, but the backgrounds of several of the sisters' spouses illustrate well the mixing of Miskito women with non-Miskito men which has been a definitive characteristic of the Miskito in general since the origins of the population in the seventeenth century. It is also understandable in this light why the present residents of Asang, who consider themselves Miskito ethnically, attribute the origins of the community specifically to the Bobb sisters and brothers along with *Dama* George; these were the original Miskito members of the village.

One sister was, of course, married to Jesús George, but another, Dora, was one of two Miskito wives (the second was named Fanny) of an Englishman, Coleman, who originally came from Cornwall. Before coming to Asang, *Dama* Coleman, as he was known, had cattle holdings and operated a general store near San

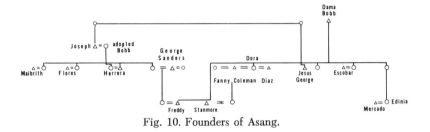

Fig. 10. Founders of Asang.

Carlos, a short distance downriver from Asang. After Coleman's death Dora married a Nicaraguan surnamed Diaz, reportedly from Managua. One of the Bobb brothers, Stanmore, who was still alive in 1965, later married a daughter of Coleman and Fanny.

A third sister married a Spanish-speaking Honduranean named Marcus Escobar, while the only child, a daughter, of a fourth sister whose husband had deserted her prior to the move to Asang, married a Spanish-speaking merchant of Jewish extraction, Clarence Mercado. (This woman, Edinia, is at present the oldest living woman in the village.) *Dama* Mercado and *Dama* Escobar are credited with introducing techniques of lumbering, house building, and rice cultivation to the village. The fifth sister, who was adopted, married a Miskito man surnamed Joseph, a cousin of *Dama* George, who also was still living at the time this study was made.

The second Bobb brother, Freddy, married the daughter of yet another foreigner who settled in Asang not long after its founding.

This man, George William Sanders, was an American Negro origi-nally from Ohio. He was involved in mahogany lumbering and also owned a chain of three commissaries along the river, one of which came to be located in Asang. *Dama* Sanders had two Miskito wives, one of whom, surnamed Herrera, had several sisters who also settled in Asang with their spouses (at least one of whom was a non-Miskito Honduranean), and a brother who married a daughter of *Dama* Joseph.

Other men with wives and children, usually single nuclear fami-lies, gradually arrived, attracted by Asang's excellent location and often having kinship ties with those already there. Most of these people were Miskito, although at least two Creole men eventually settled in the village and married Miskito women. One engages in agriculture and other economic pursuits as a Miskito; the other sup-ports himself and his family by operating a small commissary.

However, the large majority of Asang's residents are related through at least one parent either to the original Bobb brothers and sisters (including the adopted daughter), forty of whose children have remained in Asang, or to the Sanders-Herrera families (*Dama* Sanders had ten children; his wife's brother and sisters had seven-teen children living in Asang). Through the intermarriage of mem-bers of these two family groupings, both between groups and with others who have settled in Asang over the years, the village has grown to its present size.

Figure 11 presents the population breakdown as of spring, 1965. It should be noted that the age of persons above thirty-five can only be roughly estimated. The Miskito do not celebrate birthdays and generally do not pay much attention to adult age. Mothers, how-ever, usually know the ages of their young children, and young adults are also fairly sure of their age. Therefore, the population breakdown from zero to thirty-five years is probably accurate.

Statuses: Age and Consanguineal Kin

This population regulates its activities and behavior through channels provided by the social organization of the village, which we will interpret as an example of Miskito social organization in general. First of all, Miskito society contains social positions or sta-tuses in terms of which all persons are categorized. These categories are based primarily on "age" in the sense of physiological develop-ment and the social status of parenthood, and, secondarily, sometimes indicate sex. The categories are: *tukta* (child); *tiara* (adolescent girl); *wahma* (adolescent boy); *almuk* (adult). A "child" is one who has not yet reached puberty, regardless of chronological age. *Wahma* and *tiara* are those who are physiologically adult, but who have not yet established a family unit, that is, have not yet produced at least one child, preferably several, and shown adult sta-

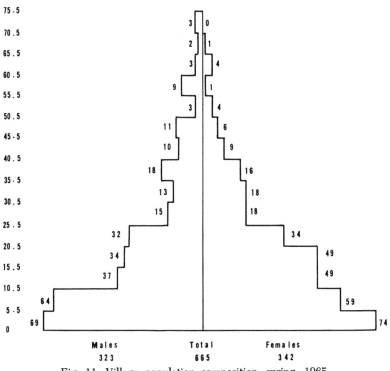

Fig. 11. Village population composition, spring, 1965.

bility in accepting the responsibilities of running a household. *Almuk* includes all those who not only have children, but have also shown themselves to be responsible householders and have indicated a serious concern with the affairs of the village.

The terminology also reflects other features characteristic of these statuses. Children as a group seem carefree, unconcerned with the worries of adults. From the point of view of older people, they form a single, sexually undifferentiated category, although sometimes there is terminological distinction between *tukta waikna,* man child, and *tukta mairin,* woman child. However, a separation is made between boys and girls in the nature of the tasks they are taught, and the children themselves tend to play in groups of the same sex.

Only those statuses referring to adolescents, *tiara* and *wahma,* are always given terminological distinction in terms of sex. It is during these years that the distinction between sexes is most important and apparent, for these are the years of courtship. It is also a period of insecurity, especially for girls. This is observed in the need for close physical contact between *tiaras.* When several go walking in the evening, for example, they inevitably hold hands, link arms, or put their arms around each other's waists. This close physical contact contrasts sharply with the usual Miskito inhibition toward physical contact in public. It may be understood as a seeking of reassurance among young women who soon expect to marry and hope for the best, but who are aware of the subordinate position and often difficult life accorded to wives in this society, and who regard men in general as potentially untrustworthy.

Almuks or adults, both men and women, share a common position in that they are concerned with managing and directing the everyday life of families and community. To a great extent their duties are complementary, so that while men kill a pig, women cook it, men cut firewood but women carry it, men cut rice and women gather it into bunches. Therefore, they form a single working category of adults.

These social positions are given a certain amount of day-by-day recognition through the use of various terms of reference and address. Within Miskito society, individuals are addressed or referred to by personal names (often used in conjunction with a kinship term as in "sister [*moini*] Diane"), nicknames, or teknonymic devices, depending on the situation. Teknonymy, the practice of referring to an adult after the name of his or her child, is regarded as the most proper or "Miskito" way to refer to persons, and is also the terminological category which tends to express society-wide statuses.

However, it is not necessarily the type of reference term used most often by everyone. Adult men and adolescent boys more often use first names, especially when dealing with other men. Women, on the other hand, prefer teknonymy. Thus, when a woman is speaking to someone about another woman, she will usually refer to her as "so-and-so *momika* (mother of so-and-so)," and when speaking of a man, as "so-and-so *popika* (father of so-and-so)." Both men and women are also referred to as "so-and-so *maia* (spouse of so-and-so)." When talking with close female friends or relatives, though, women also may use first names or nicknames when referring to absent adults, and this practice tends to give a feeling of informality to these conversations. However, women address each other directly by kinship terms.

Tiaras, wahmas, and *tuktas* are referred to and addressed by their personal names or more often by nicknames. *Tiaras* and *wahmas* in turn use personal names or nicknames when referring to and addressing others within their own social category, but are expected to refer to all adults by the proper teknonymic term. However, here again kinship terms are used in direct address to adults. Once more it is the children and *tiaras* rather than *wahmas* who are most conscientious about carrying out the practice of teknonymy. Men in general are more familiar and more at ease with the use of personal names than are women. Conzemius (1932:106) notes the same situation in the early decades of the twentieth century and attributes it to men's wider contacts in non-Miskito society through temporary jobs away from home "working in the mahogany camps, gold mines, and other enterprises, where they had to give their name in order to be distinguished from the other laborers. . . ." However, men, too, sometimes use teknonymy, particularly when speaking of "so-and-so *maia* (spouse)."

Among adults the child named in the teknonymic reference is generally the oldest, but among *tiaras* and between an adult and a *tiara* the person named is often the individual closest in age to, if not part of, the category of *tiara*. Children and adults addressing children tend to do the same, naming another child in the reference. Thus, the same individual could be referred to by several teknonymic references, depending on the speakers. For example, the woman of the household where the anthropologist lived would be referred to as "Edwin *momika*" (her eldest child) by other adults, sometimes as "Florrie *momika*" by young girls, or as "David *momika*" by small boys. As wife of the lay pastor she was also often addressed and referred to as "*Sasmalkra maia*" (lay pastor's wife).

We can also say that *tiaras* and *tuktas* give verbal recognition to their own social categories by identification of persons outside those categories through the relationship of these outsiders to someone within. The freedom of adults to refer to those younger, *tiaras*, *wahmas*, and *tuktas*, by personal names or nicknames shows a separation of society from their point of view into adult and nonadult spheres. In the same way, for one adult to use teknonymic references towards another indicates the "adultness" of the second through mention of his or her being a parent or spouse.

These separate sociocentric statuses are woven into a single social unit through the kinship system. It is via kinship that most interpersonal conduct is defined. Even in those situations, mostly of an economic character, where contract becomes the basis for interac-

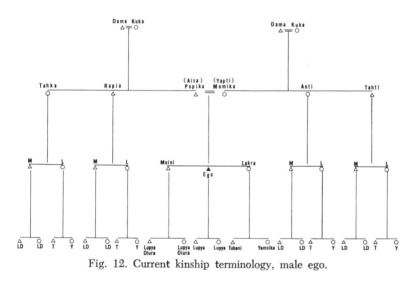

Fig. 12. Current kinship terminology, male ego.

tion, the potential impersonality and harshness of the relationships is softened by adding a veneer of kinship-based obligations (see chapter 4).

At the present time, the kinship system is characterized by Hawaiian cousin terminology with bifurcate collateral terminology in the parental generation. In other words, the terms for brother and sister are extended to all cousins, while individual terms are given to mother, mother's sister, mother's brother, father, father's sister, and father's brother. Figure 12 contains the basic terms if ego is male. If ego is a female, the terminology is changed slightly as illustrated in Figure 13.

First, it will be noted that the usage of *moini* and *lakra* by a woman is the reverse of their use by a man. That is to say, a male will address a woman of the same generation with the proper form of *lakra* and a man of the same generation as *moini*, whereas a woman will address another woman of the same generation as *moini* and use a form of *lakra* when addressing a man of her generation. A simpler way of saying this is that *moini* merely means "person of my sex and generation," whereas *lakra* means "person of opposite sex but same generation." Second, the terms for a *lakra*'s children vary depending on ego's sex. Whereas a male ego uses *yamsika* to identify his *lakra*'s daughter and *tubani* for her sons, a

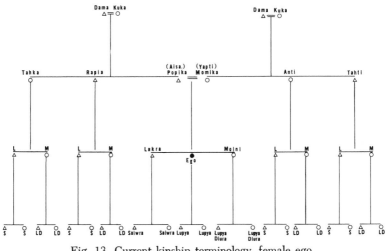

Fig. 13. Current kinship terminology, female ego.

female ego uses a single term, *saiwra*, for both son and daughter of a *lakra*. Ego, whether male or female, distinguishes his or her *lakra*'s children terminologically from the children of a *moini*. All children of the latter are termed *lupya diura*.

Some kinship terms are extended beyond the immediate range of known relatives to include a wider group. This holds true particularly for the terms for grandmother (*kuka*) and grandfather (*dama*). Proper etiquette requires a younger person to refer to and address any elderly individual as *kuka* or *dama* to indicate respect. That is to say, the terms are used to address all persons who are in a society-wide status of "elder," which may be defined as those who are generally no longer expected to carry out the entire range of adult activities. Thus, the categories of *kuka* and *dama* denote the upper limits of the general status of adult (*almuk*) although the words themselves are also kinship terms.

Another category of kinship terms which is widely used is that of *muli* or grandchild, by which term an elderly person usually addresses anyone considerably younger than himself. Again, as in the case of the society-wide use of *kuka* and *dama,* this is a kinship term used in such a way as to at least theoretically unite all Miskito within a single web of relationship.

The third set of kinship terms that is also extended to include a wider range of persons is *moini* and *lakra.* Theoretically, any children of ego's parents' *moini* and *lakra* are also by definition his (ego's) *moini* and *lakra.* This means that almost anyone of ego's own generation could be his *moini* or *lakra* because ego's parents' *moini* and *lakra* include not only their full and half siblings, but also a wide range of cousins, or, in other words, all the children of all the people that their parents (ego's grandparents) called *moini* or *lakra.* Because of the shallowness of the present descent reckoning system (not more than three generations above ego), the exact relationship between ego and the person he is addressing may not be known. However, the supposition is that at one time their respective ancestors were likely to have been *moini* and/or *lakra,* and so it is polite and respectful for persons of the same generation to address each other by those terms now, even if they are strangers. When taken to its logical extreme, this system is seen to unite all Miskito into a network of mutual "brotherhood" or "sisterhood."

In addition to indicating exact genealogical relationships in some cases or polite behavior in others, the use of *moini* and *lakra* also has a religious connotation. Traditionally, members of the Moravian church have used the terms brother and sister when addressing other church members. This practice has carried over into the mission fields, and in the case of the Miskito fits in well with the kinship-based *moini* and *lakra* terminology. Since the Moravians were the first and most successful missionaries in the area, Moravian use of these terms is widespread and has become a mark of Christianity, at least of the Moravian sort, among the Miskito.

It might be expected that similarly wide use would be accorded other kinship terms such as *tahti* (MoBr), *anti* (MoSi), *rapia* (FaBr), and *tahka* (FaSi). However, this is not the case. These terms are restricted to those persons of the generation older than ego whose actual genealogical relationship to him can be traced. The reason for this might be that, due to large families, the terms used to distinguish people of two formally adjacent generations can easily be used between people of the same biological age. For example, two Asang girls, each age sixteen, address each other as *anti* (MoSi) and *lupya diura* (Si child), respectively. However, when strangers meet there is no way for them to establish exact relationships outside of direct genealogical reckoning which is usually out of the question. If one is obviously considerably older than the other, the terms of respect between old and young will be used (*kuka, dama, muli*), or, if the two are roughly the same age, the mutual use of *moini* or *lakra* may be brought into play.

It is difficult to put an exact limit on the collateral extension of genealogically based kin ties, but in general the functioning limit would seem to stop at about third cousins. The boundary is hazy because the Miskito themselves attribute varying strength or "closeness" to kin ties, depending on the nature of the genealogical relationship. Full siblings consider themselves to be "closer" to each other than half-siblings, and half-siblings are "closer" to each other than to the children of an *anti* or *rapia*, although all these people stand in the relationship of *moini* or *lakra* one to the other. Eventually a point is reached where calculation of exact relationships fades into use of *moini* and *lakra* in the wider sense of politeness, or in the context of religious affiliation.

Geographical distance may also be a factor in determining who are "counted" as known kinsmen. If a person related to ego lives in a nearby village or in the same village, their relationship, even if rather distant, will be calculated and given recognition through use of the proper kinship terms. However, if relatives live some distance from ego's village, chances are that they or at least their children will eventually enter the category of "strangers" even if they are genealogically as closely related to ego as people in his own village. An example of this was given by an informant when she said: "When my grandfather was alive our relatives from downriver came to visit him, but after he died the visits stopped. I myself don't know these people. I'm thinking I should look them up sometime."

This geographical factor can hold even within the same village. Informants volunteered that closer ties of friendship and mutual obligation often develop between two individuals who live in close proximity as neighbors, than between them and a third party who lives on the other side of the village even though the same kinship relationships are involved and, therefore, the same obligations exist. This holds true particularly for women, whose daily round of activities includes the same kitchen, the nearest spring, the same neighbors, the same path to the plantation week after week, month after month. To walk to another section of the village on some particular errand can bring them into territory that is somewhat unfamiliar, and at such times they seem vaguely uncomfortable. In one rather extreme case, the lay pastor's wife, who was not native to Asang, claimed that in her three years of residence in the community she had never seen a small stream that ran along the west edge of the village, and that was used by women in that neighborhood for washing dishes and clothes. In this context it would sometimes be remarked to the anthropologist that, in contrast, she seemed to know all the landmarks and to feel at home anywhere in the village.

The system of kinship terms in use today has been in effect only fifty years or less. From studies by the Rev. George Heath (1927), entries in various dictionaries (Ziock 1894; Heath and Marx 1961), and data obtained from Asang informants, it is possible to reconstruct successive steps in the process of terminological change (Fig. 14).

One basic change has occurred in the loss of a terminological distinction between cross and parallel cousins. Certain of the oldest residents of Asang, people perhaps seventy years old or more, were able to define the cross-cousin terms, and said that they could remember their parents using them. It seems, however, that usage was discontinued prior to the founding of Asang since none of the younger generations know the words, much less the meanings.

One elderly informant attributed the extension of parallel terms to cross cousins to the influence of the Moravians, saying that after her parents became Christians the children were no longer taught the cross-cousin terminology. It is interesting to note that by the turn of the century, when cross-parallel distinctions seem to have been weakening, Moravians had been working on the Coast for approximately fifty years. An entire generation would have been born and reached adulthood in this period. Those who were influenced by Moravianism might well have begun to adopt the broad Moravian usage of "brother-sister" terms, perhaps with a corresponding tendency to de-emphasize the cross-cousin distinctions.

However, in light of evidence from other societies, it is likely that

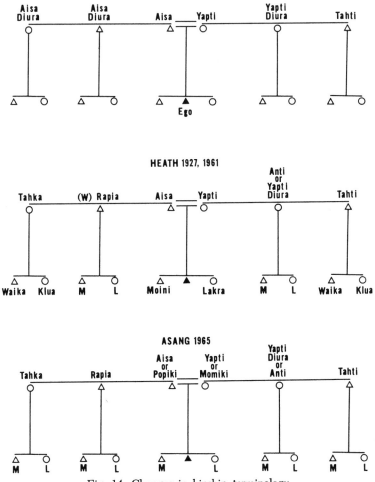

Fig. 14. Changes in kinship terminology.

factors other than missionary teachings played a role in effecting
this change. In general, it appears that when generational cousin
terminology (i.e., no cross-parallel distinctions) is found in egalitarian, nonranked societies such as the Miskito, it often correlates with
depopulation, social disruption, and population dislocation due to
Western contact (cf. Dole 1957; Service 1962:137, 139). There is
evidence on the Miskito Coast for limited depopulation due to dis-

ease in the eighteenth and nineteenth centuries (see chap. 1n20). The literature also reports missionary attempts at population resettlement around mission stations in the latter half of the nineteenth century. In addition, the turn of the century was a period of economic reorientation, and it is quite possible that the increased dependence on wage labor provided impetus for social adjustment. Unfortunately, a detailed reconstruction of pressures and reactions is not possible. Yet it seems likely that the loss of cross-parallel cousin terms and the resulting generational terminology is the result of all these factors.

Terminological changes in the first ascendant generation show several stages, the latest of which is still going on. The dropping of *aisa diura* in the category of "father's *moini*" (Br) occurred about the turn of the century.[1] The change from *yapti diura* to *anti* for "mother's *moini*" (Si) is currently in progress. At present people use both *anti* and *yapti diura* as terms of reference, but only *anti* as a term of address. The word *anti* itself strongly suggests a borrowing from English.

There are also, at the present time, two sets of terms for mother and father. The strictly Miskito terms of *yapti* and *aisa*, respectively, are not heard as often as *momiki* and *popiki*. Differential usage of these sets is not distinguishable in terms of reference versus address, but rather in the sense of formal versus informal situations. For example, the lay pastor will use *yapti* for solemn occasions such as burials or when preaching, or people will use the term when they are obviously trying to be very "Miskito," for example to impress the anthropologist. In everyday conversation, however, *momiki* and *popiki* are heard much more often than *yapti* and *aisa*.

Changes have also taken place in the dimension of generational depth. Again, it is only the oldest residents of Asang who remember the terms for great-grandparent, great-great-grandparent, and great-great-great-grandparent. These terms were reciprocal, that is, could also be applied to great-grandchildren, et cetera. Today, as older informants emphasized and independent investigation sub-

1. According to Heath (1927:81), *diura* is "an old word . . . meaning either 'moini' or 'lakra.'" Thus *lupya diura,* applied by ego to his *moini*'s children, translates as "(my) child's *moini/lakra.*" *Yapti diura* becomes "mother's *moini*." There is no evidence that *yapti diura* was ever applied to "mother's *lakra.*" Mother's full consanguineal sister was also referred to as *yapti sirpi,* i.e., "little mother." *Aisa diura* translates as "father's *moini*." As Figure 14 shows, the term was once extended to father's *lakra* (father's sister).

stantiated, the terms are not used. *Kuka* and *dama* for elders and *muli* for the very young are all that are heard.[2]

The loss of these terms seems related to the fact that at the present time it is highly unlikely that more than four generations of relatives will be alive at any one time, if Asang is at all typical. This situation in turn is the result of girls marrying at a later age. Before missionary influence became widespread, girls were married when they reached puberty, at about twelve years of age (Young 1847: 75; Crowe 1850:246; Conzemius 1932:147), and presumably soon produced offspring. It would then be quite possible to have at least four and probably five or more generations alive at the same time, depending on the average life span. Missionary influence and economic hardships have led many people to postpone marriage today until the girl is about eighteen or twenty.[3] The number of generations alive at one time is then reduced, assuming no corresponding increase in life span, for which there is no evidence. Consequently, there is not much use today for terms beyond those for grandparent-grandchild. In the few cases in Asang where there is a situation of great-grandparent and great-grandchild, the terms for grandparent and grandchild are used.[4]

Another set of status terms' has also become obsolete within the last fifty or sixty years. Again only the elders of the village remember these terms and their meanings. The words in question are a

2. Great-grandparent (child), *snawika*; great-great-grandparent (child), *usbaika*; great-great-great-grandparent (child), *plakbaika*; ancestor, *srakia*.

Several collateral terms referring to children of *waika* and *klua* and to children of grandparents' siblings have also been lost in the last half century. Asang informants did not know these terms, although the relationships in question are still counted. According to Heath (1927:83), children of a *waika* or *klua* were termed *lupyakuya*. Today these people are termed *lupya diura*, *yamsi*, or *tubani*, since their parents are now termed *moini* and *lakra* by ego. Similarly, Heath defines *aisakuya* as "[ego's] father's 'waika' or [ego's] mother's 'klua,'" and *yaptikuya* as "[ego's] mother's 'kauhkiya' or [ego's] father's 'klua.'" (*Kauhkiya* or *kauhka* was the former term for a female ego's MoBrDa or FaSiDa, i.e., the female ego's equivalent of the male ego's *waika*.) Today these people are termed *tahti*, *anti*, *rapia*, or *tahka* because, under the present system, they are ego's parents' *moini* and *lakra*. Finally, the term *dinma*, defined by Heath (1927:82) as "a man's sister's daughter's child; and vice versa a maternal grandmother's brother" is not used. These relatives are termed *muli* and *dama*, respectively, today.

3. "Boys under 18 and girls under 14 years of age cannot be married by us" (Moravian Church 1898:22).

4. Loss of kin terms for persons more than three or four generations apart could also indicate a shortening in depth of genealogical reckoning. There is no evidence, however, for or against this supposition.

series of expressions which were applied to individuals upon the death of certain close relatives, such as parents, *moini, lakra,* children, or they were used to indicate the position of an individual within his family. Only two of these terms are still in use: *plaisni,* used affectionately as a term of address to the youngest child of the family, most of whose relatives are now deceased; and *piarka,* meaning "one whose spouse has died."[5]

In addition to the ascribed statuses of kinship, age, and sex already discussed, there are several achieved positions in Miskito society which are held by only a few individuals at any one time. One of these is that of the *sukya* or shaman. There are no shamans in Asang because the villagers are very conscious of forming a Christian community. Farther upriver, however, where the church is less influential, and downriver, where contact has been going on the longest, shamans and related types can still be found. These individuals today operate mostly as curers and some are highly skilled bush doctors. In pre-Christian times they were also curers, but were thought to hold their power through contact with the supernatural rather than simply through knowledge of local herbal remedies. At that time they also were able to placate spiritual beings and claimed control over the elements to some degree.

Within the organization of the mission church, regardless of denomination, the status of lay pastor has been added to Miskito society. Among the Moravians at least, this position is called by the Miskito term *sasmalkra,* meaning teacher. There is one lay pastor per congregation. An individual achieves this position after completing a period of instruction at the church training institute downriver.

The final position to be noted is that of village headman or *wita.* This post had an earlier counterpart in the person to whom individuals would refer quarrels for settlement. Now it is seen mainly as providing a channel for formal interaction between villagers and representatives of the national Nicaraguan government. The headman may continue, however, to settle local disputes if people re-

5. Other terms, no longer used, include: *sukrika,* used between parents who have lost a child; *wailankra mairin,* younger sister to older when a parent has died; *kamkabaira,* one *moini* to another after the death of a third (*moini* or *lakra*)—the term *ungabra* was also used in these circumstances; *raukasaura,* a child whose parents and *moini* have died (literally, badly orphaned).

The reader should also consult Heath (1927:80–85) for an extensive list of kinship terms and definitions.

spect his judgment. The job today is obtained from the government, although the village may replace the incumbent headman with another, if the new candidate's qualifications satisfy the government. The basic prerequisite for the post is the ability to read, write, and converse in passable Spanish.

Groups

The social structure of Asang is composed of three types of groups: *taya,* the *kiamp,* and the nuclear family or household. All these groups are kinship based. *Taya* is a general term referring to all persons considered to be ego's relatives. This includes people resident in Asang and elsewhere. *Taya* can be best described as a loose kindred, since it includes all living descendants of ego's father's parents and of their siblings and half-siblings, of ego's mother's parents and of their siblings and half-siblings, and of ego's great-grandparents, both maternal and paternal, (who are usually deceased). *Taya* thus includes all living relatives to a distance of third cousin from ego. It is interesting to note that those *taya* who are traced to the great-grandparental generation are more often traced to the women of that generation, that is ego's great-grandmothers, than to his great-grandfathers.

The *kiamp* involves only part of the *taya,* specifically, all living descendants of a pair identified by the last name of the male, as, for example, the Bobb *kiamp.* From ego's point of view, he is a member of his father's *kiamp,* as will be his children as they continue use of his name. However, anyone whose father was not originally from Asang, but whose mother was, a not uncommon situation, will also be considered members of their mother's (i.e., mother's father's) *kiamp.* For example, Prida, a young girl whose mother is from Asang, but whose father came from Wasla, a Miskito village downriver, commented that Wasla people consider her to be of her father's *kiamp,* while Asang people consider her to belong to her mother's as well as to her father's *kiamp.* She herself acknowledges both. In such cases, however, the father's surname, and thus his *kiamp,* are still the official marks of family and personal identity.

Currently there are twenty-seven *kiamps* recognized in Asang. More specifically, there are twenty-seven surnames each of which, note, is held by several people who are adults or near-adults and who are related consanguineally. The minimum unit is a father and his adolescent child or children, or, should the father be deceased, the children alone, provided that they are approaching adulthood.

Potential new *kiamps* are introduced to the village when an Asang woman marries a non-Asang man who then takes up residence in Asang, and whose family has not been represented previously. As long as this couple is childless, or has only one or two small children, the family is not considered to represent a new Asang *kiamp*, because only the husband represents the name consanguineally as an adult there. (The wife will always belong to her father's *kiamp*.) Only after this individual's family is well established, with the children well past the dangers of babyhood, will he begin to be recognized as representing a new *kiamp* in Asang. Currently there are seven such new or growing units in the village.

The size and generational depth of any one *kiamp* depends on the number of sons born to the family. If boys are born and reach adulthood in each generation, the *kiamp* continues to flourish, "as new banana shoots branch off the parent stock," as one informant put it. However, if no sons are born, the *kiamp* cannot endure, but will end "as a tree is cut down" with the death of the last daughter.

However, no Asang *kiamp* extends lineally beyond ego's great-grandparents. This genealogical depth ties in with the custom of not mentioning the name of a deceased individual in ordinary conversation, which serves to limit genealogical calculations effectively since new members born into a family rarely learn of specific deceased ancestors beyond grandparents, possibly great-grandparents. Thus, when people refer to the Bobb *kiamp* they trace its origin to *Dama* Bobb, the deceased father of the five sisters and two brothers (all deceased except one brother). But the *kiamp* name really is held only by those people surnamed Bobb who are alive today. This includes *Dama* Stanmore Bobb, his children and sons' children, and the daughters, sons, and sons' children of Freddy Bobb.

Presently the Bobb *kiamp* covers three generations of living adults, and contains nine units of father and children, along with the sisters of these men. Five *kiamps* cover two adult generations. One contains two father-child units, two contain three such units, one (Joseph) contains five units, and one (Sanders) contains seven father-child units, in addition to sisters of the fathers. Twenty-one of Asang's *kiamps* cover only one adult generation today. Fifteen of these have only one unit of father-children, three have two such units, two contain three units, and one contains five father-child units, along, of course, with any sisters of the men.

Within the village the oldest and largest *kiamps*—specifically the Sanders, Joseph, and Bobb—are conceptualized geographically to some extent (Fig. 15). At present not all members of these *kiamps* live in the general area thought of as being their *kiamp's* territory. Marriage has scattered some *kiamp* members widely throughout the village. Yet due to a prevailing tendency for daughters and, increasingly, sons, to set up housekeeping near the residence of their parents if at all possible, many of *Dama* Sanders' children and grandchildren still live toward the northern end of the village, where the original Sanders home was located. South of the Sanders',

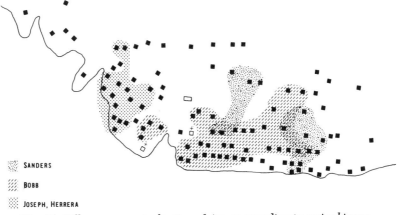

SANDERS

BOBB

JOSEPH, HERRERA

Fig. 15. Villagers conceptualization of Asang according to major *kiamps*.

where their parents first built their homes, are found many sons and daughters of the original Bobb sisters and brothers. Technically, of course, only the brothers and their descendants carry the name of Bobb today. The children of the Bobb sisters carry their respective father's names—George, Escobar, Coleman, Diaz, Mercado.[6] However, here again along with the official *kiamp* tie, named for non-Asang men, some of whom were also non-Miskito, the link with the Bobb sisters, original Miskito settlers of Asang, is also remembered. Through a similar process the section still farther south, beyond the churches, is heavily settled by Joseph *kiamp* members (*Dama* Joseph's wife was a Bobb by adoption), and by descendants of *Dama*

6. *Dama* Mercado's wife, *Kuka* Edinia, is considered a Bobb in this general sense by the villagers because her mother, one of the Bobb sisters, was deserted by her husband (Edinia's father) before the move to Asang, when Edinia was still a child.

Sanders' in-laws, the Herrera sisters and brother (who married a Joseph). See Figure 10.

Newer, generally smaller *kiamps,* whose original members came to Asang after it was founded in order to marry Asang women or as relatives to those already there, are not accorded geographical locations as readily. Rather, through affinal ties to the older *kiamps* which originally divided Asang among themselves, they are likely to be considered with one or another of the established groups. For example, the sons and daughters of *Dama* James Kittle belong to the Kittle *kiamp.* Yet because *Dama* James' wife is a daughter of *Dama* Coleman and Dora Bobb, villagers place the Kittle *kiamp* with the Coleman and, ultimately, the Bobb in terms of its position in the community (the Kittles live at one end of the Bobb complex). Consequently, although twenty-seven *kiamps* are currently represented in Asang, residents still view the community to a large extent in terms of the original division of the village between Bobbs (with Josephs) and Sanders-Herreras.

As with *taya,* the *kiamp* functions only as a reference group. It serves no corporate purpose. It does not hold property, officially adjudicate disputes, nor hold ceremonies.[7] Yet to function simply as a reference group can be important for the structuring of society. As we have seen, Miskito postnuptial residence rules favored matrilocal residence. In a matrilocal residence group husbands enter as strangers from other villages. By stressing affiliation with his father's or his mother's father's *kiamp,* ego is emphasizing ties with his nonlocal relatives. In this way the concept of the *kiamp* serves to unite people of various villages who cannot be united through sheer geographical proximity as is the local residence group. The *kiamp* would seem to be most functional, therefore, as long as the matrilocal pattern is maintained. As the following pages will illustrate, this marital residence pattern is changing today in Asang, and there is some hesitancy now to marry outside the village. As a result, *kiamp* ties at the intervillage level are fewer, and the primary function of the *kiamp* becomes less and less significant for the overall structuring of Miskito society. Rather, as village endogamy increases, the *kiamps* are becoming more and more localized. However, both *kiamp* and *taya* ties still provide the necessary contacts for obtaining food and lodging in other villages when traveling.

7. Neither is there any reference to *kiamps* or their equivalent in the ethnohistorical literature.

Compared with *taya*, however, the *kiamp* even today provides a stronger reference group both within Asang and between villages. The concept of *taya* involves only a general feeling of kinship, while the *kiamp* is a special group of relatives. An even more select kin group is the nuclear family or household. This group is strictly a local residence group compared with *taya* and *kiamps*, which have both local and nonlocal aspects.

The custom of uxorilocal postnuptial residence was still remembered and generally adhered to by the older inhabitants of Asang (see chap. 1n17). However, analysis of preferred postnuptial residence patterns over the years leaves no doubt that matrilocality as a result of uxorilocal marital residence is no longer the rule. The original settlers of Asang followed the preference for matrilocal residence on the village level in that the husbands of the Bobb sisters settled in the new community, rather than taking their wives elsewhere. The same can be said for the husbands of the Herrera sisters.[8] The same practice was observed several decades later by the children of these early settlers, although from this point on, village endogamy was becoming prevalent. Consequently, identification of marital residence patterns must include not only movement between villages, but also house location within Asang.

Intravillage marriage was particularly popular between children of *Dama* Sanders and the Bobb sisters, whose families were the first to reach maturity in Asang. A reconstruction of the Asang settlement pattern as it may have looked about 1930, when this first Asang generation was reaching marriageable age, shows that seven out of the approximately twenty marriages which had taken place by then were between Sanders sons and daughters and those of the Bobb sisters. (One Sanders daughter married one of the two Bobb brothers.) One couple left the village. Five of the remaining six built homes immediately adjacent to, or in the near vicinity of, the home of the wife's parents. However, one husband, a son of *Dama* Sanders, set up housekeeping closer to his parents' home than to that of his wife.

The thirteen additional marriages of this period involved eleven children of Bobb sisters and two Sanders who either brought new spouses to Asang (in ten cases) or married recent newcomers to the village (three cases). In all cases, however, residence was in Asang.

8. I am not sure whether *Dama* Sanders' wife lived in Asang prior to their marriage, or whether the Sanders' residence was neolocal.

These marriages introduced five new women to the village and an equal number of new men. Without exception the husbands new to Asang settled close to their wife's parents' home, as did those already resident in Asang who married Asang women. In the cases where new women entered the village, the couples set up residence in the general area of the husband's parents' home, although not immediately adjacent.

If the village is viewed again about 1950, twenty years later, sixty-two new households are found.[9] Thirty-four of these marriages were between Asang men and Asang women. Analysis of residence patterns among these intravillage marriages now shows almost twice as many of the new couples establishing households in the vicinity of the husband's natal home, rather than in that of the wife's. Five of these couples took up residence with the husband's parents, who were elderly and needed assistance in running the household. In one case two married brothers returned to their parents' home. About 18 per cent of the new households were located approximately equidistant from both sets of parents.

Twenty-eight marriages involved spouses entering from outside the village. Of these, sixteen were between Asang women and non-Asang men, while twelve involved Asang men and non-Asang women. Of the sixteen households established by husbands entering Asang, ten were located in the vicinity of the wife's parents' home (none actually took up residence in the home). Six, however, were located by themselves, on the edges of the community. Six of the twelve new households formed by Asang men and non-Asang women were also located by themselves, at some distance from the husband's natal home. Four, however, were placed adjacent to the husband's parents' home. Two of the wives entered already existing homes where the husband's first wife had died. Seventeen Asang residents, four men and thirteen women, left the village upon marriage. One case involved a couple. The other fifteen went as spouses of non-Asang individuals.

By 1964–65, twenty-one new households had been added to those mentioned above. Except for one case, the remarriage of a widower, they all involved young adults who represent the third generation to be born and raised in Asang. In two-thirds (fourteen) of these

9. Not included here are five cases of deserted wives, four married to non-Asang spouses and one to an Asang man. I am not entirely sure where the original postnuptial residence was located in these instances.

marriages both spouses were from Asang. The remaining seven involved spouses who were entering the village. Residence for the couples who have married within Asang is markedly virilocal (69.2 per cent). In seven of these cases residence is under the same roof as the husband's parents. In one instance residence is with the young man's older sister and her family, with whom he had lived for some time prior to marriage. However, in most cases it is expected that these newlyweds will eventually build homes of their own, and we can anticipate that these will probably be located either in the vicinity of the husband's parents' home or on the edges of the community where more space is available. Only if parents are elderly is it likely that the couple will remain with them. This particularly holds true if older siblings have already married and left the household.

One intravillage couple resides with the wife's parents. Two other couples took up residence close by the wife's home. One young man has built a new home at some distance from both families of in-laws, while one couple rotates between their natal homes, spending a few nights at one home, then at the other.

A similar rotation system is used in a case where the husband is from the nearby village of Karisal. A few days are spent in Asang, a few in Karisal. In the three additional intervillage marriages involving Asang women and non-Asang men, residence is uxorilocal. In two cases residence is with the wife's family, in the other the new couple built their own home nearby. Two marriages involved Asang *wahmas* and non-Asang women. In both cases residence was in the home of the husband's parents. The widower's new wife, also a non-Asang woman, took up residence in his home, located adjacent to that of his parents. One *tiara* left Asang for her husband's village.

The above data is presented in Table 1. Upon inspection it readily becomes apparent that postnuptial residence in Asang has moved away from matrilocality on several counts. With respect to the community as a whole, village endogamy is definitely a major development and seems to be increasing. However, in those cases, now in the minority, where non-Asang men enter the village as husbands, residence is still predominantly uxorilocal, although some couples have preferred to build at some distance from the in-laws. For marriages between Asang residents, and also in those cases where non-Asang women entered the village, residence is becoming increasingly virilocal, although here again neolocal residence may also be found.

In general the people of Asang are quite aware of the trend towards village endogamy, and are somewhat defensive and self-righteous about the virtues of such a practice. Their attitude is that if you marry a local person you know what you are getting. When non-Asang men marry into the village, informants asserted, you can

TABLE 1

Trends in Marital Residence Within Asang

Husband's village	Wife's village	Number[a]	Percentage	Household Location		
				Uxorilocal	Virilocal	Neolocal
1930						
A[b]	A	9(1)	47.4	8 88.9%	1 11.1%	
N[c]	A	5	26.3	5 100.0		
A	N	5	26.3			5 100.0
1950						
A	A	34(2)	54.8	10 29.4	18 52.9	6 17.7%
N	A	16(12)	25.8	10 62.5		6 37.5
A	N	12(3)	19.4		6[d] 50.0	6 50.0
1965						
A	A	14	66.7	3[e] 23.1	9 69.2	1 7.7
N	A	4(2)	19.0	3[f] 100.0		
A	N	3	14.3			3 100.0

a. Corrected for number of individuals leaving Asang after marriage, as shown in parenthesis after figure.
b. A=Asang.
c. N=non-Asang.
d. Includes two cases of remarried widowers whose new wives joined their husbands' existing homes.
e. A base of 13 is used since one couple rotates between in-laws' homes.
f. A base of three is used since one couple rotates between villages.

be sure they will steal, fight, drink, and probably desert their wives. It is a fact that four of the five deserted Asang women currently living in the village were married to and deserted by non-Asang men. On the other hand, there are over twenty other non-Asang men married to Asang women who have not deserted their families. Insecurity concerning potential desertion still remains though, since the plight of a deserted wife is indeed severe.

By the same measure it is felt that marriages involving non-Asang women are no better since, one is told, it is a surety that any "strange" woman who enters Asang society will quarrel a lot and be "proud," i.e., unfriendly and uncooperative. Similarly, parents prefer that their daughters marry within Asang because if they reside elsewhere there is no way to help them if marital problems develop. According to Asang *wahmas*, local girls are preferable because they are dependable, competent, and have "good sense."

When Asang was smaller protective measures were sometimes taken, with respect to potential newcomers to the village, in an effort to select spouses, particularly young men, who would fit into Asang smoothly. A *wahma* who wanted to marry into the village would be taken aside and spoken to by the men of the community who would point out the village customs and emphasize what would be expected of him as a responsible husband and village adult. Such admonitions prior to marriage are still customary, as we shall see, and are carried out within the context of the obligation felt by the Moravian church to maintain a Christian atmosphere in Asang. Not long after its original settlement, the village was converted to Christianity. The need, still strong today, to distinguish between outside "heathen" and local "Christian" living so as to protect this new and valued status presumably began at the same time, and has underlain much of Asang's defensiveness and sense of moral superiority. Whether other villages are equally defensive I cannot say. The significant point is that the people of Asang proudly feel that they are unique in this respect.

The decision regarding postnuptial residence is made by the husband, and there are reasons other than the ideological which can influence his actions; having a house or other property in Asang is often mentioned. Traditionally all property—animals, trees, as well as personal goods—was destroyed at the death of the owner. This is no longer done and at least some Asang men have preferred to stay in the community for property reasons. The availability of food or of good plantation land is another commonly mentioned factor. Several of the non-Asang wives are orphaned and have no strong family ties to keep them in their own villages or challenge their husbands' wishes to stay in Asang.

Once begun, endogamy probably has been facilitated through sheer population expansion, which in terms of numbers alone has made mate selection within the village increasingly possible. Consequently, along with pressures that have made it ideally more desirable to find a spouse locally, it has in fact been increasingly possible to realize that ideal.

Yet the problem of finding an acceptable spouse involves considerations not only of locality but also of genealogy. One factor behind Asang's village endogamy has been the increasing willingness of young people to place locality above kinship considerations in the choice of a spouse. Concurrently, there has been a change in kinship term guidelines for marriage partners and, in a sense, readjustments in people's opinions as to who does or does not constitute an acceptable spouse from the point of view of kinship. Consequently, there have been a number of cases over the last two generations in which marriages have taken place between Asang residents who, in the views of many of the villagers, were too closely related to be respectably married.

To judge from the information recorded by Conzemius (1932: 146) and Heath (1927:82), and completely substantiated by informants, cross-cousin marriage was the rule until approximately the early decades of the twentieth century. Up to this time the children of brothers or of sisters, i.e., the children of *moini*, were not to marry. *Moini* were felt to be too closely related, and this closeness carried over to their children. If the *moini* were brothers, they and their children held the same surname; if sisters, each served as a surrogate mother to the other's children.[10] The resulting ineligibility of these cousins was expressed by the reciprocal use of the term *lakra* between them if they were of opposite sex. It was believed that if *lakra* did marry, the children of the union would be deformed.

On the other hand, as Conzemius (1932:146) notes, "the children of brother and sister [i.e., of *lakras*] are not considered blood relatives, and a union between such cousins is the common, and originally perhaps the only, marriage allowed. Unions of this kind are still encouraged to this day [late 1920's] for it is felt that family ties are strengthened thereby." These potentially marriageable cousins were designated terminologically by the reciprocal term *klua*. Ideally speaking, according to rules of matrilocal marital residence, these persons would not be resident in the same village prior to marriage, whereas parallel cousins, the children of *moini*, would.

For reasons which are not entirely clear, but which probably are rooted in pressures emanating from contact with the outside world,

10. The practice of the levirate and sororate (Conzemius 1932:146) also made it possible for children of *moinis* to be, in some cases, half-brothers and sisters.

the terminological distinction between *klua* and *lakra,* i.e., between cross and parallel cousins, was gradually lost sometime around the turn of the century. All offspring of opposite sex of brothers and/or sisters now address each other as *lakra* (see Figure 14). However, the prohibitions against marriage with a *lakra* or, to state it another way, against marriage between the offspring of *moinis,* remained.

For the first few decades of Asang's existence, the prohibitions seem to have been followed, apparently without much difficulty. The village, as we have seen, was more or less divided between two groups, the Bobb brothers and sisters and their offspring, and the Herrera siblings and their children. There do not seem to have been significant genealogical ties between Bobbs and Herreras prior to their mutual settlement in Asang, and the marriage of many of the sisters to non-Miskito men further assured that the offspring of these two groups would not be related. Consequently, intermarriage between individuals of Bobb and Herrera background, respectively, did not violate marriage rules, and occurred often. The fact that both groups were resident within the same community, and that the new couples continued to reside there, does not seem to have been important for its own sake. Suitable spouses were also found outside Asang, and among newcomers to the village.

However, beginning with the following generations, i.e., the grandchildren of the original settlers, marriages which broke the standard prohibitions took place. Villagers express their disapproval of most of these marriages (at least twelve so far, including almost 30 per cent of the most recent marriages), by pointing out either that the couple stand in the relationship of *lakra,* and thus by definition should not marry, or that the grandmothers of both were sisters, i.e., *moini* (referring usually to the Bobb sisters), and that it was bad for the children or grandchildren of *moini* to marry. This is simply another way of saying that the prospective spouses were *lakra* in the sense of first or second cousins. In one case the grandfathers of the couple were *moini,* and the same standards applied (Fig. 16a).

The community was particularly aghast at a marriage where the grandparents were brother and sister, thus, in traditional terms, making the spouses technically *lakra* in the sense of full siblings, since the girl's father and boy's mother, as children of a sister and brother, respectively, were technically marriageable under the earlier system, i.e., were *klua* (Fig. 16b). The marriage of a man to his *moini's* (in this case first cousin) daughter was also severely criticized.

Divergence from the former system is particularly noticeable in situations where children of a brother and sister, who before stood in mutual relationship as *klua*, i.e., as potential spouses, are no longer seen as such. Today, as we have noted, the term *lakra* has been extended to cover these cousins, and, consequently, they should not marry. There was one such case in the village complicated by the fact that the girl became pregnant before marriage.

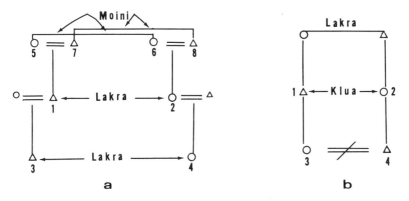

Fig. 16. Currently disapproved marriages. a, Children (1 and 2) and grandchildren (3 and 4) of *moinis* (5 and 6; 7 and 8) are *lakra* and should not marry. b, Since 1 and 2 were potential spouses under the traditional system, 3 and 4 are potential siblings and therefore should not marry.

However, the marriage was vehemently opposed by the village on the grounds that the potential spouses were too closely related. Not only were they *lakra*, it was pointed out, but their respective mother and father, as brother and sister, held a common surname.[11] Eventually the couple left the village for a gold mining community in the interior.

Occasionally, derogatory comments were also made to the anthropologist about other villages which did allow marriages between persons in a similar relationship. In the views of the young people concerned, marriage with a local person is preferable for various reasons, as was noted above, even if he or she is technically off-

11. This suggests that identification of family membership through use of family surnames is rather new since marriage between the children of a brother and sister was preferred formerly.

limits in the eyes of the older members of the community. The parents of the prospective couple, who come most sharply under attack from the rest of the village, argue that it is impossible and unwise to stand in the way of young people who presumably love each other. In certain cases, where the difficulty lay in the fact that grandmothers were *moini*, parents resorted to the defense that the grandfathers in these instances were non-Miskito, hence the amount of objectionable relatedness was reduced by half. Furthermore, they emphasized, although marriage to a *lakra* is said to cause deformed children, none of the children born to these couples has been deformed.

Some young people, however, make an effort to avoid marrying relatives, and eventually may look outside the village for a spouse. A typical case is that of Bertram, who described at some length his difficulties in finding a suitable wife. He noted, first of all, that many people in Asang marry relatives, and that this shows lack of "respect" for them. Then he went on to describe how he had first thought of marrying an Asang girl, but her father was his *tahti* (mother's *lakra*), so she was ineligible (note that under the traditional system, this match could have been approved). He then decided on another Asang *tiara*, but was informed that she was his *lakra* because their grandmothers had been *moini*. Bertram finally married a girl from a neighboring village, but brought her to Asang to his parents' home.

Occasionally marriages have taken place between cousins, but the relationship was not known before the marriage. In these cases there is considerable criticism of the apparent breakdown in socialization technique which allowed children to grow up without knowing their relatives. The general uncertainty about who constitutes a proper marital partner is illustrated by the fact that after discussing the various problems of marriage these days, many people would ask the anthropologist what she thought was most advisable.

The root of the difficulties seems to lie in the fact that whereas kinship categories formerly offered mutually exclusive guidelines both for prohibitions and preferences in the choice of a marriage partner, kinship today indicates only prohibitions. Factors other than kinship—property holdings, the desire for personal security, romantic love—now form preferential guidelines which can, and in some cases do, conflict with kinship considerations.

It is felt that the *wahma* and *tiara* who are contemplating marriage should be fairly close in age, with perhaps three or four years difference between them, the boy being older than the girl. *Wahmas* usually marry at anywhere from twenty to twenty-six years of age while *tiaras* are considered eligible from about sixteen to twenty-two or twenty-three. The age at marriage has increased from earlier days when girls in particular were betrothed by their parents while still children, and married shortly after reaching puberty: "A girl at a very early age, between eight and nine, is betrothed to a young man, who at once takes up residence in the house of her parents, whom he assists until . . . (she) is old enough to be married, when, without any ceremony, they are recognized as man and wife" (Pim and Seemann 1869:306–7; cf. Esquemeling 1893:253; Conzemius 1932:145, 147).

Certain aspects of this system, however, clashed with the values held by the missionaries, and the current arrangement of allowing girl and boy to make their own decisions may again be due to their influence: "The former custom among the Indians, of giving away their girls, while still in infancy, to men, is not permissible by us, and we should use every means in our power, to prevent and suppress this heathen custom. We are however not opposed to a friendly mutual agreement among the parents" (Moravian Church 1898:22).

Economic factors also are involved, at least at present. Some young men today are having second thoughts about marrying during the present depression conditions. The lack of money to buy clothes and food and generally to support a wife is a fact to be seriously considered.

In Asang, opportunities for courtship are numerous. Sunday provides an excellent occasion for *wahmas* and *tiaras* to survey the field in church. After Sunday morning service, if it is dry season, young people from one of the neighboring villages, San Carlos, Krasa, or Santa Izabel, will come over to watch the Asang *wahmas* play baseball with *wahmas* from another village. This takes place in the cleared area behind the village. The young people are dressed to perfection with the girls particularly being conspicuous for wearing shoes and their best dresses, and perhaps even carrying a furled parasol. There is little mixing of the sexes; instead, groups of girls keep more or less to themselves and groups of young men likewise cluster together beneath the orange trees at the edge of the playing field. Although actual conversations between *wahmas* and *tiaras* may be limited, eyes and ears are busy.

After the baseball game and, for some, another church service, the afternoon and part of the evening are devoted to *kihrbaia* or strolling. This is a favorite time during the week when people relax at home, visit relatives, or walk casually around the village. Groups of *wahmas* and *tiaras*, maybe two boys and a girl, or four or five boys and two girls, will be seen also strolling casually through the village. Single couples are hardly ever encountered. Actually, any late afternoon or evening after the work of the day is completed is a favored time for strolling and for *wahmas* to walk by the homes of girls in whom they are interested. Sunday strolls are most important because they allow visiting between villages.

Everyday chores also permit considerable boy-girl interaction. When the *tiaras* carry noonday food to men working in the plantations, for example, they linger long enough to joke and flirt. Also many subtle messages can be exchanged with glances and swift hand signals as boys and girls meet in the course of their daily work. In general, flirting is carried on quietly without trying to attract too much attention.

When a *wahma* becomes seriously interested in a girl he will indicate his intentions by sending her letters, buying her small gifts, or even giving her "medicine" to bewitch her. This last is described as a pleasant smelling liquid which will make her think of her suitor when she smells its fragrance (cf. Conzemius 1932:145). This procedure is considered to be slightly out of order since the girl's feelings are manipulated, possibly against her will.

If the suitor's attentions are foiled by angry parents, he may resort to serenading his girl at night. This requires rudimentary knowledge of guitar playing, possession of a guitar, and knowledge of the traditional Miskito love songs, plus the ability to compose impromptu verses praising the particularly charming features of the loved one. Some Spanish songs are also sung at these times. In pre-Christian days the serenading was accompanied by a bamboo flute, but this type of instrument is no longer found (cf. Conzemius 1932: 112).

The body of Miskito love songs is extensive, and generally unknown to non-Miskito who sometimes claim that the Miskito have no indigenous music. The following lines may give an indication of the nature of this poetry:

Kati painkira uli aula	The full moon is rising
Touan kanra ingni dauki	Making the town bright
Upla manus yangra wise	Everyone tells me
Yawon wol kli aisabia apia	We will not speak together again.
Sarikira iwi luki	Disconsolate I sit and think
Kankara ni iwi lukamna	Above all else I will sit and think.
Lalma tininiska mairin	Wandering lady hummingbird
Naiwa mamunisna	Today I sing your praises.
Naha paiaska kra wina	With this blowing breeze
Yang mai lukisna	I am thinking of you,
Prais mai alkra.	Precious thoughts sent to you.

Final permission to marry a girl is obtained by the suitor from her parents. In the early days of missionary influence the betrothed couple were not permitted to speak with each other, but this is no longer practiced. If there is severe opposition to the match, the couple can elope, but this is dangerous, particularly for the girl, since she runs the risk of being disowned by her family, and, should the marriage encounter difficulties, she may not be able to count on help from them.

In theory, it is required that the couple be married before indulging in sexual activities, but in practice the number of "shotgun" weddings shows that the theory remains just that. Yet it is embarrassing to a girl's family if she becomes pregnant before marriage, especially if they are active in church affairs and thus should set an example for the rest of the village. Sex is an area of extreme reticence on the part of the Miskito, especially among women. Men are more casual about the topic among themselves, but not in mixed company. According to Schneider's report (1890:63), such shyness is also the result of Christianity.

In addition to matters of genealogy and locality that were discussed above, there are personal characteristics to be considered when choosing a spouse. For the girl an ideal husband is a young man who has a reputation for making good plantations and "planting many bananas," is interested in raising chickens and pigs, brings her good cloth, and doesn't drink or chase other women. The last point especially is an area of tension, for it is considered proper for a young man to run around before marriage but to settle down afterward. Some *wahmas* find the transition difficult. A *wahma,* on the other hand, professes to be attracted by a girl who has "good sense," that is, who doesn't do "foolish" things, and who can handle household chores adequately—as expressed in the phrase "make *wabul* without lumps." Each *wahma* repeatedly emphasizes that whereas other young men are attracted by a pretty face or a shapely figure, he himself is more interested in a sturdy girl who can keep the home in order.

Aside from these areas of proficiency, there can be problems of color and church affiliation. Families who consider themselves Christians, even if only nominally, want their children to marry other Christians, preferably within the same denomination. The lay pastor, not surprisingly, also discourages marriages with nonchurch members, as well as interfaith unions. Most adults concede that to have both Moravian and Church of God denominations represented in the same family is asking for trouble. Generally it is the parents who are more concerned with this than the young people them-selves, and, consequently, interdenominational marriages occasion-ally do occur. There were two cases of Moravian–Church of God marriages in Asang at the time of this study.

This is in line with the general feeling that if the young couple is satisfied with their choice the parents should hesitate to ultimately forbid it. Yet considerable pressure may be brought to bear on the young couple. For example, there was much concern among the relatives of an Asang *tiara* whose family was officially Moravian, but who wished to marry a non-Asang *wahma* with an Iglesia back-ground. A much better spouse, she was told, was a young man, the son of a Moravian lay pastor who once lived in Asang, who cur-rently worked at the mines in the interior. But Cecilia did not wish to wait, and was married with the grudging consent of her parents. Her husband's parents insisted she would have to join the Iglesia congregation, but Cecilia felt she could resist that. However, the couple took up residence in the husband's village at his request in order to avoid pressures from Cecilia's relatives, who wished him to become Moravian.

The area of color is one in which young people are more involved. There is an underlying current of feeling that dark skin is "bad" and light skin is "good," although just what is good or bad about it is hard to say. Some families encourage their children to marry lighter-skinned persons rather than darker, in order to have lighter-skinned grandchildren, and *tiaras* and *wahmas* also tend to take this into account. One informant indicated that for this reason marriage with non-Miskito peoples, for example with Spanish-speaking Nicaraguans, was desirable. However, she emphasized that there was then a greater chance that the couple would not live in Asang. Given the alternatives of Asang residence or a mixed marriage with a lighter-skinned foreigner, residence would be more important, she felt.

Once marriage is decided upon, there are two steps to be taken: (1) the meeting with the Moravian Helpers (elders of the church) and lay pastor, and (2) the civil ceremony required by the government and conducted by the village headman. These two events are conducted during the same evening. It is important to note that the church meeting is held regardless of whether any of the party is Moravian or not. The atmosphere is more one of secular admonishing than denominational preaching. The following excerpts from field notes set the scene for an understanding of village marriage activities:

> This evening three Asang couples were married. Procedures began in the afternoon when I typed out the marriage certificates for the headman. This was the first time civil marriages were performed in Asang. Heretofore it was necessary for villagers to go to San Carlos for the civil ceremony, since before 1964 the headman was an *Agente Policia* only and did not have the authority to marry. In 1964 he was appointed *Juez de Policia,* and is now empowered to conduct civil ceremonies as well as to register births and deaths.

> In the evening the three couples, their parents, the lay pastor, and the Helpers assembled in the church. The men (including the grooms), as usual, sat on one side, the women (including the brides) on the other. The grooms looked very unconcerned, and the brides appeared painfully shy. The lay pastor proceeded to conduct a session of admonition on the proper behavior for husbands and wives. This was done in a solemn way, but informally, for he came down from the altar area and paced up and down in front of the people concerned. The usual herd of curious children was removed from the church since this was "grown-up business."

> The lay pastor first told the young men to respect their wives and not to leave them—a long discussion on this point. They

were married for life, he said, not for only a few years. He
commented that marriage isn't easy and that they couldn't run
around any more. He emphasized that now the men belonged
to their wives' families; that their wives' homes, their parents,
their *moinis* and *lakras* were to be the concern of the new husbands. He talked to the *tiaras* too, but for a shorter time, admonishing them to obey their husbands, to iron and cook, and
not to refuse to perform these wifely duties. Sometimes husbands turn out bad, he said, but it was the wife's duty to put
up with these things, and to pray to God for help if it got too
difficult. He also reminded them that it was proper to bring
family troubles to the attention of the Helpers (see chapter 5)
if necessary. Since the *wahmas* were not formal members of the
church, although the young women were, these three couples
could not be church-married until the boys were confirmed, if
this should ever happen. The lay pastor told the *tiaras* this, and
stressed that both should join the church. The emphasis with
the women was on seeking God's help in their marriage; for the
men on not leaving their wives; for both on the fact that now
the respective families were one.

Before this speech the lay pastor had asked each *wahma* by
name if he were satisfied with what he was doing, and each
said yes. After he had asked this of one *wahma* he would ask
the *tiara* and then the parents of both. In each case verbal as-
sent was registered—public acknowledgment that this was
being done with the consent of all concerned.

After the lay pastor had finished speaking he invited the
Helpers to add any comments. Ceferino spoke at length on living together in harmony, and Augusto stressed the importance
of believing in God and living according to His word. After
Augusto finished, Gregorio tried to persuade some of the
women Helpers to say something, but they were too shy.

After the church meeting, the civil ceremony is conducted:

At the headman's house the rafters were full of bunches of
rice. A few notables, i.e., some of the men and the anthropologist, sat on a bench along one wall. The *tiaras* stood in the door-
way at one end of the room and the ubiquitous little boys
crowded wide-eyed at the other door. Someone had a radio
which was playing Latin music. The lay pastor sprawled in a
chair while the headman, having extracted the bride and

groom from the separate corners in which they were self-consciously trying to hide and gotten them to stand side by side in front of the main table with the witnesses, read the marriage certificate while leaning casually on the table with one leg crossed over the other and a flashlight at a precarious angle in his hip pocket. When he reached the point of pronouncing them man and wife he persuaded them, with some difficulty, to hold hands. After the reading everyone had to sign the certificate. One of the witnesses couldn't write, and after a bit of a struggle the lay pastor managed to guide his hand and obtain a signature. This considerably amused the groom. The headman gave the bride her copy of the marriage certificate—the groom does not receive one. The parents of both parties were absent.

There was no celebration of any kind afterwards. Rather, the bride and groom joined the rest of the group as they headed back to the main part of town. On the way home the *tiaras* made the groom walk beside his bride, and they also walked with her. Gradually the newlyweds fell behind the main body of people. In the dark the groom put his arm around his new wife's shoulder and once playfully tried to throw her off a log bridge. As soon as light hit them, they separated. At the bride's home, where they will reside, the young woman went inside, while the groom remained outside talking with a group of young men.

When times were more prosperous, it was not unusual for refreshments to accompany the marriage celebration, rolls and "coffee" made of burnt maize being provided for the entire village in one account (Siebörger 1881:254). Sometimes animals were slaughtered for weddings, too (Grossman 1940:32). Now, however, money is scarce and no or very little partying is done. Certainly no animals are slaughtered for feasting, and marriage ceremonies now are not generally village affairs. An exception to this may be a church wedding, which can be held only if both candidates are confirmed. There were no church weddings conducted in Asang while I was there, but I was told that this is an appropriate time for greater festivity.[12]

Church weddings are not to be entered into lightly. Nicaraguan

12. The account by Siebörger of rolls and maize "coffee" being served in honor of a marriage referred to a church wedding.

law requires only a civil ceremony, and there is general compliance with this rule. In other words, to be "civil married" is to be officially married not only in the eyes of the government, but also in the eyes of the Miskito. There were only two cases in Asang where men were living with women in free union, a point of pride to the village in general, since it is felt that free unions are more common in other villages. Both men had been officially married before to other women, but the marriages failed. The red tape for an official divorce requires traveling to Puerto Cabezas as well as money, and I know of no Miskito who has officially obtained a divorce. Rather, if the marriage fails, the couple merely separates, and it is understood that if they take other spouses and must live in free union, it is not really their fault.

The Moravian church, however, frowns not only upon divorce, but also on desertion—the usual Miskito "divorce"—and those Miskito who are "church-married" or who are contemplating it are well aware of the pressure for permanency. Thus, if a couple does have a church ceremony, it is not at all unlikely that they have been civil-married for some years and have several children. In other words, the marriage appears to be permanent. To be church-married carries with it considerable prestige, at least among the members of the congregation, but it is not a necessary condition for membership or even for active work within the church.

Prior to missionary influence families were sometimes polygynous with the number of a man's wives being limited only by his ability to maintain them (Hamilton 1901:130). Judging from the literature, as many as four to six wives might be supported by one man, although two was more often the case (M.W. 1732; Mierisch 1893: 31; Schneider 1890:62). Conzemius notes, however, that polygyny was not very common and was "generally limited to men of rank, as sorcerers" (1932:149; cf. Pim and Seemann 1869:308; Wickham 1895:206; Grossman 1940:36). All wives lived under the same roof, each with her own fire, and cooked for herself and her children. The husband ate wherever he preferred. Frequently wives were sisters or orphans (Conzemius 1932:149; cf. Heath n.d.).

The eldest inhabitants of Asang remember the days of polygyny. However, today all complete families in the village are nuclear, although more than one nuclear family may live in one house. At the time of this study forty-nine out of ninety households in Asang contained only a single nuclear family. Thirteen households included a single nuclear family along with various other relatives. Ten households were composed of two nuclear families, the second in all cases newlyweds, while three households included two nuclear families with additional relatives (in two cases parental families with newlywed couples; for the third see Appendix A). One household contained three nuclear families (two sets of married children, one, a middle-aged son, the other a newlywed daughter, with their spouses and children, in addition to the parental family), while one household included three nuclear families along with assorted relatives. Thirteen households did not contain a nuclear family, but partial families of widows, widowers, or deserted mothers. Appendix A notes in more detail the composition of Asang households, particularly those containing persons other than nuclear family members.

The raison d'être of the family is to raise children. Children are the only form of old age social security as far as parents are concerned, and are also seen as the successful issue of a union between the two affinal families. Only then do the two families as represented by the two sets of parents-in-law consider themselves *taya* or relatives. Until a woman produces children the marriage is likely to be rather unstable, and may even dissolve. Furthermore, we have noted previously that only when a woman has borne several children does she become sociologically an *almuk* or adult, to be addressed by the proper teknonymic term. Actually, teknonymy of several types emphasizes the importance of the child as a focal point for family solidarity. The "so-and-so *momika (popika)*" terms are one expression of this, but the widespread use of *muli yapti* or "grandchild's mother" as a term of reference and address between parents-in-law and daughter-in-law after birth of a child to the daughter-in-law shows a similar emphasis between generations.

If a woman does not conceive, there is a good chance that the marriage will dissolve, or that the husband will sire illegitimate children (cf. Conzemius 1932:150, 152). The two or three men in Asang who were particularly known for their extramarital adventures were all childless by their present wives. This sort of activity is considered morally poor behavior, but understandable under the circumstances.

It is considered proper that the illegitimate children be the father's responsibility. If the mother of the child is married, she fears the wrath of her husband and the scandal that will probably ensue. It is reported that infanticide occasionally occurs in these situations.

Also, it is generally agreed that the child will not be loved in his stepfather's home. Better by far, people say, that in this situation the child be raised by his real father. This places the father's wife in a personally embarrassing position. One Asang woman is raising three children under these circumstances. However, another wife, newly married, refuses to care for a child fathered by her husband in a neighboring village before their marriage. If a deserted woman bears illegitimate children she will raise them herself, if possible. Although her situation is not considered an example to emulate, it is understood, and the ultimate blame is placed on the deserting husband who, in a sense, has forced her to be available to other men if her sexual needs are to be met. One young woman in the village who has several children has never married, but maintains her own household near that of her mother. This situation is deplored by the village at large.

The children born illegitimately, through either free union or adultery, are not themselves particularly penalized. People accept two categories, legitimate and illegitimate, and are rather matter-of-fact about both of them. A person is simply in one or the other category, depending on the relationship between his parents, for which he is in no way responsible. Illegitimate children carry their biological father's surname.

Families in Asang are large. During her span of child-bearing years a woman is likely to have anywhere from four to twenty children. Of the thirty-five women living in Asang who had completed their families at the present time, twenty-eight, or 80 per cent, had borne from seven to twelve children with the mode falling at ten. Not all these children reached adulthood, however. The mode for number of living children falls at eight for these same women, 60 per cent of whom lost children.

The first five or six years are the most critical in a child's life. Within the village as a whole, 92 per cent of all deaths occurring for reasons other than old age involved children up to about six years of age; 41 per cent of this group were stillbirths. Asang people attribute this to the stresses and strains of the hard physical labor performed by women in the plantations and in the household during pregnancy.

Births are spaced about every two years. Women feel that it is too difficult to handle several very small children at one time, and say that if children are born with less than a year between them, one will probably die. Birth occurs at the home of the woman's mother or another female relative, and she is assisted by the women of the household and other relatives.[13] One woman in the village has a reputation as a midwife and at times charges for her services "like a real doctor." There is a hospital within two or three days travel, but this is used only in emergencies.

A general practice carried over from pre-Christian times, though not followed by everyone, is the calling in of a special friend or relative, someone whom the family wishes to honor, to cut the umbilical cord of the newborn. This individual, either man or woman, becomes the child's *lapia* and is henceforth "counted" as a relative. The same obligations of respect, duty, and privilege accorded to consanguine and affinal kinsmen are extended to this ritual relative, including a ban on marriage between individuals who stand in a mutual *lapia* relationship or their children. The duties of the *lapia*, or his wife if the *lapia* is a man, are to care for the mother and child for the first few days after birth, cooking food and washing clothes.

When a child is born it is necessary to register the birth with the headman and obtain a birth certificate costing five cordobas (ca. U.S. $0.70). This registration also officially establishes the child's name. It is felt that each child should have a name which is unique. No name should be repeated in the village, and parents also try to avoid selecting a name held by friends living in other villages. It is common for parents to ask a foreigner to name their child, and it is necessary for the person so honored to suggest possible names until one is found that is both new to the village and "sounds right."[14] According to Conzemius (1932:106), this is an old custom.

When the child is anywhere from a few months to several years old he may be baptized by the parson on one of the latter's periodic visits. Baptism sometimes, though not necessarily always, leads to the creation of another set of ritual kin ties—those of the *libra*. The term *libra* is a carry-over from pre-Christian times when it referred to a type of fictive kin relationship created between two people of the same sex who were friends, but not relatives. The two could

13. In order to assure easy births in the future, young girls are often urged not to eat certain "dangerous" foods—liver, beef stomach, chicken crop—that are suggestive of or contain restrictive membranes or obstructions.

14. Women's names almost always end in i(consonant)a or ia; men's often end in (consonant)o or io, or in a consonant.

"become *moini*" by mutual agreement, exchanging articles of clothing or ornamentation to seal the bargain and following kinship obligations wherever possible. This is still done, but the process is termed *moini takaia* ("to become *moini*"). The term *libra* is now used within the Moravian church, at least, for the Christian status of godparent.

It is not required that a *libra* be found for the child being baptized, but if the parents do so decide, they must ask a person who is already a communicant member of the church. The individual is often a relative and usually a woman, although a couple may also sponsor the child. The *libra* undertakes to provide the child with white clothing for the ceremony, and holds or stands beside the child while the parson performs the baptism. Afterwards the *libra* is regarded as *taya* by the child's family, and takes an interest in his development and training. As with *lapia*, *libra* and their children may not marry.

Theoretically the *libra*'s main function is to provide social security should the child's mother die. If this happens the *libra* is to care for the child in accordance with the promises made to the parson in the baptismal ceremony. The status of godparent is relatively recent, however, and in actuality the mother's death usually means that either the maternal grandmother or an *anti* (MoSi) will assume care of the child.

The position of *libra* is considered to be more important at the present time than that of *lapia*, presumably because in a community with a strong Christian ethic a Christian-based status is more prestigeful than one which dates from pre-Christian times. In both cases, however, the status at the present time is verbal rather than real. The role of *lapia* is declining while that of *libra* in the Christian sense is not yet fully developed. Neither relationship contains the complex of socio-economic-political ties which often characterize the *compadrazgo* relationship found among Hispanic Latin Americans (Mintz and Wolf 1950).

Children grow up in a permissive atmosphere surrounded by numerous relatives. Older siblings or mother's younger, unmarried sisters may care for youngsters, carrying them to church and tending them if the parents are busy. Grandparents also act as babysitters and older women are often seen carrying a grandchild slung in a length of cloth on their backs, the ends of the cloth tied around the waist to leave the hands free. After work, the father may take the youngest for a walk about the village, or play with the newest baby on the porch steps. The youngest child always receives the most attention and is especially loved and petted, being the "last of the line."

There is not much disciplinary action involved in child raising. Loud threats and scoldings are tried long before actual physical punishment is administered, although occasionally, when they have finally gone a bit too far for even their parents' extensive patience, children get sound spankings. Generally, though, parents say they cannot discipline because of their great love for their children. As a result, children, especially boys, lead fairly free lives and soon develop attitudes of independence and self-assurance which usually get them out of any scrapes they get themselves into. Such independence and self-confidence are essential for the egalitarian nature of Miskito society. Adult men in particular continue the attitude that "no man is my master." Women, on the other hand, are quite definitely subservient to their husbands.

It is permissible in Miskito society to give a child to someone else to raise. If children are born too close together or the burden of caring for them becomes too great for the parents for economic reasons, a *libra, anti* (MoSi), grandmother, or *tahka* (FaSi) may care for the child instead. There are other situations, too, where an individual may be called upon to raise another's children. The person most pitied in Miskito society is the orphan. The term is applied whenever one of the parents has died, but the situation is regarded as most serious when the deceased is the child's mother. In situations of this sort, children are usually reared by their maternal grandmother, or, in her absence, by a mother's sister. If neither of these individuals is available, another relative on the maternal side will care for the children. The father's family is not usually expected to concern itself with the orphans. If there is a *libra*, she might be expected to look after children in such a situation; this is sometimes the case, but not a general rule. The institution of the *libra* in this context is too new. Rather, mother's relatives fill the gap. In pre-Christian times, informants noted, if a mother died while raising a very young child the baby was killed as well. Other children were taken in by a maternal relative or by a *lapia*.

Similar procedures govern the situation created when a man or woman remarries after the death of the first spouse. The new wife is not usually willing to care for her husband's children by his first

wife, and a new husband doesn't want the responsibility of caring
for the children of his wife's first husband. In both cases, the children are given to a relative of the mother. The general feeling is
that the unit of a mother and her children, or by extension maternal
relatives and children, is the stable and basic one. This practice is
in keeping with the ideal structure of a matrilocal society where a
stable core of related women live continuously in the same village.
Husband-father's relatives, on the other hand, would be scattered
in other communities.

The relative importance of maternal versus paternal relatives is
also given concrete expression in other ways. Evidence for the pre-

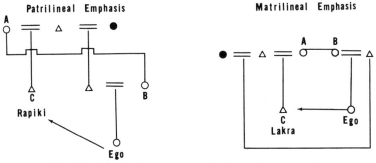

Fig. 17. Patrilineal versus matrilineal emphasis, case 1.

dominance of the female line is provided by an analysis of certain
kinship situations. Due to the trend towards village endogamy in
Asang, there are cases where ego can calculate his genealogical position to the same set of relatives through both maternal and paternal lines. It is significant, then, to note which side is emphasized.
Generally it is that of the mother.

Figure 17 illustrates one example where a female ego addresses
a male relative (C) as *lakra* when he could also be her *rapika*. This
unusual situation is the result of the marriage of a father and son to
two sisters (A and B). As the figure illustrates, the relationship between ego and C is that of *lakra* only when calculated on the matrilineal side.

Figure 18 illustrates a second case where ego (male) addresses
a male relative as *waikat*, that is, "husband of my *lakra*." The critical relationship here is that of ego vis-à-vis his *waikat*'s wife (A).

If the relationship is calculated through the paternal line, the woman becomes ego's *lupya diura* and her husband would be his *dapna*. However, if the relationship is calculated through the maternal line, the woman becomes ego's *lakra*, and her husband his *waikat*.

Finally, in a third example (unillustrated), ego, an adult male, could refer to a child as *muli* through her relationship to him through the female line, or as *lupya diura* through her relationship to him via the male line. He chooses to call her *muli*. His choice of terms, however, is influenced also by the fact that there is a considerable difference in age between himself and the child. In situa-

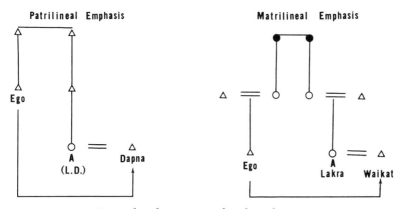

Fig. 18. Patrilineal versus matrilineal emphasis, case 2.

tions where several kin or affinal terms may be applied, relative age is a common factor in deciding which should be used. For example, Figure 19 illustrates a case where ego (female) addresses another woman (A), as *rapiki maia* (my father's brother's wife), but is addressed in return as *moini*. On ego's maternal side, the mothers of both women were *moini*, thus making them *moini* also. On ego's paternal side, A married ego's *rapia*, and thus became her *rapia maia*. Since ego was quite young when this marriage occurred, she prefers that the difference in age (10–15 years) dictate her mode of address. A, on the other hand, prefers the closer consanguineal term.

E called A *tahti maia* (father's sister's husband) even after her marriage to his *moini*, until she had children. Then she addressed him as *maisaia* (husband's *moini*) (Fig. 20). Here the achievement of an adult social status through children allowed her to address another adult on an equal footing with an affinal term. Before she achieved this status, she used a consanguineal term.

Although a nucleus of related women provides much of the focus and stability of Miskito culture, within each nuclear family the husband-father is unquestionably the head.[15] When visiting another

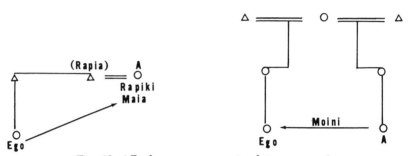

Fig. 19. Affinal versus consanguineal terms, case 1.

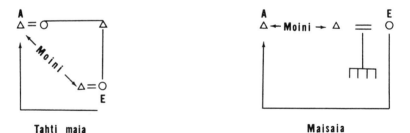

Fig. 20. Affinal versus consanguineal terms, case 2.

village or just strolling within Asang, the wife remains a step or two behind her husband, indicating his authority. The husband feels it is his privilege to come and go, and generally do as he sees fit, and the wife is not expected to object, at least not publicly. The only area where equivalence between the sexes is formally attempted is that of church affairs. Both men and women hold positions of re-

15. There is no satisfactory information in the literature indicating the existence of former lineages in Miskito society. A detailed reconstruction of past changes in Miskito social organization is beyond the scope of this work.

sponsibility within the Moravian church, and when it is necessary to hold a church meeting both men and women are expected to attend. However, no one really expects the women to participate, and they generally do not. The men say that they are letting the women "play" at being church leaders, presumably in accordance with the wishes of the missionaries who deplore the "servant" status of Miskito women.

An incident during a Sunday School service illustrates the point. During the service all those owning Bibles are invited to rise and participate in a round-robin reading of the Scripture for the day, verse by verse. Usually only men rose to participate, although some women own Bibles too. On this occasion, however, at the proper point in the service a young woman rose along with the men. She was ignored and cut off whenever her turn came; after a few minutes she grumpily resumed her seat.

Her behavior was unusual and in part was a reaction to the presence of the anthropologist, with whom she was good friends. Like me, she was unmarried, although in her late twenties. An earlier marriage had failed because of her inability to conceive. A childless, husbandless woman in Miskito society is extremely marginal, and she felt her plight keenly. The presence of another unmarried, childless, rather independent woman, who, in contrast, enjoyed the respect of the village, was a source of considerable satisfaction, but also frustration to her. Her behavior in church on this occasion was an indication of her wish to be seen as a responsible member of the community, bolstered to overt action by the presence of the anthropologist, who, however, at no time during her stay made an effort to participate in the Bible readings.

Within the operation of the household and related activities, there is a nominal division of labor between men and women. Men are expected to chop wood, clear plantations, and build houses, but not to carry water, wash clothes, or cook. These are women's duties. In actuality, women are fully capable of almost every type of task either at home or at the plantation. A husband's periodic trips to other villages, not infrequently when there is an onerous task such as weeding the rice to attend to at home, his absences while working downriver (see next chapter), or, more seriously, desertion by her husband, forces many women to learn to take care of themselves and their families almost singlehandedly.

The contrast between men and women in Miskito society can be summed up with a few observations on general behavior. Men as a group are casual, laughing, and independent. They do not complain much about daily matters, except for the recent loss of land in Honduras. They joke readily. Women, on the other hand, usually have something to complain about—health, overwork, general poverty. Women don't joke as much, are more serious, and give the impression of hard and steady work. Men have definite periods of free time, too, after they return from the day's work at the plantation, and they enjoy longer respites from their work by occasional visits to other villages. Women's work, in contrast, is endless, and they rarely have a chance to enjoy a change.

Statuses: Affines and Ritual Kin

The interfamily unity produced by marriage is based on the creation and maintenance of a series of affinal ties identified terminologically. Between parents-in-law and children-in-law a single term, *dapna*, is used reciprocally. After the birth of a child, however, *dapna* is replaced by *muli yapti* (grandchild's mother) when parents-in-law address or refer to their daughter-in-law. *Dapna* is extended to a spouse's parents' brothers and sisters, except that between a man and his wife's mother's brother the mutually reciprocal term *swikat* is used.

Within the same generation, several ties are recognized. *Lisang* is used by parent-in-law to parent-in-law after the birth of a grandchild has united their families and made them relatives (*taya*). *Lamlat* is used only by women to address or refer to a sister-in-law, that is, a brother's (*lakra's*) wife or husband's sister (*lakra*). *Waikat* is used only by men to address or refer to a brother-in-law, that is, a sister's (*lakra's*) husband or wife's brother (*lakra*). *Masaia* is used by both men and women to address or refer to a person of the opposite sex related through marriage, i.e., ego's (male) wife's sister (*moini*) or his brother's (*moini's*) wife, or ego's (female) husband's brother (*moini*) or her sister's (*moini's*) husband.

All four of these relationships involve only one marriage bond. If more than one marriage tie is included, the relationship is not significant. For example, the husbands of two sisters do not consider themselves to be directly related. Instead they refer to each other as "*masaia's* (wife's sister's) spouse."

Since affines become relatives, the same respect is due them as is due consanguine and ritual kin. To show respect for an individual means not to gossip about him and to address him by the proper kin term, not by name alone. However, some affinal relationships, being particularly delicate, require more careful patterning of behavior. There are two approaches to this problem—avoidance behavior and joking behavior.

Traditionally avoidance has been practiced between sons-in-law and mothers-in-law. The early Moravian missionaries complained that it was difficult to hold services in an Indian's home because son-in-law and mother-in-law were not permitted to be in the same house (Lundberg 1858:113). Heath notes that "a man and his mother-in-law must not speak to one another, and according to the strictest usage must not see one another" (1927:85). Conzemius mentions that this custom was found among the Miskito of the upper Río Coco, but not in other parts of the Coast (1932:148–49).

In Asang, mothers-in-law and sons-in-law as well as daughters-in-law and fathers-in-law may practice avoidance if it is necessary to preserve family peace, but only after the birth of a child. This new individual is the concern of both parents and grandparents and, therefore, the object of potential conflict between them.

Another relationship of similar strain may occur between a *libra* and/or *lapia* and the child's mother. Again it is proper to practice avoidance if necessary. The only other relationship where avoidance may be used is that between *masaias* (cf. Heath 1927:85). Sometimes, however, instead of avoidance, *masaias* will enter into a joking relationship, showing unusual familiarity with each other in slaps on the back, joking, and teasing.

Between other in-laws, friendship and cooperation is usual. The test of this statement is found in those households containing more than one nuclear family. The general pattern of cooperation as it affects the women—who are the ones most likely to be in each other's presence during the day—is based on rotation of tasks. Every girl or woman in the household takes daily turns at cooking, washing dishes, and preparing food for cooking, but each wife is responsible for tending to the personal needs of her husband and children.

In such households, daughter-in-law and mother-in-law are most likely to clash. This relationship was not covered traditionally by avoidance rules, probably because in days of stricter uxorilocal residence these two individuals would not live in the same community. Today, however, they are increasingly found together as *wahmas* bring their brides home, at least for a while. In some cases friction between wife and mother has provided the necessary impetus to get a *wahma* started on building his own house. On the other hand, if mothers and daughters-in-law get along well it provides a point of great pride and solidarity between the families.

The ties between father-in-law and son-in-law are usually expressed in actions relating to plantation work and food. Each man takes care of his own plantations, but if one family runs out of rice or beans, the head of the other family will contribute a hundredweight or two. In the same way, after a man has finished harvesting he may help his son- or father-in-law in exchange for a gift of produce. *Dapnas* also assist each other in house building and pig butchering. Between *waikats* a genial friendship is often found, expressed by mutual borrowing of personal items, exchange of cigarettes, and gifts of shoes. *Waikats* also aid one another in cooperative family activities such as house building. Finally, in time of need, a man will approach a *moini, waikat,* or *dapna* for assistance.

The same type of friendships are also found between women. A *moini* or a *lamlat* is the person from whom to borrow or the one to ask to mind the children. *Lamlats* may share hair oil, go walking together, or give each other gifts of cloth. As noted above, the relationship between *masaias* can be either one of joking or of avoidance. Avoidance is the more extreme position today, implying as it does that there is some disharmony in the relationship. A *masaia* relationship based on respect and proper fondness, however, may find the man giving the woman gifts of shoes or a dress, or some item from his travels, or even clearing a plantation for her. She in turn might wash and iron for him, especially if his wife has recently had a baby or if he is single. If there is a considerable difference in age between the two, the girl may address him as *papa,* implying that the man is concerned about her welfare from a fatherly point of view while she reciprocates with daughterly affection.

The respect that should be found between relatives of any kind, consanguineal, affinal, or ritual, is given further expression through the widespread custom of food sharing. The rationale behind the sharing of food is generosity and a show of concern for the well-being of the other family or individual. Proper Miskito hospitality requires that food be offered to anyone, relative or stranger, who is in the vicinity when food is being prepared or eaten. Older residents reminisce about the "good old days" when travelers approach-

ing the village on the river had only to call out as they neared the
bank, and a pot of *wabul* or some boiled bananas would be dispatched to them immediately. This is no longer done, however, and
damas and *kukas* criticize the younger generation's stinginess.

Still, food sharing remains as an integrating mechanism for village
society. There is a constant exchange of small amounts of extra food
between relatives and neighbors every day. A cup of coffee and an
extra flour tortilla, or some *wabul* may be sent to the house next
door anytime. Sunday morning and evening are especially emphasized as appropriate for food exchange, and the observer is struck
by the unusual number of children hurrying here and there with
covered plates and teapots. Not every family follows the Sunday
schedule, but many do. Portions of the catch are also distributed
after a successful hunting or fishing expedition, or when a cow or
pig is slaughtered. There is no particular set of rules regarding what
portion of the animal is to be distributed to what relative. The only
consideration is that the piece of meat be large enough to indicate
proper generosity on the part of the giver.

The role of women as guardians of the social core is given direct
expression and support in the custom of food sharing. Although in
the theoretical division of labor it is the man who is responsible for
providing food for the household, it is the woman who is responsible
for distributing it among relatives. Not surprisingly, it is usually to
other women that food is sent, and when food is sent directly to
men, it is quite likely that they will be related to the giver on the
maternal side. A compilation made from numerous specific instances of Sunday food sharing showed that the persons most often
mentioned as receiving food from ego (female) are: parents, specifically, mother; *moinis*; *lakras* on the mother's side; married daughters; *antis* (MoSi); husband's mother's *moinis*; *libra*; *lapia*; *lamlats*;
masaias; and the lay pastor. Similarly a husband, home after a successful hunt, requests his wife to send pieces of meat to her *moinis*,
mother, and *lakras* (that is, his *waikats*), and also to his *antis*
(MoSi), *kuka* (grandmother), *tahkas* (FaSi), *lapia*, and *libra*.

Meat distribution also contains its subtleties. Meat can be distributed either fresh or cooked. When fresh, it is sent from the
woman of one house to the woman of another with the understanding that the latter will cook it and feed her entire family. When
cooked meat is given, it is designated for a specific individual, who
is often a man. The rationale behind this is that a woman may not

sit down and eat a piece of meat in front of her family without being compelled to share it with them, but a man may. This symbolizes in a nutshell the independent status of the man compared with the kinship-conscious woman.

The generous distribution of fresh meat sometimes conflicts with the realities of living in an economy based partly on cash (see chapter 4). There is often a felt conflict between sending a lesser amount of cooked meat to one or two individuals and selling the difference for money. The problem is especially acute in times of depression like the present, when the temptation is to sell as much meat as possible in order to obtain some of the scarce cash. Since cash is limited, however, people tend not to slaughter as much in the first place in order to maintain the social security of owning cattle. Generosity suffers as a result.

There are a few times during the year when people outside the scope of kinsmen are included in food distributions. This occurs at Christmas, New Year, and Good-Friday-Easter. I was told that a few people celebrate September 15 (Nicaragua's Independence Day) in this way, but most villagers do not. On the first three occasions, however, a supply of food is prepared, and anyone who stops to visit may eat until the food is gone. An alternative is to send invitations to special friends, or, especially at New Year's, a cash collection might be raised from the entire village in order to buy a cow for a community feast. Donations of firewood, manioc, and bananas are also made, and the entire feast is prepared in the cooking shed that belongs to the Moravian church. While the women maintain the fire and prepare the side dishes, the all-important job of cooking the meat is done by men. Men also distribute the portions of meat to the villagers. Every family is entitled to a serving whether it has made a donation or not.

These community feasts are enjoyed greatly, but the depression has put a damper on what used to be a much grander operation. While the banana business was booming, the New Year's feast at Asang claimed river-wide fame, and people attended from all the nearby (usually smaller) villages. In those days Asang inhabitants were wealthy; they could easily afford to buy several head of cattle from anyone interested in selling, and the necessary flour, sugar, or salt from the commissary, to feed any and all who came. Now, however, there is no money, and without money no extra food, and without extra food, no extravaganza. The point is simple: when

work is plentiful and money "cheap," people can indulge in generosity, but when work and money are scarce generosity becomes a
luxury. Hence the current New Year's celebrations are attended
only by Asang people, and the food supply is rather low.

The New Year's community feast does bring to focus certain social aspects of food use which emphasize village solidarity rather
than family ties. A general agreement among the villagers to supply the town beggar with food illustrates the same pattern. This un-
fortunate individual is an elderly Nicaraguan widow who has lived
in Asang for many years with her daughter, who has been deserted
by her husband. It is generally agreed that this woman needs help,
and everyone gives her what they can spare as she makes the
rounds. Another example of this feeling of Asang unity was the
habit of families giving a gift of food to the anthropologist when she
visited them. The gift was usually presented along with a statement that Asang people will do this for a stranger, whereas another village might not be so generous.

Food also serves as an indication of solidarity within the Moravian congregation of Asang. According to the regulations set up by
the Moravian Mission Board, each congregation is charged to provide a plantation for their lay pastor's use.[16] In addition, many members of the Asang congregation send gifts of food to the lay pastor's
household after a successful hunting or fishing expedition, or if they
have prepared some special delicacy for their family. A certain es-
prit de corps has been created and is maintained within the congregation as a result of this extra attention to the lay pastor, since once
again it is felt that other congregations are not as thoughtful.

Generosity as applied to the church is not simply a carry-over
from the general kinship ethic of generosity, but contains an element of Christianity as well. For example, the lay pastor will request contributions of food to feed a group of visiting Moravian
young people from another town, and state the request in terms of
it being a Christian thing to do. The case of the indigent widow is
also often explained by reference to Christian charity rather than
to the general Miskito ethic of generosity. In reality, however, these
two systems of generosity are blended into a single behavior pattern.

In our earlier discussion of the problem of defining Asang, it was

16. "The people shall cut a plantation for the evangelist every year, the
latter being responsible for its upkeep" (Moravian Church 1928:77).

suggested that in the sense of social organization it was difficult, if indeed at all possible, to identify a bounded entity called Asang. Rather, ties stretched from village to village, uniting friends and relatives into a complex of interpersonal relationships. The nature of these ties and the frequency of interaction between peoples of different villages, however, vary, depending on changing conditions.

Many of these changes have been noted previously in the chapter and are repeated here briefly for emphasis. The trend towards change in marital residence pattern from uxorilocality to village endogamy has reduced the number of intervillage ties and will continue to do so as the village becomes increasingly defensive. Yet young people still greatly enjoy Sunday visits to other villages, and these excursions are still an important part of the courtship procedure.

The impact of economic depression apparently has served to decrease intervillage contacts. The once widely popular New Year festivities at Asang no longer draw visitors from other villages, partly because money is scarce and luxury foods are unobtainable, but also because intervillage festivities carry psychological overtones of gaiety and lightheartedness which no longer exist. These have been replaced by feelings of deprivation and depression which, people say, make them disinclined to visit since they are only reminded of what used to be and no longer is.

On the other hand, one of the effects of Christianity has been to increase intercongregational ties. It is a popular diversion among the young people to travel from village to village within the church district in order to conduct services, ostensibly for proselytizing purposes. Just as important, however, is an excuse to visit another village and see and be seen in such a public place as church. Throughout the church year there are also a series of church conferences held at different villages, which bring together people from several districts and serve as forums for the exchange of news. Much of the popularity of these conferences is a reflection of the opportunity they afford to travel and visit. Girls and women, particularly, anticipate the chance to get away from the village which conferences afford them. Men can readily come and go as they seek work or just relax, but women do not often have an opportunity for relaxation and travel.

Summary

The intent of the preceding pages has been to describe the various groups and statuses which compose the social organization of Asang. By way of chapter summary, we can note several of the distinguishing characteristics of this system.

The most obvious feature which strikes the investigator is the use of kinship as an explicit rationalization for much daily activity. Although there is no functioning corporate kin group above the level of the nuclear family, the notion of showing respect for all one's relatives forms the basic code for proper behavior. The constant use of kinship terms and teknonymy in reference and address, together with generosity, particularly in the form of food sharing, are daily reminders of the importance of the kinship ethic. Certain forms of cooperative work, especially house building and slaughtering, are also areas where kinsmen, both consanguineal and affinal, are expected to work together.

In many respects, however, the emphasis on kinship is only a veneer. For example, the changes which have occurred in kinship terminology have made kinship increasingly inoperable as a guide in the choice of a marriage partner. Similarly, many forms of village cooperative activity really operate on a contractual basis, as the chapter on economics will illustrate. Village political organization and especially the system of social sanctions are only partially affected by kinship, while religion is organized through the framework provided by foreign mission churches.

Given so many major areas where kinship apparently does not have a function, it would seem surprising that so much of the kinship ethic is still found. The differential roles of men and women in maintaining Miskito customs becomes significant in this context. Women continue to handle the traditional side of Miskito life. They continue the public usage of kinship terms and teknonymy and retain charge of food distribution. Men, on the other hand, reflect the increased amount of involvement with the non-Miskito world which has also come to regulate those areas of Miskito culture where kinship no longer functions. So far, the separate roles have been more complementary than conflicting; hence the continuation of a strong traditional kinship ethic.

4

Economic Orientations

THE EARLY YEARS of the twentieth century saw both the founding of Asang and the beginning of foreign capital investments in exploitative enterprises—bananas, lumber, and mining—on the Coast, primarily by United States concerns (see Figure 3). The Miskito, including the residents of Asang, quickly became involved in these operations, and the economic fortunes of American businesses were felt by Asang families as well as by those of company officials.

The Nature of the Economic System

The lure of the Coast for American companies lay in the opportunities for profits through the sale of coastal resources on the American and world markets. For the Miskito, the major advantage lay in the chance to obtain items of foreign manufacture—clothes, tools, cooking utensils, et cetera—which had become cultural necessities for them over the preceding centuries. Two avenues were open for acquiring these goods: jobs with the companies themselves, which yielded wages and/or commissary privileges, and sale of local resources, generally foodstuffs, to company camps for the cash necessary to purchase the desired foreign items.

The economic history of Asang is basically an account of the development and collapse of foreign enterprises and the adjustments made by the Miskito in response. In the eyes of its residents, the developments of the twentieth century are viewed primarily in terms of the availability of hard cash and its purchasing power at commissaries. "Good" times are those when money and goods are readily available, even if considerable effort is entailed on their part to obtain the means to buy. "Bad" times, like the present, are periods when cash and the means to obtain it are scarce, and purchasing power is curtailed accordingly.

However, it is important to note that during difficult periods people do not lack the means for survival, even for a fairly comfortable life, from the point of view of an outside observer. Currently in Asang, for example, there is enough to eat, sufficient clothing to wear, and decent shelter. The occurrence since the turn of the century of several periods of decline in job opportunities and related activities in response to local situations and the world market conditions has necessitated periodic returns by the Miskito to self-sufficiency. Consequently, traditional skills of hunting, fishing, gathering, and agriculture have been maintained to a large degree, serving as a cushion to ease the jolt when foreign companies folded, and providing subsistence and material necessities until commercial jobs were available once more. However, in the opinion of informants, this is at best a stopgap measure regardless of how much there is to eat, and life will not be psychologically satisfying until cash and well-stocked commissaries return.

The maintenance of an economy which has faced in these two directions, first through the more or less simultaneous operation of traditional skills and barter of natural resources, along with limited opportunities for wage labor, during the eighteenth and nineteenth centuries, then by the cyclical alteration of traditional activities with wage labor and cash sales during the twentieth century, has served to keep the Miskito linked with, and thus influenced by, the fortunes of international trade. Yet at the same time, they have remained outside this wider realm conceptually. Their orientation has not been towards profit-making in the market sense, but towards obtaining items which spell security and psychological satisfaction, whether they be honey and wild game from the bush or machetes and shoes from the commissary. Like many other peoples living on the fringes of the wider commercial and industrial world, they participate *in* a market economy, indeed depend heavily upon it, but are not *of* that economy since they do not understand the mechanisms behind its operations sufficiently to "economize." Specifically, the people of Asang fail to allocate their limited cash and numerous, highly valued wants and needs so as to get the maximum benefit from their resources. We shall illustrate this point further below as it applies to the management of the consumption of rice and beans.

A major hindrance to the development of a sophisticated market mentality, especially in the twentieth century, has been the fact that cash for the Miskito either has been almost totally absent, as during a depression, leaving virtually nothing to allocate, or so abundant, during a boom in frontier exploitation, that it is almost impossible to spend all that is earned. This insecurity in a vital area of their economy has prompted the Miskito to put considerable overt emphasis on the monetary sector. In contrast, traditional economic activities are carried out quietly and unobtrusively.

The earliest remembrance of market opportunities by Asang informants concerns the situation at the turn of the century, when Asang was founded. The picture presented is one of access to wage labor at the gold mines in the interior to the south, near the headwaters of Río Coco and Río Prinzapolka tributaries, and at lumber camps (pine, mahogany) near what is today Puerto Cabezas. One of the favorite gauges of prosperity used by the Miskito is the type of food utilized at any particular point in time, and in this respect informants noted that these early Asang residents also enjoyed quantities of wild game "morning, noon, and night"—a delicacy that is considerably more scarce today as population increase in Asang and along the river has pushed game farther into the bush. Flour tortillas were made with flour purchased from commissaries, one or more of which has existed in Asang ever since the days of *Dama* Sanders, but rolls and biscuits were not yet baked as they are today. Rice and beans were available in the store, but were not used by the Miskito. This information can be summarized by noting that in the early years of the twentieth century wage labor and commissary goods were available and used to some extent, but traditional subsistence activities also formed an important part of the economy, and commissary items were not used as extensively as in later years.

Much the same situation existed during the 1920's, with jobs available in mahogany camps along the Río Coco and to the south, at the mines, and in banana operations directed mainly by the Standard Fruit Company, and centered at Puerto Cabezas and the territory to the west of that town as well as farther south along the Río Grande and Río Escondido. Asang residents go into few details of these years, however, since the traumatic months of the Sandino Affair or, as it is described by informants, "the time of the bandits," claim most of their attention.

Briefly, as we have noted above, the period 1927 to 1933 saw the attempt by the Nicaraguan patriot Augusto Sandino to stem the "Yankee imperialism" of United States economic and political intervention in Nicaraguan affairs through guerrilla warfare against U.S.

Marines (cf. Macauley 1967). In 1931 major guerrilla offensives were aimed at the east coast against the Standard Fruit Company holdings west of Puerto Cabezas. Part of the operation entailed movements of Sandinistas along the Río Coco, and local villagers, including the inhabitants of Asang, were often robbed and terrorized; some were murdered by the unruly fighters. For several months Asang families abandoned the village, and under the leadership of *Dama* Sanders, who was headman at the time, lived in the bush. Operations of American lumber, banana, and mining companies were halted, at least temporarily (a reflection of the depression as well as of Sandinistas), and the lack of jobs along with depredations to plantations, livestock, homes, and commissaries made life difficult. The fear and general upset of this period is vividly remembered, along with lighter moments such as the excellent hunting in Honduras during the sojourn there, and having to resort to clothing made of bark cloth which stretched when it got wet in the rain, and shrank when it dried.

Hardships of the "bandit" period were quickly eased by the banana boom beginning in 1935 and lasting until about 1942. This is the "golden age" against which the present Asang residents measure the effects of current depression. Both sides of the Río Coco as far as the rapids were covered with banana plantations worked and owned by Miskito men, each of whom had several plots, with technical assistance in clearing and irrigating from the Standard Company. A string of barges carried the fruit to Cape Gracias a Dios, or, if the river was too low, natives took the produce to Waspam by dugout. Payment was made through company checks, which noted the number of stems purchased from an individual and the price paid. Checks were then cashed at company commissaries for merchandise and cash. The major trade center was San Carlos, where, according to a former commissary employee, U.S. $30,000–40,000 worth of merchandise would be sold per month. The goods available were United States imports, and, as in preceding decades, American dollars were used for currency until Nicaraguan currency was substituted by order of the Nicaraguan government.

Hurricanes, plant disease, depredation from the Sandino era, and World War II combined to bring an end to Standard's operations in the early 1940's. But while the banana boom lasted, the Miskito lived well. Traditional subsistence activities were largely neglected —only small plots of maize and manioc were tended. Bananas were plentiful and "English food" purchased from the commissaries (flour, sugar, salt, canned goods) was eaten in quantity. Yards of cloth, clothing, axes, machetes, saws, cooking pots, sewing machines, soaps, and trinkets were all readily available. Church collections were large; holidays were festive. There was much visiting between villages and partying with friends in the evening. People were happy and, as they put it, "ate much meat," both figuratively, in that meat eating implies festivity in general, and literally, in that cattle for community festivities and holidays could be purchased at will from private Creole and Miskito owners.

When Standard left the downgrade began. A private coastal concern, located at Waspam, continued to buy bananas from the Miskito, but did not continue to assist them technically, so that quality, and thus a market, declined. Still, some income was possible, and the commissaries, many of them, including Asang's, now under the direction of the new banana company, continued to stock a range of goods. During World War II employment as rubber tappers could be found with an American rubber company operating on the river, while in the 1950's a new lumber company started operations in the area between the river and Puerto Cabezas. This company and other lumber concerns also were operating across the river in territory under dispute between Honduras and Nicaragua. A mahogany lumbering operation worked the region near Asang, and provided not only jobs for Asang men, but a market for sales of agricultural produce, in particular rice and beans. As we shall see in more detail in the following pages, rice and bean production in Asang developed slowly during the earlier decades of the century, until at present it consumes the major part of the agricultural year and provides a food staple as well as a cash crop. However, it was not until the end of the Standard period that rice and beans began to fill these roles significantly.

The demarcation of the Río Coco as the Nicaraguan-Honduranean border in 1960 ended both lumbering and commercial banana operations, since in both instances what were now Honduranean land and resources were no longer available to Nicaraguan-based companies. Deforestation and the decline in fruit quality also contributed to ending these activities. Presently only the interior mines offer long-term employment opportunities, but there are many applicants for the relatively few jobs. Sale of rice and beans to Waspam, Puerto Cabezas, and the mines, which provided some income in the 1950's and early 1960's, has fallen as companies have closed, and an agricultural cooperative in the mines area has taken over much of the market remaining there. There is some demand for chicle for an American chewing gum manufacturer, but nothing that can begin to compare with the banana boom of the 1930's and the early 1940's. Cash is scarce, and those commissaries which have not closed stock fewer goods. Less luxury food can be eaten, fewer new clothes bought. Church contributions are low, and holidays such as Harvest and Christmas are quiet. Visiting and partying in the evening is largely a thing of the past. The residents of Asang have fallen back to more traditional subsistence activities, eat much of their cash crops, see little money, and complain heartily about their miserable existence. A feeling of deprivation and isolation is dominant.

Although a division may be made for heuristic purposes between those economic activities directed towards interaction with the wider market economy and those concerned only with local self-sufficiency, these two orientations are combined into a single system in the lives of the Miskito. The most accurate approach for depicting the operation of the system as a whole would require a diachronic analysis covering conditions both during a period of economic prosperity, when opportunities to acquire cash and purchase foreign goods are many, and during a period of depression when outside resources are greatly diminished. Unfortunately, only the latter period was observed in the field.

At the present time the people of Asang acquire the material items essential for existence through a combination of slash-and-burn agriculture, fishing, hunting, gathering, craft production, raising of domestic animals, and, for a few, wage labor outside the village. With the exception of wage labor, which provides cash and manufactured goods alone, all these activities provide cash, although only in limited amounts today, and foodstuffs and material items consumed directly by the villagers. It is important to note, though, that foodstuffs and material items produced directly by these activities provide more of the total subsistence base today than do purchased items.

Hunting, Fishing, Gathering, and Crafts

To judge from the earliest accounts, hunting of deer, monkey, peccary, fowl, and manatee, together with fishing, turtling, and gathering of various wild fruits provided a major portion of the subsistence of the indigenous Coastal populations in pre-Columbian times (Dampier 1703:33, 35; M. W. 1732; de Lussan 1930:285–86) and throughout the centuries of contact (cf. Roberts 1827:93, 96, 108, 150; Young 1847:21–22, 77, 107; Cotheal 1848:237; Stout 1859: 183, 184). Hunting and fishing are specified as men's activities (cf. Cotheal 1848:237; Anonymous 1885:419; de Lussan 1930:286), and it seems likely that both men and women engaged in garnering various resources of the savannah and bush, both for food and for craft activities.

As was noted in chapter 1, during the eighteenth and nineteenth centuries, products of hunting, fishing, and gathering provided the Miskito not only with food, but with materials for barter at trading posts. The expert fishing ability of the Cape Gracias natives led to their employment by the buccaneers as strikers for pirate voyages (Esquemeling 1893:chap. 8; de Lussan 1930:286; Wafer 1934:xviii, xxiii, 4n1). In later years tortoise shell was an important trade item. The Caribbean shores of Central America, particularly the stretch known as Tortuguero, Costa Rica, are nesting sites for several species of sea turtle, and the entire littoral provides excellent opportunities for sea turtle fishing (cf. Carr 1967). From April to September Miskito men and boys regularly traveled to Tortuguero and to the Miskito Cays, a series of small offshore islands near Cape Gracias, to obtain supplies of shell for trade (Roberts 1827:52, 108; Cotheal 1848:238; Stout 1859:184). Turtle meat and oil were used at home and exchanged with interior peoples for forest resources not available on the seacoast.

The savannahs at that time abounded in deer, and skins provided another major trade item. Similarly, sarsaparilla and other medicinal herbs, India rubber, various gums, fustic or dyewood were obtained from the bush for exchange with traders (Roberts 1827; Young 1847; Cotheal 1848).

In the early twentieth century Conzemius noted that fishing in the ocean, lagoons, and rivers for several species of fish, manatee, turtle, crustacea, and mollusks provided "a very large share of the food supply" as did hunting of deer, peccary, monkey, iguana, and various birds (1932:65, 73, 79, 80. Cf. Mueller 1932; Grossman 1940:34–36). He also noted the use of numerous wild fruits, leaves, honeys, and grasses both for food and for household purposes.

Because of Asang's inland, riverine location, products of ocean, lagoon, and even savannah are not directly available to the villagers. They do, however, make use of river and bush products, although at present it cannot be said that hunting, fishing, and gathering provide a major share of subsistence. This is due partly to distance from the coast proper, with its more abundant sea resources; partly to a decrease in the availability of local game through population increase and greater agricultural activity in the area; and partly to the availability of other foods which can be obtained with less effort. Wild game is still considered to be the best form of meat, far superior to that of domestic animals. However, not every man goes hunting today and those who do, go only periodically, often for Saturday relaxation. A major hindrance to hunting is the considerable distance that must be traveled today before game can be found, a sharp contrast with conditions fifty years ago when abundant game roamed the bush near Asang.

Hunting is usually an individual activity, although several friends may travel together, and is still restricted to men. No woman ever hunts. Guns and dogs to flush game are the necessary equipment. In addition, some hunters employ a thin bone whistle to attract the game. Some also believe that poor hunting will result if a woman should see this whistle. Peccary, several species of wild fowl, armadillo, various species of deer, iguana, parrots, and pigeons are killed for food, while jaguars, which often come close to the village, are hunted because of their depredations to young domestic animals, especially pigs, and to dogs. Jaguar skins are sold to traders. The people of Asang do not kill monkeys because of their resemblance to humans, but claim that other Miskito are not always so squeamish (cf. Conzemius 1932:77–81). If several men cooperate to kill an animal the meat is equally divided. As previously noted, part of the hunter's bag will be distributed to relatives.

As with hunting, fishing for Asang residents is now considered a form of recreation, providing food which, like wild game, is held to be exceptionally good eating. Given the proximity of the river and the fact that women and children fish as well as men, comparatively more fishing is done than hunting, and fish are an important source of protein. March and April, the heart of the dry season, are the best fishing months. In addition to a half dozen types of freshwater fish, crabs, clams, snails, and river turtles are also caught with a variety of techniques. Men fish individually in streams with palm wood bows and reed arrows tipped with a piece of sharpened iron

—a reworked umbrella rib, for example, or thick wire. Occasionally the juice of crushed *basala* vines (*Seriania inebrians*) is thrown into the water first to stun the fish (Conzemius 1932:70). Men also dynamite river fish with materials smuggled home from the mines, although this is officially illegal. Men, women, and children fish from dugouts with a hook, purchased from the commissary, and line, often made of silk-grass fiber fastened to a thin bamboo rod, using worms, ripe plantain, or the fruit of the pejivalle palm for bait. In the dry season women and children trap river fish along the shores with wide drag nets, and night fishing from dugouts, using pine torches for illumination, is also popular. This can be done only on moonless nights, however, when, according to the Miskito, the fish are sleeping and can be easily caught. On moonlit nights, fish, like people, are said to stroll about enjoying the night, and therefore are too alert to be caught.

In some villages, particularly those located above the rapids, families erect dry season fishing camps on the broad gravel beaches along the river. This custom is reported in historical sources and probably was practiced in precontact times as well. Crude shelters consisting of support poles and a thatched roof provide shade, and a few hammocks and iron cooking pots provide the necessary furniture. Asang residents do not practice this dry season move, but camps can occasionally be seen at other villages (cf. Wickham 1895:208).

At Asang a favorite Saturday activity in the dry season, especially among girls and women, is to "beat the lagoon." A group of several dozen, armed with large, conical, vine-woven baskets and conical fiber nets, travel to one or more of the long, narrow lagoons created by the ever-changing river. Beginning at the open, river end of the lagoon, the wading, splashing women drive the fish towards the banks, where, crouching in the muddy grasses and muck, some women trap the fish by hand while others behind them catch escaping fish in the baskets and nets. Whenever a fish is caught, it is killed with a quick bite at the back of the head and strung on a length of vine wrapped around the fisherwoman's waist. When the entire lagoon has been combed in this fashion, the expedition is over. Each woman keeps her own catch, but will later distribute some fish among relatives and send a few to the lay pastor.

A wide range of wild honeys, fruits, and seeds are gathered casually in the bush as people come and go about their tasks, and are eaten as between-meal snacks. Of the dozen varieties of wild honey collected during the dry season, especially in March, one may be sold at the commissary, while the others are used as sweeteners or watered down as beverages. Some households maintain a hive of stingless bees in a large bamboo joint suspended from the house porch roof. It is claimed that overindulgence in drinking honey will make a person dizzy (the Miskito term, aptly enough, is *blah*).

Among the numerous wild fruits and seeds that are consumed are Spanish plum, piñuela, the fruit of the tamarind tree, guajinquil, monkey apple, locust tree pods which make an excellent beverage, the fruit of the nancito, sapodilla or naseberries, and the fruit of a species of cacao (*Cacao pataste*) (cf. Conzemius 1932:90–91).

A number of forest products are used around the home also. Annatto provides food coloring and is applied to the face for protection against the sun. Wild flowers are popular hair decorations among *tiaras*, and hair oil is made from the seeds of fruits of the hone or oil palm. Most of the hair oil supply in Asang is traded from farther downriver where the oil palm is more common. The juice of a type of sour orange (*taitap*) is used to scrub floors and tables, together with "sandpaper" of rough leaves. *Taitap* is also applied as a bleach to bark cloth as the cloth is beaten over a log bench with a grooved mallet of palm wood (Fig. 21). Bark cloth is made from the inner bark of a tree closely related to the rubber tree (Heath 1950:32), and used today for sheets. In times of extreme hardship, as during the Sandino period, bark cloth was sometimes cut and sewn into European-style trousers, shirts, and dresses.[1]

Gourds and calabashes are used as water carriers. Five varieties of *sani*—thin, flexible strips of tree bark—are invaluable for tump lines and for tying everything from roofing thatch to small packages of food. Imitations of hemp rope are woven from *sani* if none is available in the shops. Large bijagua leaves are used for wrapping food packages and as umbrellas in a sudden downpour. Formerly they were used as plates, but have been replaced now by commissary goods. A bluing agent is made from a species of grass when the commissary is out of commercial preparations, and a kind of

1. Before the turn of the century bark cloth served as sheets and clothing, particularly for women, who wore a bark-cloth wrap from waist to knees. Under missionary influence cotton wraps and then calico dresses replaced the bark cloth (Sapper 1900; Grossman 1940).

soap is obtained from seeds of the soapberry tree if the store's shelves are empty. A handy broom is made with a few handfuls of a wild shrub. Silk-grass fibers are rolled into an extremely durable thread, if, again, manufactured thread is not available from the commissary. A pierced thorn makes a serviceable needle, as does a filed sardine can opener.

Rafts are made from bamboo, which, as was noted in chapter 2, is also widely used in house construction and in rice-drying platforms. Bed bottoms are commonly made of split bamboo and cov-

Fig. 21. Beating bark cloth. Note grooved beater, specially carved log, and sour oranges used to lighten color of cloth.

ered with a cloth mattress stuffed with the fibers surrounding the seeds of the balsa tree. Various hardwoods, especially mahogany, cedar, nancito, and rosewood are used in the manufacture of cooking spoons and stirrers, tables, chairs, stools, dugouts, paddles, mortars, and pestles. As has long been done, dugouts and paddles may be sold for several hundred cordobas to peoples living along the seacoast where the forest hardwoods are not found (cf. Roberts 1827: 119; Young 1847:11). For most people torches of pine provide the only light on dark evenings. A few families have kerosene lamps, and the Moravian church owns three Coleman lanterns, but there is difficulty now in getting fuel. Baskets of various sizes, from a few inches to several feet in diameter, are made of withes, vines, and twisted fibers (Fig. 22).

Chicle collecting provides a source of limited income for those who care to engage in it. The work is feasible since Asang is located fairly close to the forested interior where the proper trees are found. Men, singly or with several friends, travel into the bush for periods of a week or so, collecting and processing the sap. All work is done at a centrally located camp where temporary quarters are erected for eating and sleeping and for boiling and congealing the sap to

Fig. 22. Basket weaving.

form gray, sticky blocks of gum. A week's cutting today yields about one hundred pounds of chicle, which is considered a poor yield, and apparently is the result of continuous tapping. In addition, the supply of trees is becoming low, since tapping eventually kills the tree. Each man works independently as a *chiclero*, selling his supply either to local commissaries or directly to a small processing plant downriver. He keeps what profits remain after deducting the costs of provisions while in the bush. Chicle collecting is a dangerous activity, though, since a fall from a tree can mean prolonged hospitalization and high bills, and not all Asang men are willing to take the risk.

Small amounts of cash may also be obtained through the manufacture and sale of rubberized sacks to seacoast peoples. A yard or two of cheap cotton cloth is tied to a rectangular pole frame supported at a convenient working height by forked stakes at the corners (Fig. 23). A thin mixture of latex and sulfur is spread over the cloth by rotating the frame manually. Several applications are made, each being allowed to dry thoroughly before continuing. After four or five layers have dried, the piece is removed from the frame, trimmed, and folded; the seams are glued with rubber to

Fig. 23. A piece of cotton fabric tied to a pole frame is coated with a mixture of latex and sulfur to make a waterproof sack.

form a large sack. These waterproof carryalls are in wide demand for travel throughout the Coast.

In brief, it becomes apparent that the natural resources of bush and river furnish the inhabitants of Asang with a variety of foods, useful working materials, and occasionally the means to earn a few cordobas. However, the main source of cash today, such as it is, comes from the production of rice and beans as cash crops. Let us turn, then, to a consideration of agricultural practices which provide the major source of subsistence among the Miskito today.

ECONOMIC ORIENTATIONS 123

The Agricultural Cycle

The earliest ethnohistoric sources (M.W. 1732; de Lussan 1930: 280–86) note that sweet manioc, yams, bananas, plantains, maize, sugarcane, and cacao formed a significant part of the Miskito diet. These crops were raised on plantations often located some distance inland from the relatively unfertile seacoast. They continued as staples during the centuries after contact.

Agriculture did not provide material for trade, but did provide products strictly for local consumption. Furthermore, the sources agree that agriculture traditionally was women's work. This division of labor proved exceedingly adaptive to the conditions of culture contact experienced by the Miskito in that men, not responsible for sedentary tasks associated with horticulture, were free to roam the Coast hunting, fishing, and engaging in various activities associated with the means for obtaining items of foreign manufacture. It was not until the advent of commercial banana production in the twentieth century, followed by production of rice and beans as cash crops, that agriculture provided a means for cash as well as for subsistence. Concurrently, men became involved with agriculture. However, women still take greater responsibility for the daily plantation chores, such as weeding, while men's agricultural work centers more on briefer periods of clearing and, together with women, planting and harvest.

At the present time, in addition to rice and beans, several varieties of bananas and plantains, manioc, and other roots are the major crops. Maize, sugarcane, and pineapple are cultivated on a smaller scale, as are cacao, pejivalle palm, and various fruit trees. As Table 2 indicates, the introduction of cash crops has added considerably to the agricultural calendar. The yearly schedule of agricultural activities is a compact program, especially for women, with only one brief period of rest between the end of rice harvest in November and the beginning of bean planting in January. Not surprisingly this interval is eagerly anticipated as a holiday.

According to a Food and Agriculture Organization report (Taylor 1959:63), the land along both banks of the Río Coco is composed of brown alluvial soils of 5 to 8 kilometers average width, extending up to 20 kilometers wide in some areas. West of Leimus, i.e., in the direction of Asang, land is held to be practically flood-free except for small areas flooded for short periods. Texture of surface soils is commonly sandy loam, clay loam, and silty clay. Drainage is reported as good to fair, and the soils in general are held to be "highly fertile for humid tropical conditions" (Taylor 1959:74).

At Asang, informants consider the Honduranean bank of the river to be considerably more fertile than the Nicaraguan side, which on the whole is much higher ground. Honduranean land, both that fronting the river and that extending inland, is flooded annually during the rainy season, as are portions of the Nicaraguan

TABLE 2

ANNUAL CYCLE OF AGRICULTURAL ACTIVITIES IN ASANG

	Cash Crops	Subsistence Crops
Dry season		
January	Clear plantation and plant beans	
February	Weed beans; clear and	Clear and burn
March	burn rice plantations	plantations
April	Harvest beans	
Rainy season		
May	Plant rice	Plant maize, manioc, banana, and plantain
June	Weed rice	
July	Weed rice	
August	Weed rice	
Wet and dry		
September	Harvest rice; plant small bean plantation (optional)	Harvest maize; manioc ready for use
October	Harvest rice	
November	Harvest rice	Second maize planting (harvest Jan.–Feb.)

side, specifically the land lying upstream from Asang between the river and the stream which drains into the main channel in front of Asang (Fig. 6). However, land behind Asang and the downstream Nicaraguan bank stands above the flood line and is dependent on rainfall alone for moisture in addition to foregoing the annual alluvial soil deposits which are a by-product of flooding.

Prior to 1960, Honduranean land was cultivated extensively by Asang residents. The World Court's boundary decision, however, officially closed this territory to them, although to the best of my knowledge villagers may continue to cultivate if they obtain a permit. The people of Asang, though, consider permits insult added to injury. Consequently, except for periodic raids, often at night, to "steal" food from the old, now uncared for plantations, the Honduranean land is no longer used. The subversive night trips are occasioned by fear of the local Honduranean police, who now maintain stations at intervals along the river, and who occasionally harass Nicaraguan Miskito encountered by day in Honduranean territory by taking their produce or impounding a dugout and generally intimidating them with threats of further retribution.[2]

There is much hard feeling expressed in the village about the loss of this good land, and bitter complaints are voiced concerning the relative poverty of most of the Nicaraguan soil. Honduranean land reportedly could be steadily planted for up to ten or fifteen years. Nicaraguan plantations, on the other hand, wear out after one or two years, and give poorer yields even during the first year than did the Honduranean plots.

Plantations are cut today along the Nicaraguan bank of the river upstream from Asang, along all nearby creeks and their tributaries (waterways provide the major mode of transportation), and to a limited extent, on the downriver side of the village. The pattern of land utilization depends on the soil quality of individual plantations and on the type of crop planted. The basic practices adjust crop rotation and field fallowing with annual (beans, rice, manioc, maize) versus perennial (bananas and plantains) crops, and burned (rice, manioc, maize) versus unburned (beans, bananas, plantains) plots (Table 3). Thus, annual crops requiring burned land, i.e., everything except beans, cannot be planted in banana or plantain plantations since burning would destroy the perennial banana and plantain plants. Therefore, only beans are planted in banana and plantain plantations, while rice, manioc, and maize require separate plantations. Maize sometimes is planted with rice. Beans may be planted in separate plantations too.

Rice is planted preferably in wet, low lying areas directly along the river, while beans are planted in dryer soil. Both rice and bean plantations are generally planted for one year followed by one or

2. Nicaraguan Miskito villagers cultivate land on the Honduranean bank without incident in regions downriver from Asang. The difficulties experienced by Asang villagers are strictly local matters involving members of the Honduranean police stationed at a post not far from Asang.

two years fallow before they are replanted in the same crop. Sometimes, however, rice is planted in a bean plantation that has just
been harvested. This procedure is followed by at least one year's
fallow. The same holds true for (Christmas) bean plantings in a recently harvested rice plantation.

Manioc and other tubers are planted in stonier ground and can
be grown several years in succession in the same place followed by
a year's fallow period. Banana and plantain land also is used continually for several years. Rice or maize is then planted for one or
two years on this land, but not beans. After a year or two in rice or
maize, bananas and plantains can be replanted.

Plots are measured in terms of tas and hectares. A tas, theoretically, is a plot 50 meters square; four tas equal 1 hectare. People

TABLE 3

PATTERNS OF LAND UTILIZATION

	Major Annual Crops		Perennial Crops
	Plant 1 year fallow 1–2 years	Plant several years fallow 1 year	Land used continuously
Unburned field	Beans		Banana and plantain
Burned field	Maize Rice	Manioc	(New banana and plantain plot)

claim that they pace off the 50-meter distance, but in actuality, although most plantations approximate a square shape, they cannot
be guaranteed to be exact multiples of 50-meter-square units. Plantation size also varies with the crop. A 1-hectare plantation is considered large; plots of several tas are more common.

Families keep many plantations going at once. The various plantings held by an average family include: manioc, 1 or 2 tas; other
tubers, one-quarter tas, often none; maize, 1 or 2 tas plus some
planted with rice; banana and plantain varieties, three or four separate plantings of up to 1 hectare each, plus abandoned Honduranean plots still "raided"; pineapple and sugarcane, very little pineapple, and perhaps 1 tas of cane; rice, one-half to 1 hectare; beans,
1 or 2 tas; fallow land, several tas; on loan to relatives, several tas.

If more land is desired, it is simply a matter of clearing new bush.
The land fronting on the river is fully cultivated, since it is the best

on the Nicaraguan side, but land is still available along the creeks towards the interior.

Land per se has no money value—to buy or sell land is inconceivable to the Miskito. It is free for the taking. Once cleared, however, it "belongs" to the person who cleared it. He alone has the authority to direct its use as a productive unit. An "owner" will either plant the plot for his family's use or, if he does not need the land immediately, may loan a plantation to another for a season at no charge. However, the borrower may plant only rice and/or beans on the borrowed land. He definitely may not plant bananas or plantains, for to plant these perennial crops is to claim "ownership" for himself by denying the original owner use and authority over the land for several years, in effect for the productive life of the plot. Such a procedure is "playing smart" (*smart pulaia*), meaning to take advantage of someone else. This is contrary to the Miskito code of showing proper respect to one's fellow man, especially to kinsmen, and it is usually a male relative—a brother, *waikat*, uncle—who has loaned the land.

In actuality, however, "stealing" land by planting perennials is a frequent cause for quarrels. This is particularly the case after the death of a family head, when relatives will scramble for possession of the various plantations, and he who first plants bananas or plantains on the contested land wins it through sheer occupancy. Underlying this behavior is the restricted amount of alluvial soil available today, the lack of clear-cut inheritance rules in general, and the fact that obtaining the means for subsistence in Asang today is a problem faced by all family heads, but on the whole is solved individually. Kinship *ties* provide channels to other individuals who are most likely to be of assistance when help is needed, but ethics of kinship *behavior* often form only a veneer for public view. As we shall see below, private practice often involves contract agreements, and not infrequently is opportunistic.

Although the technology of planting, weeding, and harvesting is the same for all crops in that work is done by hand with only digging sticks and machetes as tools, there are variations in procedure that highlight the sociological aspect of plantation work. Specifically, production of rice and beans involves group labor on a scale not found in the cultivation of maize, manioc, bananas, and plantains. This is predicated in part on the fact that in the eyes of the people of Asang today, rice and beans are economically much

more important than any other crop since they are to provide the
necessary cash for commissary purchases. Consequently, the work
surrounding their production acquires much greater social-psycho-
logical importance than do other agricultural labors. However, from
the point of view of an outside observer, group labor may also be
seen simply as another form of technology required by the need to
plant relatively large areas in a short period of time so as to assure
even growth.

The yearly agricultural cycle begins in January with bean planting. The season is opened with the congregational planting of the
lay pastor's bean plantation. It is incumbent upon all Miskito Moravian congregations to provide rice and beans and other foodstuffs
for the use of their lay pastor (see chapter 3n16). This obligation
is handled as each congregation sees fit, but without special ceremony, by providing either produce itself, or cash to buy the necessary items. In Asang, produce is supplied, and it has become traditional for the members of the congregation to plant and harvest the
lay pastor's rice and bean plantations before beginning work on
their own.

The origins of Miskito bean cultivation and utilization are not
clear. Beans have been a Central American staple for centuries, but
ethnohistorical documents do not mention their use on the Coast
until the 1930's (Moravian Church 1890–1956:vol. 14, p. 107; Moravian Church 1903–1954:vol. 33; Conzemius 1932:63; K. Hamilton
1939). However, the Rev. Theodore Reinke, who worked with the
Miskito from 1905 until 1914, mentioned in a personal conversation
that at that time the people of Wasla, on the lower Río Coco, grew
beans on the river flats during dry season. In any case, utilization
by the Miskito was certainly not widespread. The people of Asang
recalled that "beans," the English term is used today, were available for purchase at commissaries around the turn of the century,
but were not bought. They also noted, although without being able
to specify details, that use of beans and bean planting techniques
were introduced to them in the early years of Asang's existence by
"Spaniards" from the interior who came to trade. There are two
main varieties of beans grown at the present time, red and white.
In addition a tan spotted bean and a quick growing *cuarenteno* or
forty-day variety of both the red and white are raised. The basic
red and white are by far the most common.

A bean plantation is cleared, but not burned; the covering of dead weeds acts to prevent new weed growth until the bean plants are big enough to handle weed competition. Planting is mostly women's work. Armed only with digging sticks, and keeping a sharp lookout for thorns and coral snakes, the barefooted women pierce the weed cover and drop exactly four beans into each 2-inch-deep hole. Holes are spaced approximately 15 inches apart in no particular order.

Most people plant both red and white varieties of both regular and *cuarenteno*. Sometimes each type, red or white, is planted in a separate plantation; sometimes one plot is divided into halves and each half planted in one variety. Bean plantations are not large, averaging only 1 or 2 tas.

Bean planting, along with the planting of rice, is an occasion which involves considerable interfamilial cooperation and a carefully calculated system of payment for services. Each household lets it be known which morning or afternoon they are planting, and the day before relatives and friends are approached with requests for aid. The day of the planting itself carries an atmosphere of festivity, as up to twenty-five or more women and children travel together to the plantation where, laughing and joking, they quickly plant the cleared area under the direction of the plantation owner. When they return to the village about noon (or evening if it is an afternoon session), each receives a leaf-wrapped package of food, called *bian pata* (bean food), prepared in a flurry of activity at the plantation owner's home by his wife and her female relatives. It is a point of pride among the cooks to produce a tasty bean food, but the current depression has limited the amount of "luxury foods," especially sugar, salt, and flour, that can be purchased. Thus, the women are often apologetic as they present packages to the returning workers because they feel they are not living up to the usual standards for festive foods. The family feels particularly humiliated if meat, pork or beef, is not included since meat is symbolic of the real meaning of food distribution.

In addition to providing their field help with food, the family owning the plantation automatically acquires an obligation to assist in turn every family who helped them with their planting. This return or exchange of labor is called *pana-pana*, and is based on the following principle. Plantation ownership and plantation work is basically the responsibility of each nuclear family. Therefore, when there is a chore, such as bean planting, which requires additional help, those who agree to assist in the work are working overtime. That is to say, their assistance is requiring from them labor which is in addition to their own work on their own plantations. Hence they must be recompensed for their efforts. Bean food is one method of payment operating at the level of kinship generosity and the subsistence economy, but this extra labor is also given cash value and thereby placed within the money economy. As part of the monetary system, there is need for payment either in cash or its equivalent in pounds of meat, or, as is most often the case at the present with cash so scarce, in returned labor or *pana-pana*.

There appears to be a close relationship between the means available for payment and the interest in "hiring" and being hired as extra help. The usual method of payment today is that of returning labor. However, informants emphasize, this puts the individual in the position of getting his work done only by involving himself in more work, whereas if cash can be used as payment, ego can get his work done by simply handing out money. Then, because he will gain money, he agrees to work temporarily for someone else.

During the banana period when cash was plentiful, people readily hired extra labor to help with banana work, paying in cash at a fixed rate per period of time expended, e.g., C$2.50 for one morning's work planting. People were willing to be hired because of the cash they would earn. They point out that by both hiring extra help and thereby keeping his own plantations well tended, and serving others as hired help himself, an individual was assured of plenty of cash—first from the quantity and quality of fruit he could sell, and second from his cash earnings from services to others.

The situation today reveals that while cooperative labor is still required—particularly at the busy and relatively short period of time allotted for planting beans and rice—people are not as anxious to be hired, since it is no longer possible to obtain cash by hiring out. Although an individual will probably be involved in no more physical work than before, psychologically he feels unsatisfied because there is no hard cash involved.

It is important to note the relationship between bean food and labor exchange or its cash equivalent. As we noted above, they are, in effect, two separate payment systems operating on different levels. The agreement to work for another is entered with the principles of cash payment forming the basis of the contract. It is, in other words, strictly a business deal. The presentation of bean food functions to cover or soften the impersonal economic transaction by making it an acceptable social relationship as well, based on the concept of generosity towards kinsmen and friends, with thanks expressed by food sharing, the institutionalized method for indicating mutual concern. Thus, by distribution of bean food to plantation assistants, the laborer's work is put into the category of a generous deed performed out of consideration for the well-being of the plantation owner and his family, who return the labor-gift with its equivalent in food in order to express their thanks. In this way the individualistic nature of a cold cash business deal, which threatens the existence of the kinship aspect of society because of its strong ego-orientation, is given a veneer of sociability so that it will not be as disruptive.

We also mentioned that meat forms an essential part of bean food. For practical reasons, such as potential spoilage, meat must be consumed at once. When it comes in large quantities, such as a pig or cow, this necessitates sharing between families. Thus, meat becomes symbolic of interpersonal ties, and because it carries this significance, is considered an essential element for bean food.

It is tempting to argue that the labor exchange principle itself is a manifestation of this ethic of generosity and cooperation. In fact, the people of Asang sometimes become eloquent on just this point, explaining to the stranger that the Miskito, especially the Asang Miskito, operate under the *pana-pana* principle because they have strong feelings about the virtues of helping each other. The shallowness of this ethic, at least when applied to labor exchange, becomes apparent, however, when it is necessary to weed beans. Instead of applying the principle to quickly clear the fields of weeds, the women of each family, at most the female members of a single household, labor tediously, complaining constantly, working sometimes for weeks to clear away weed growth. When asked why they do not obtain help, the answer is a sigh, and a statement to the effect that if money were available, laborers would be hired, but without money no one will consent to work. This reaction strongly suggests that labor exchange will be tolerated as an emergency measure for planting, because a nuclear family or single household cannot plant the necessary amount quickly enough to assure even growth and ripening. Without such cooperation every family would lose individually, but if it is possible to get along without hiring help on this basis, people will do so.

One final aspect of *pana-pana* should be noted. Although plantation work is seen basically in terms of individual and family responsibility with a considerable amount of a "what's in it for me" attitude behind the sociability of cooperation, the fact that cooperation does occur, irrespective of the motives, provides an area of unity which the people of Asang stress when dealing with non-Asang elements. That is, there is at least a sentiment of mutual aid and community unity that is verbalized to the anthropologist, to the missionary, sometimes even to Miskito of other communities. It is a point of village pride and of unity towards the outside which is emphasized whenever the political Asang comes into the open.

Bean harvest occurs in April, at the end of the dry season. This is a time of considerable concern for should the rains begin a bit early the crop will be destroyed. One or two good soakings will turn the fields into stinking masses of rotted beans. There is greater risk in raising beans than rice because only if floods are exceptionally heavy can the rice crop be lost, and in this part of the river floods are rarely that severe. On the other hand, the bean crop can easily be completely destroyed. People claim that because of potential loss they are a bit reluctant to plant too many beans. It is not unusual for close relatives, *moinis* for example, to help each other with bean harvest, but food is not prepared in payment for their assistance.

Harvesting beans requires two separate operations—pulling, which is women's work, and whipping or threshing, which is done by men. In pulling, each unit of four bean plants is pulled up by the roots and a vine is wrapped around the roots to make a compact unit. The package is then laid on the ground to dry for several days. The prevalence of thorny weeds makes this work rather uncomfortable. After three or four days the bean pods are dry and can be whipped. There are two techniques used for threshing. On a hot day, when the pods will be dry, six or seven men, armed with long poles, beat huge piles of bean plants placed on a ground covering of cloth and leaves (Fig. 24). The hard dry beans are then placed in barrels and the stalks thrown away. This technique is used to harvest the lay pastor's plantation because of the large number of men involved. For individual plantations, the men of the family build a raised platform of bamboo and leaves and beat the dried bean plants against the floor of the platform, letting the beans fall through the cracks in the floor onto a cowhide.

In addition to the main bean crop some families plant a smaller crop in September in order to have beans for Christmas festivities. Beans from the regular harvest are too hard to use by then, and have probably been completely consumed long before anyway. Only a small Christmas crop is planted because of the risks of wet weather.

Production depends mainly on the quality of the soil. Anywhere from four to as many as twelve "bags" per tas can be expected, or an average of about eleven quintals per family per year. A "bag" in

Fig. 24. Village men thresh the lay pastor's beans.

this sense includes beans as they come from the field with whatever chaff has gotten mixed in, and weighs less than a quintal, although the volume is roughly the same. At present, beans, like rice, are in reality a food staple as well as a cash crop, but to the Miskito they are seen as a money crop rather than a subsistence crop. Thus, approximately half of the harvest, specifically red beans, is sold, or rather exchanged, at a set rate (currently 20 centavos per pound) at the commissary for necessary goods. White and spotted beans are used largely for local consumption, although red are also eaten in quantity. The effects of the discrepancy between consuming beans as food, but viewing beans as a cash crop, will be considered after the following section on rice, since both crops are regarded in this manner, and their ultimate utilization is part of a single pattern.

While beans are growing and women are weeding, men are kept busy preparing plantations for the major annual planting period at the beginning of the rainy season in early May. Unlike the preparation of bean plantations, which are cleared, but not burned, rice, manioc, maize, and new banana plantations are both cleared and burned, and plumes of brown-gray smoke are a common sight against the constant blue of the dry season sky. Of all these crops, it is rice that receives most attention, both in conversation and in the need for group labor. As with beans, this concern reflects the importance of rice as a cash crop, and the necessity of planting a quantity in a short period of time.

There are several varieties of rice, and several categories for classifying the varieties. One distinction is made in terms of shades of hull color—red, white, and black. Another category is based on length of growing season—four-month, five-month, or six-month. Still a third is made in terms of supposed origin—Miskito and Chinese. These systems are often combined thus: Miskito, four-month, white; Chinese, five-month, red and/or black. (Five-month also can be white as can six-month.) Red and white are the usual classifications used. Black and six-month are not grown in quantity.

Like beans, the extensive utilization of rice by native Coast peoples appears to be quite recent, although rice as a New World crop dates back to early colonial times when it was introduced by the Spaniards. On the Coast, rice cultivation is mentioned as early as 1780, although it is not clear whether natives or foreigners are cultivating it (Anonymous 1885:423, 425). Roberts notes rice production by Negroes and Black Caribs in the area of the Patuka river in Honduras and west (1827:155, 274). Rice was also available from missionaries during the nineteenth century (Moravian Church 1849–1887:vol. 24, p. 244; cf. Wickham 1872:266).

The first clear references to native rice cultivation known to me are found in the *Periodical Accounts* of the Moravian Church for 1862 (p. 518) and 1877 (p. 287) (Moravian Church 1849–1887). However, not until the late 1920's does locally produced rice begin to figure prominently in the Coast economy, apparently as a result of missionary efforts to ameliorate economic conditions (Moravian Church 1890–1954:vol. 12, pp. 235, 396; Moravian Church 1903–1954:vol. 27, p. 5; K. Hamilton 1939). Conzemius notes that at the time of his visit rice was "rarely cultivated and has been introduced recently . . ." (1932:63). Only after the decline of Standard Fruit's banana operations in the early 1940's did rice cultivation, along with bean production, become commercially important to the Miskito, who found a regional market for their crops at the gold mines, lumber camps, and administrative centers of the Coast.

According to informants, the "Miskito" variety of rice was introduced to Asang by *Dama* Mercado, who brought a small amount from Honduras.[3] At first, they recall, he planted it in too high and dry a spot on the Nicaraguan bank, and only a handful was harvested. The next year, aided by *Dama* Escobar, he planted at a lower, wetter spot, and did well. *Dama* Mercado gradually gave rice to others as the supply increased, and reportedly carved the first mortar for the village. With considerable humor, informants recalled how one *kuka* tried at first to boil rice in the hulls. When they harvested one hundred pounds, they said, it seemed like a lot. Origins of Chinese rice are not remembered beyond statements that the name refers to Chinese traders who may have introduced it. There is no Miskito word for rice; the English term is used.

All varieties are planted in May, as soon as the rains have begun and the soil is loosened. While rice was new to the Asang Miskito, it is said, only women actually did the planting. Now the division of labor is such that men dig holes with the digging stick while women and children plant. Rice is planted much closer than beans, the holes being only a few inches apart. As with beans, the seeds are not covered with soil. It is felt that the rains will serve to close the holes and prevent animals from eating the seeds. Again, as with beans, rice planting is done cooperatively in half-day sessions. A nuclear family may have up to four rice plantations, each requiring a separate planting. Red rice is often planted alone in one or more "big" plantations of as much as 1 hectare each. A smaller planting, often half red and half white, may be planted in the smaller, recently harvested bean plantation. Maize may be planted in this smaller plantation among the rice if a separate maize plantation isn't planted, but maize is not planted in the larger rice plantation.

The labor exchange system of mutual aid is utilized until all

3. One informant specifically pinpointed the Patuka region in Honduras as the source of rice. A visitor to the Patuka area about 1926 or 1927 noted that rice grew well in swampy areas (Altschul 1928:381).

planting is completed, and food packages, still called *bian pata* or "bean food," again are distributed to the laborers.

Rice often requires two weedings since it takes four to six months to grow. Weeding in the rainy season is miserable work: mud, mosquitos, and *pus* flies (small, stinging gnats) must be tolerated, and back strain from the endless bending is common. Smudge pots offer some protection against insects, and girls wear trousers under their skirts for greater comfort. Weeding is done individually by each family or household, sometimes with the help of close kinsmen and in-laws on the *pana-pana* basis. Most often, though, it is "self-self"— wife, sometimes husband, and unmarried children working for weeks on end, laboriously cutting the weeds from between the rice stalks with a machete. If money were available additional workers could be hired at the rate of C$2.50 per day's work (early morning to noon). The owner of the plantation would also be expected to provide a light refreshment such as sugarcane water about 11:00 A.M. If cash is not available and help is needed, meat can be given in lieu of money—2½ pounds for one day's work (one pound equals C$1).

Today, since cattle are not numerous, people are loath to kill an animal just for this, although sometimes it is the only solution. For example, Ricardo had planted 2 hectares in rice and had only his wife to help with the weeding, which was particularly slow and difficult since most of the weeds were fine grass. He finally killed a cow and distributed the meat in 2½ or 5 pound lots to anyone who wanted it in return for promises of one or two days' weeding. People were eager to obtain the meat, and he had no difficulty disposing of it. Note, however, that before he began to distribute meat to potential laborers Ricardo serviced all those who wanted to pay cash for meat. Only the non-Miskito residents bought in this way: the school teachers, the Creole commissary owner, and the anthropologist. This was the only such "emergency" case for the season.

Harvest extends from late August into November with September and October as high points. Small plantations are harvested by the nuclear family or household, but larger ones may require help. Therefore, harvest workers are recruited, but instead of working on the emergency labor exchange system, most laborers take wages in produce. Specifically, half the number of bunches or bags of rice harvested by an individual are given to him as pay. If cash were available it would be preferred, but in its absence produce, which serves as cash today at the commissary, replaces it. It is not difficult to recruit help when produce is the method of payment because there are "poorer" people, widows and deserted mothers, for example, who are eager for the extra rice. Labor exchange does not help these people as much because no matter how often they assist others, they can only obtain return help for work on a plantation which is of set size and therefore of limited production. If payment is in produce, however, the amount of rice a woman can earn is limited only by her energy and her time.

Five to ten people, usually girls and women, may help with harvesting. Since they will not return home until two or three o'clock in the afternoon, they are fed at the plantation rather than at the plantation owner's home. Food is prepared at home by the women of the family and then about noon is carried along the slippery paths to the plantation. Again women feel prestige pressure to prepare good food for the plantation helpers.

Harvest techniques vary. Rice can be reaped by the bunch (*buns* in Miskito), defined as a double handful of stems. Men cut the stems while girls and women strip the leaves from the stalks and gather them into bunches. A woman can harvest anywhere from five to ten bunches in one day's work. When the stems are dry and bent, near the end of the harvest season, the rice stems are broken just below the head without pulling the stalk.

As with beans, handfuls of stems may be whipped or beaten on a platform of bamboo and banana leaves, allowing the grain to fall onto a cowhide (Fig. 25). Heads may be stripped into a shirt or a pail also. A woman can whip three or four bags worth and a man eight to ten bags in one day. A bag contains the grain plus any chaff that has fallen through.

About two months after the main harvest, the plantation may be reharvested by the family to reap any rice that was still immature at the time of the main harvest. Some people prefer to save this rice for seed since it is thought to have a thinner hull.

Back at the village women and *tiaras* are busy from August through November threshing rice. Before being threshed, the bunches are spread on roofs or high bamboo platforms to dry in the sun for a few days. The dull, rhythmic thump, thump, thump of mortar and pestle are heard constantly, alternating pleasantly with the faster tap, tap of bark cloth beating which is also done at this time of year. Usually one girl threshes at a time, but for amusement, or to show off, two or even three will work in unison at one mortar. A few chickens always scurry about picking up fallen grains. The rice yield varies tremendously with soil quality and care given to plantations. From 2 tas it is not impossible to obtain as high as 600 bunches, but this is rarely done. A conservative average figure might run from 150 to 300 bunches from 2 tas, or, since one bunch of unhulled rice weighs about 6 pounds, 900 to 1,800 pounds of unhulled rice. This is equivalent to 600 to 1,200 pounds of hulled rice.

Rice, like beans, is utilized in two ways—as a cash crop, or in

Fig. 25. Handfuls of rice stalks are beaten against a bamboo platform, and the grains fall to the cowhide below.

today's depression as cash itself, and as food. At least half the crop is eventually exchanged for food, cloth, and miscellaneous items at commissaries in Asang, Santa Izabel, or San Carlos. The rest is kept at home for food, and is hung in bunches from the house rafters until needed.

Rice is usually eaten simply boiled with beans, a concoction known by the English term "rice and beans." Sometimes beans are boiled separately and then fried in lard before being ladled on top of a plate of boiled rice. Ground rice, prepared in small, hand-cranked mills purchased at the commissary, is made into a thin gruel or, occasionally, baked into small cakes, sometimes mixed with coconut.

The supply of both rice and beans does not last the entire year. To a great extent this shortage is the result of the two situations mentioned above which often conflict. In reality, rice and beans form a major part of the Miskito diet today. However, the people of Asang conceptualize rice and beans mainly as instruments for obtaining cash or foreign goods rather than as food. The discrepancy between the fact that rice and beans actually are basic to subsistence today and the perception of rice and beans as serving primarily as a cash crop serves to deplete the annual supply quickly.

Rice and beans are called English food by the residents of Asang, indicating that they do not consider them entirely part of Miskito culture. It is not unusual to find a family eating a full plate of rice and beans while at the same time complaining loudly about the lack of food, meaning either that they feel they are missing traditional Miskito food (wild game or the higher quality produce once grown on Honduranean soil), or that they are nostalgic about the once abundant foreign foods no longer readily available because of the depression. If it is pointed out that they are having enough to eat, the investigator is met with a condescending glance, and it is explained that rice and beans are to be used for money, not food. Consequently, whenever a piece of soap, some flour, or sugar is needed, a child is dispatched to the commissary with a pan of rice or beans to exchange for the desired item. However, as long as there is a supply remaining, rice and beans also form the basis of the two or three meals eaten by the family every day. Eventually the time comes when no more rice and beans are left to eat because they have been sold, and vice versa.

In theory rice and beans between them should neatly cover the needs of the year. Rice harvest takes place in September-October, and the supply should last until the April bean harvest. Beans should then carry over until the new rice harvest in September. The flaw in the system is perhaps twofold. The insightful village philosopher claims that lack of planning is to blame. The Miskito are "ready-made poor," as he put it, because they do not budget time, needs, and quantity of marketable produce. He points out that families prefer to sell their rice and beans as goods are needed with no concern for restraint today in order to have something for tomorrow. We can add that the same reasoning applies to the consumption of rice and beans at home. Other family heads argue, in turn, that the problem lies in limited production. They cannot handle the weeding that extra planting would require without hiring help, they say, and there is no cash to hire extra help, so what can one do?

Both arguments appear to be legitimate. To the people of Asang there is little point in planting more of a cash crop if there is no market for it. To grow more in order to have more to consume at home is illogical to them because rice and beans are not grown for food, but for cash. To grow more in order to have a larger quantity for exchange in kind at the commissary is not considered sensible, either. Commissary stock is low, people complain, and so is the price paid for rice and beans. Although in past years, informants noted, rice brought as much as 30 centavos per pound and beans sold for up to 50 centavos per pound, today rice and beans bring only 18 centavos and 20 centavos per pound, respectively. "Why spend more time for such a small return?" they ask. That is the way to "lose." What is wanted is a ready market for rice and beans, a higher price per pound, actual cash paid for their produce, and a well-stocked commissary. Then, informants claim, they would gladly plant more, and be able to handle the extra work because money would be available to hire help. In brief, when the advantages of the market economy are good, Asang villagers are eager to participate as fully as possible. When the market is depressed, however, only limited effort is made to obtain the limited advantages still available. Thus, although beans will bring 35 centavos per pound in Waspam and Puerto Cabezas, little effort is made by individual growers to get them there directly. One informant put it aptly: "When I have less money, I work less." For the Miskito the index to the presence or absence of suitable market conditions is basically the availability of hard cash. This will determine production of rice and beans.

However, the point concerning absence of planning of what supply is available is also relevant. The traditional Miskito subsistence economy contained bananas, plantains, and manioc as staple foods, all of which are available year round on a day-to-day basis. Long-range planning is not required to keep a supply available. Rice and beans, on the other hand, are harvested all at once and their use, whether as food or exchange, must be conserved and planned if they are to last for the desired period. This is not done. Immediate needs of food and commissary exchange are met fully, under the philosophy that "when the rice (beans) is gone, it's gone." Other foods—meat, fish, manioc, banana, plantain—will be available to hold over until the next harvest, and bush materials can replace salt, soap, et cetera, if necessary. Another factor behind the lack of planning is that during the banana period just prior to today's depression money and goods were overabundant, and hence no decisions concerning their allocation were required. At present, in contrast, so little cash can be obtained that there is not much point in being concerned with its distribution. In other words, the Miskito simply have never had to learn to economize. Consequently, by April many families have run out of rice. In order to replant rice in May and also have some for bean food, they must buy rice back from the commissary with the newly harvested beans at a greatly increased price, currently C$1.00 per pound. This puts an extra strain on the bean supply, so that it too is quickly finished. The result is a period without rice or beans during the months of the rainy season while the new rice crop is growing.

In addition to rice and beans and along with domestic animals, fish, and forest products, serving as a backstop during the lean period in rainy season are the agricultural products that have formed the traditional Miskito food supply. These include sweet manioc and other root crops (eddoes or yautia, sweet potatoes, varieties of yam), several varieties of bananas and plantains, maize, sugarcane, cacao, coffee, pineapples, and squash. In the overriding concern with the rice and bean crops, these cultigens and the work connected with them go almost unnoticed. Planting, weeding, and harvesting of these crops is a nuclear family or household affair, and extra help is normally not needed.

Manioc is first mentioned by the buccaneers, and was undoubtedly cultivated by Coastal people in aboriginal times. It formed an agricultural staple particularly for those living along the seacoast proper, for of all the cultigens noted in the early literature, manioc fared best in the savannah areas close to the sea. Although people farther inland also raised manioc, they relied more heavily on bananas and plantains. This distinction held throughout the centuries of contact, and remains today (Roberts 1827:115; Conzemius 1932: 61–62; Grossman 1940:20).

Currently in Asang, informants noted that manioc production and consumption has increased since the 1960 border decision forced them to rely more on poorer Nicaraguan soils. Manioc is planted in late April or early May before the rains begin. The plantation is cleared, burned, and thoroughly cleaned of debris. Then stems from the previous year's harvest are cut into two or three slips and placed horizontally in the ground. By September the manioc is ready for use and roots are pulled as needed for immediate consumption. By the following March or April, when the plant begins to flower, the roots are too hard for eating. Hard roots are ground, soaked, strained, and dried to make starch. When roots are no longer edible the plantation is either cleared on the surface of all stems, reburned, and left to regrow, or just the leaves are cut from the old plants leaving the stems to regrow a new leaf set. In either case, a new edible root growth is obtained which serves to provide manioc through the growing period (May–September) until a new plantation is ready to be used.

When a supply of manioc is needed, the selected stems are cut off near the ground, placed cut-end down in a hole, and covered lightly with dirt. They will take root and remain viable to serve as slips for next year's planting. The roots themselves are then pulled, and the nodes are cut from the main root and placed into baskets to be carried home.

Of the other root crops used in Asang eddo or yautia is next in importance. The same planting and harvesting technique is used except that stems are cut into quarters for planting, and planting occurs after the rains have begun, rather than before. Unlike manioc, eddoes can be stored, and after being harvested can be placed in baskets and kept on the house rafters for up to a year. Small quantities of sweet potatoes and yams are also raised occasionally (cf. Conzemius 1932:63).

Manioc and other tubers are eaten boiled or baked. Manioc is also made into a soured beverage, a *bunya* as any soured drink is called. *Bunya* can also be prepared from bananas, plantains, or the fruit of the pejivalle palm, and its consumption is noted in the literature beginning with the buccaneers. More festive manioc preparations include a kind of sweet cake made of ground manioc mixed with sugar, lard, salt and then baked, and a fused cylinder of ground manioc mixed with lard and salt, wrapped in a leaf, and baked.

As late as the early decades of the twentieth century a fermented beverage called *mishla* was still drunk. *Mishla* was prepared from masticated manioc, plantains, bananas, or pejivalle fruit with sugarcane or pineapple added to hasten fermentation (cf. Roberts 1827: 129–30; Conzemius 1932:99). The beverage was prepared on all social and ceremonial occasions until its use was stopped by missionaries. Rum and chicha have taken its place as intoxicants.

Along with manioc, varieties of plantains and bananas have formed the basis for Miskito subsistence for centuries. As far as the people of Asang are concerned, whereas rice and beans are considered "English food," banana and plantain are the traditional Miskito staples. Their use as a major food is mentioned consistently in the literature, beginning with the buccaneer accounts. Whether plantain and banana are pre- or post-Columbian is still unsettled. It is generally accepted that banana was brought to the Indies by the Spanish, although it has been argued that banana may also have been introduced in pre-Conquest times (Robertson 1927:19, 55n). The case for plantain is unclear. Sauer argues strongly for its pre-Conquest introduction (1950:526–27; 1952:56–7, 60). On the Miskito Coast both banana and plantain were utilized in the seventeenth century.

Of the varieties of Musaceae planted by the Miskito today, the Gros Michel, dwarf banana, and plantain are the most common. There are in addition other varieties which are not as plentiful, some having fruit only several inches long, others with reddish pulp. When a new banana or plantain plantation is begun, it is started in late May or early June, in the beginning of the rainy season. Fruit begins to form after about nine months, and in a year is ready to use. Plantain and banana plantations are kept in continuous production by the simple procedure of tending the shoots sent out from the parent stalk. Most families maintain as many as four separate banana and plantain plantations in various stages of production and also cut fruit from deserted plantations. Although the Gros Michel once formed the cash crop during the golden age of Standard Fruit's activities, today the fruit is used for home consumption only, a stem of green fruit being cut whenever needed. People note also that Nicaraguan soil is too dry and stony for optimum banana and plantain yields, and complain that fruit that was once fit to feed only to livestock when Honduranean soil was cultivated is now eaten by people, too.

Bananas and plantains are prepared in a variety of ways. Ripe bananas are eaten raw, are baked, or are made into *wabul*, which is simply a mixture of boiled fruit mashed with water or coconut milk and stirred smooth with a knobbed wooden staff several feet long. *Wabul* is the staple and traditional Miskito beverage, especially for riverine groups. It provides a warm and satisfying drink, and no Miskito meal is complete without it. Green bananas are either boiled whole or made into *wabul*. Ripe plantains may be cut into strips and fried, may be boiled or baked whole, or may be made into *wabul* or porridge. Green plantain is fried or boiled. One variety, known as *plas*, also provides a kind of vinegar, which is prepared by straining the ripe fruit and placing the bottled liquid in the sun for a few days.

Many Asang adults can recall the practice of preserving bananas and plantains. A pit several feet deep was dug and lined with leaves. Green bananas and plantains were peeled, packed into the pit, and covered with leaves and dirt. In this way a supply of bananas and plantains could be kept up to a year or more without spoiling, and provided insurance against the ravages of floods and hurricanes. When the pit was finally opened, the light-colored fruit turned black on exposure to the air and reportedly produced a horrible odor until washed and cleaned, hence its name of *bisbaia*, literally, "to stink." The preserved fruit could be dried into a kind of flour, mixed with meat, or made into *wabul*.

In Asang only one elderly, very conservative woman had a cache of *bisbaia* near her home in 1964–65. Others, although they no longer make it, reminisce enthusiastically about its flavor. Grossman (1940:17) describes another storage technique whereby bananas are cut into long slices, dried in the sun, and then stored until needed, at which time they are mashed into a flour. This is not done in Asang.

Maize has played a small but constant role in the Miskito diet. Buccaneer accounts (cf. M. W. 1732) note its preparation as a beverage, and it is so used today in Asang, although most of the maize raised by villagers is fed to animals. In general, however, as Conzemius noted, "maize or Indian corn, . . . which forms the staple food practically all over Central America, is sparsely cultivated by the Miskito . . ." (1932:63). It is possible for Asang residents to obtain two crops per year. The main planting is done about May and harvested in September, while a second crop is planted in November-December and harvested about January-February. Harvest dates may vary somewhat, since if people are busy, the matured ears may be doubled, or bent down on the stalk, until time permits their harvest. Separate maize plantations, on high, dry ground, may be cleared and burned, or maize can be planted among the rice.

Maize is most used in the form of beverages: *pinol,* made by mixing milled corn, which has first been toasted, with hot water and, if available, sugar; *pusol* or *pozol,* made from boiled kernels mashed and then strained; *atol,* made from mashed green corn. It is also eaten green, roasted on the cob, or parched and then ground and fried in cakes. Several kinds of tamales are made from green corn mixed with lard and from cornmeal prepared from kernels softened by boiling with ashes, then mixed with meat and rice. In either case the mixture is wrapped in leaves or husks and boiled or baked.

Sugarcane, cacao, coffee, squash, and pineapples are raised for local consumption today, but in small quantities. On rare occasions tomatoes and watermelons may also be planted. Village elders claim that pineapple and sugarcane were raised in greater abundance in the early days of the village, but that it was difficult to keep ahead of the depredations of mischievous boys, whose numbers increased as the village grew. To be sure, today's young men fondly recall their furtive boyhood excursions to sugarcane and pineapple plantations in the bush, but an equally plausible reason for the decline in production of these crops is that *mishla,* which used pineapple and sugarcane for flavoring and to hasten fermentation, has been suppressed by missionaries and is no longer made (Roberts 1827:129–30; Conzemius 1932:99). Today only small amounts of pineapple are eaten; sugarcane juice is used as a sweetener, and the sections are sucked as confections.

Many families lost considerable holdings of cacao and coffee trees as a result of the *traslado* and have not bothered to replant in Nicaragua. Cotton plants can be found growing near homes in Asang, but cotton is no longer cultivated. Conzemius (1932:50–51) notes that the younger generation at the time of his visit was not continuing the art of weaving and that cultivation of cotton was only desultory. Today all cloth is purchased at the commissary.

In addition to plantations in the bush, many families also tend small gardens near their homes. The gardens are fenced with wood, bamboo, or wire as protection against wandering livestock. These plots are crowded with a variety of plants and provide a small supply of papaya, avocado, granadilla, chile peppers, and herbs. Young cacao, coconut, calabash, and citrus trees may be tended here too and later transplanted to bush plantations or kept in the village. The numerous citrus trees in the village furnish a grand abundance of oranges, sour and sweet limes, and grapefruit in season. These fruits are eaten on a first pick, first eat basis by the villagers; children in particular help themselves freely. The individuals who own the trees complain about this disrespect for their property, and grumble that although other people don't want to bother to plant and tend trees, they have no compunction about eating the fruit. Those with fruit remaining near the end of the season occasionally sell small quantities to other villagers.

In spite of the apparent wide variety of foods available, Miskito meals have a certain similarity from day to day. Generally two main meals are eaten, one in the early morning shortly after dawn and the other in the late afternoon after return from the plantation. At noon a light refreshment, often liquid, may be taken. The main meals revolve around rice, beans, manioc, bananas, and plantains. A piece of meat or fish, or perhaps a flour tortilla, is a treat and not available every day. A typical meal includes rice and beans, boiled green bananas or baked plantains, boiled manioc, perhaps a small fish, coffee or *wabul*.

Animal Husbandry

Although today most of the daily food supply is obtained through agriculture, a not insignificant amount, especially protein, comes from hunting and fishing, and the raising of domestic animals. As with agriculture, animal husbandry and the utilization of meat in general contains elements of both subsistence and cash economies.

To judge from the historical documents, domestic animals have never been accorded great attention by the Miskito. Compared to reports of agriculture and fishing, the literature is practically silent on the matter of animal husbandry. Mention of domestic animals is first found in the late eighteenth and early nineteenth centuries, and these sources note that domestic animals were neglected. Horses and cattle were allowed to roam the savannahs untended, while pigs, chickens, and turkeys fended for themselves in the village. Cattle herds were constantly being depleted by indiscriminate slaughtering for festivals and by the custom of settling disputes, especially charges of adultery, by shooting each other's livestock (Porta Costas 1908:262, 272; Roberts 1827:137; Young 1847:15; Mueller 1932:23; Grossman 1940:31–34).

The people of Asang continue the pattern of neglect. Horses, cattle, pigs, chickens, turkeys, and an occasional muscovy duck are raised by the villagers, and numerous "sneaky, repulsive curs" (Conzemius 1932:59) are constantly kicked out of the way as well. A few cats are also kept as mousers. This livestock, however, is left to take care of itself for the most part.

However, lack of careful attention does not mean that animals are not valued. In contrast to plantations which are "owned" by the head of the nuclear family for everyone's benefit, domestic animals are individually owned by children as well as adults. It is by the sale of pork or beef, or, more likely of a chicken or turkey, that an individual can obtain the means to purchase personal items he or she desires. Cloth for a new dress, earrings, a bright new bandana, "sweet" (perfumed) soap can be obtained in this way without drawing on family property such as rice and beans. Yet little attention is given, particularly to cattle and horses, on a daily basis.

In Asang, horses are used for transportation only when it is not possible to travel by river, most commonly during rainy season when the river is in flood. They are often ridden without a saddle (cf. Conzemius 1932:59); an old sack, some bark cloth, or an old pair of trousers being used in its place. The villagers' horses, approximately thirty-five head, graze much of the time in the cleared area behind the settled portion of the village. However, few families own horses, and if a horseless individual wishes the use of an animal he simply borrows another's, not necessarily with permission. If the owner should scold, people say, the blame lies on him for being angry or "proud."

Cattle are kept mainly as an emergency source of money, and, because they represent wealth, are also prestige items. However, they receive almost no care from the owner, and roam the bush often dying of old age. Villagers claim that cattle holdings have been drastically reduced within the last thirty years. This is attributed to the effects of the Sandino Affair, when "bandits" destroyed the herds for their own use. Consequently, informants feel, cattle are in very short supply today. If a tally is made family by family, it quickly becomes apparent that, in fact, many families have no cattle, or only one or two head at the present time. Guerrilla fighters probably did deplete cattle holdings, but unless other factors are involved natural reproduction rates should have restored the size of the herds by now.

Another possibility, although villagers themselves never suggested it, is that during the prosperity of the banana period a disproportionate number of animals were slaughtered to provide meat for extravagant holiday celebrations. Included in all the reminiscences about the banana boom are accounts of the ease with which cattle could be purchased, and the frequency of celebrations involving beef. Villagers stress the relative lack of such meat-eating festivities today as an example of the deprivation of depression. Continued butchering for special occasions, even if on a limited basis, would have kept the number of cattle low ever since. Whatever the reasons, cattle are not very numerous at the present time. There is also a problem of pasturage now, since the Honduranean savannahs are off limits and there is not much grazing area near Asang on the Nicaraguan side of the river. This, too, could be a factor in keeping the herds small.

Partly because of scarcity, the slaughter of a cow today is rather unusual. Three animals were killed during the year 1964–65. One was purchased by the Moravian congregation for the annual village New Year's festivities. The second was slaughtered by its owner to provide meat as payment for rice weeders in an emergency situation. The third was sick and the owner feared total loss if the animal died. The depression situation also dampens people's willingness to slaughter. Cattle are potential cash, and the feeling is that since there is so little cash in circulation these days, you lose if you slaughter because no one can buy meat except with rice or beans. Consequently, cattle simply roam the area and, except for one or two families who may occasionally milk a cow, are not utilized.

Pigs are more numerous than cows and today provide the main source of meat. Again, however, slaughter of a pig rarely occurs without special cause. In addition, there are sufficient "special events" that the number of pigs owned by a family, usually a sow with litter, generally will not permit killing merely to provide variety in the family diet. For example, the average family would wish to slaughter a pig on the following occasions: to feed bean planters; to feed rice planters; in an emergency, to feed rice weeders; and to feed visiting relatives at Christmas-New Year. Another animal might be sold to a less advantaged relative who needs meat for bean food. A few more are also lost each year to jaguars. It is noteworthy that since most of the events requiring slaughter of a pig are concerned with rice and bean cultivation, the consumption of pork is probably higher today than ever before. According to Conzemius (1932:59), in the early decades of the century, when, as we have seen, rice and beans were little used, "pork [was] rarely eaten by the Indians. . . ."

Every family can afford to own a few pigs because, along with the ubiquitous chickens, they serve as garbage disposals, quickly clearing the village of the leftovers from meals and the debris from food preparation. Little food is lost in this system, since practically all uneaten vegetable matter is converted into meat.

Fowl, being smaller animals, are not reserved for use on special occasions as much as are pigs and cattle. Chickens are raised for eggs and meat. Eggs are occasionally eaten and are used as exchange items (one egg equals 25 centavos) within the village and occasionally with the commissary barges. Chickens will be killed for family use as well as for bean food. If an important visitor such as the Moravian parson or doctor visits the village, a chicken may be sent to him as a mark of respect and concern for his comfort. Chickens and especially turkeys are sometimes sold to people living downriver and serve as a minor source of income.

In the early decades of Asang's existence, elders reminisce, the killing of a large animal, either domestic or wild game, meant that everyone in the community received a gift of meat. Today, they complain, if you want to eat meat you must buy it or kill your own. The modern generation counters these accusations of selfishness, grave charges since meat distribution is symbolic of respect for kinsmen and sociability in general, by stating that the village is far too large to give meat to everyone today. But because of general poverty, they continue to give meat to relatives (although they prefer to sell as much as possible for cash). Furthermore, they emphasize, wild game is never sold (which is true).

Subsistence activities are basically the concern of each nuclear family, which fends for itself, hiring others to help on a contract basis only if necessary. However, as we have seen, there are households composed of more than one nuclear family.[4] In these situations, the head of each nuclear family retains private ownership of his agricultural produce and livestock. From this supply he contributes food to the common meals in rotation with other family

4. Reciprocal food exchange with relatives who live in separate households has been discussed in chapter 3. It forms the third arena for economic distribution, following nuclear family and extended family pooling of produce.

heads. One day his rice is used, next day the others'. When salt, soap, sugar, or lard is needed from the commissary, the families again rotate in supplying the necessary rice or beans for exchange. Personal items such as clothing are purchased from each family's private supply. If one family runs out of rice and beans before the other they will continue to eat the common meal, but cannot use any of the other's produce to buy such goods as salt or soap. There are no problems when it comes to supplying manioc, bananas, and plantains, since these are constantly available.

There can be friction in such households if it is felt that one family is selling its rice and beans too quickly and therefore will not be able to contribute enough to the common food supply. Each household reaches its own agreement on this matter. Families also take turns killing livestock for household use.

Nuclear family households may enter the production and distribution pattern of the joint household when a young, unmarried *wahma* begins his own plantations. Many *wahmas* start their own rice and bean plantations before marriage in order to have some spending money or its equivalent. They then reach an agreement with their parents as to the size of their contributions to the household food supply. In these situations, however, considerable laxity is allowed, some indulgent parents permitting their sons to keep all the produce of their own plantations or requesting only a token amount for the household.

Wage Labor, Commissaries, and the Cash Economy

Wahmas also earn spending money by collecting chicle, cutting lumber, or going to the mines for several months, sometimes years, as a sort of youthful fling before settling down to serious adulthood in the village. Family heads also resort to these methods to get extra cash in the periods between planting and harvest when plantation work is largely turned over to the women.

Note that it is only men who enter into contracts of one sort or another with the outside world. Women remain in the village. Men's more numerous outside contacts give them a certain psychological advantage over the more conservative women, who have not seen as much of the non-Miskito world. On the other hand, as was indicated in chapter 1, women's relative conservatism plays an important role in maintaining Miskito customs and cultural identity.

Work as *chicleros* has been discussed previously. No prior contract is needed to gather chicle. The current buying price for the sticky, gray blocks determines whether an individual feels it worth his while to tap.[5] Lumbering, in contrast, is undertaken through contracts between groups of eight or ten men, friends and/or relatives, who agree to provide a certain number of board feet for non-Miskito buyers on the coast. One contract, by way of example, was for a group of ten Asang men to prepare and deliver 12,000 board feet of mahogany at 75 centavos per foot to a merchant on the coast.

Fig. 26. Two teams of sawyers cut planks from a prepared log.

Several weeks are spent in the bush, laboriously felling trees and sawing lumber, using an elevated pit saw technique which may have been introduced by missionaries (Moravian Church 1890–1956:vol. 10, p. 239). A scaffold, approximately 7 feet high is constructed, and a log, which has been previously squared so as to have two opposing sides, placed flat-side down on the scaffold with ends projecting (Fig. 26). Two teams of two men each, one on the ground and one on the log, saw along marked lines with a double-

5. Chicle collecting provides the major source of cash for people in the rapids area of the river where, because of transportation difficulties, rice and beans cannot be raised commercially.

handled saw. Each team handles one end of the log, working towards the center. After all marked lines are sawed from the end towards the center, the center section is cut and the slabs of lumber removed. Profit from the sale is equally divided after food and transportation expenses have been deducted. The 12,000-feet contract group hoped to clear C$550 per man, which, they felt, would soon be spent on tools and clothing for the family.[6]

Lumbering can also become a communal activity, either for a community project—building the church or a new medical clinic—or to help an individual who has suffered extreme hardship. When Rodolfo was severely injured in a bush accident it was obvious that he needed hospitalization regardless of the high cost of such treatment. His brother, Chester, undertook to pay the bill. Various approaches were considered including carving a dugout for sale downriver or raising additional rice and beans for sale. Finally an agreement was reached between Chester and the hospital whereby Rodolfo's bill would be considered paid if a certain amount of lumber were cut for hospital use. Chester turned to the community for assistance in this task, and for several weeks teams of men sawed in the bush while women carried the boards to the river. Chester then prepared a raft, loaded the lumber and 600 pounds of beans which he hoped to sell downriver, and set off. Several days later word reached the village that while traveling at night his raft struck floating debris. Food, clothing, the beans, and some of the lumber were lost. Chester was reportedly headed for the mines to try to earn back what he had lost.

The gold mines in the interior are the best place to earn money now (cf. Parsons 1955a). Many single and even married men have sought work there, sometimes remaining for part of a year, sometimes for several years. Men may alternately work at the mines and return to Asang several times throughout their adult lives. Some, however, never return, although they periodically may send food, clothing, and/or money back to relatives in the village. Some do not show even this much concern, and are eventually considered lost as kinsmen. Most, however, especially the young men, work at the mines on a temporary basis as part of a youthful spree that takes

6. Tools and men's clothing are among the more expensive items for a Miskito family. The following list is representative of the materials needed and the cost thereof: machetes, C$16.50; ax, C$22.50; work shoes, C$22.00; dress shoes, C$50.00; shirt, C$20.00.

them wherever there is a job. But since there is currently a surfeit of labor at the mines and all other major businesses have folded, young men are gradually drifting back to the community and returning to plantation work. Approximately forty Asang men are currently employed by three mining companies.

Mine labor has both positive and negative features. The high rates of disease discourage some men, and separation from wife and family is also a matter to be considered. On the other hand, mining offers greater social security benefits than any other type of contractual work; if a worker is injured or killed while on the job, expenses or an indemnity are paid by the company. Miskito men are quick to learn about such things as mine equipment and airplanes (travel to the mines is generally via air from points downriver), and entertain the folks back home with animated accounts of these operations.

When all other sources are unavailable or unproductive, gold prospecting may be tried. The smaller creeks and streams contain gold in small amounts, and panning may yield a few flakes. Output is small, however, and no one works long or hard at panning.

Opportunities to earn cash within Asang are also limited. There are a few spare-time craftsmen in the village—two shoemakers, several barbers, and a pipe carver. (Barbers don't always charge for their services.) Several women earn supplementary money by taking in sewing. Extra work for the Moravian church may yield a few cordobas; the lay pastor paid cash, C$2.00, to those women and *tiaras* who helped to sweep the churchyard in preparation for the parson's visit.

Opportunities to spend cash are similarly few today, much to the dissatisfaction of the villagers. Commissaries have been located in Asang since the days of *Dama* Sanders. At the height of the banana boom several shops were in operation.[7] Today there are two in the village; one, the smaller of the two, owned and operated by a Miskito man of the Bobb *kiamp*; the other purchased from the banana company by a Creole gentleman, Mr. Miller, who married an Asang woman and settled in the village about ten years ago.

Commissaries are the principle source of foreign items, and shop

7. The terms shop and commissary are used synonymously throughout this study to refer to any type of general store. Commissary does not refer only to a company store, although during the banana boom some commissaries were run by the Standard Fruit Company.

ownership is a position of high prestige among the Miskito, primarily because it indicates that the proprietor is a man of the "modern" world. Generally speaking, however, stores run by non-Miskito succeed better than Miskito attempts. Asang men feel that, in spite of the prestige involved, operating a shop is bound to be a losing business because of the demands that kinsmen will make on the shopkeeper's resources by efforts to borrow cash, and the expectation of goods on credit or as gifts. An attempt several years ago by a son of *Dama* Sanders to operate a small store in the community failed because of the extensive credit he extended. At the present time, the Miskito, Augusto Bobb, who has been in business for little more than a year, is experiencing these difficulties. Because of his Miskito wife, Miller is also subject to demands of Asang kinsmen, but he is able to avoid them more successfully than Bobb, partly because of his own non-Miskito background, and partly because he makes a conscious effort to maintain a slightly aloof position in the community in order to ease the strain on his business. Miller also noted that Miskito commercial ventures were often in difficulty because of their incomplete understanding of the workings of the market economy.

There is no competition between the two Asang shopkeepers, and they charge the same for their goods. For Augusto Bobb the store is an adjunct to his plantation work, and although business is slow these days, he still has the prestige of ownership. There is also sufficient income for him to keep his family well fed and better dressed than most other village family heads, thus making him a figure of envy to some. Miller does not engage in agriculture, although he raises a few pigs and chickens, but depends entirely on his shop for his family's subsistence. His style of living is modest, however, and his needs easily met by the store. Actually, Miller's residence in Asang is for personal rather than business reasons. People claim that for this reason he is lax in trying to maintain a diversified stock. In reality, Miller is able to earn more from the buying and selling of rice and beans as a middleman between Asang producers and coastal consumers, than from the sale of stock per se.

Villagers patronize both shops, although they often go to Miller first since his is the older and larger of the two, at least in floor space. But since Miller's stock is often limited, both in quantity and variety, potential customers turn to Bobb, although his holdings are generally equally as low.

The lack of goods in Asang shops is a source of much disgruntlement on the part of the villagers. Miller, for example, will travel to the coastal towns an average of twice a year for sugar, flour, salt, lard, yard goods, manufactured men's clothing, quinine pills and various patent medicines, cigarettes and tobacco, canned goods, soaps, writing materials, kitchen utensils, hair ornaments, nails, files, et cetera. Upon occasion he will buy several additional quintals of flour, sugar, or salt and tins of lard from the commercial barges. However, not infrequently, the Asang shops are sold out of these items. Villagers then travel to the neighboring communities of San Carlos or Santa Izabel (a half day's venture at best), where, because they are educational and administrative centers for the region, shops are more numerous and somewhat better stocked.

They may also wait for the barges which run on approximately bi-weekly schedules. The latter alternative is risky, though, since Asang is close to the end of the line for barge travel (the rapids are not far off), and items may be sold out again. Also goods bought from the barges and the other towns are generally more expensive than they are in Asang.

People also grumble that they cannot exchange their rice and beans for cash alone at Miller's and Bobb's commissaries, but must take goods in exchange, and the selection is invariably poor. If change is required in the transaction it may be given with a few coins of small denomination, but also in kind, for example, beans as change for a transaction paid for with rice. If they have sufficient resources of change, barge operators will exchange rice and beans for cash, as will shopkeepers at San Carlos and Santa Izabel. Not infrequently, though, the barges also must exchange in kind.

In spite of deficiencies in stock and ready cash, Miller is somewhat redeemed in the eyes of the villagers because, along with Bobb, he is willing to extend credit to select individuals and families, whereas credit is not available to anyone on the barges or in other communities. Those who are not so favored, however, grumble accordingly, while those who are want a larger stock selection. However, Miller does not approve of extending credit as a general business principle. "People always assure me that the debt will be repaid," he said. "*Lukpara*, they say . . . that is, don't worry, don't think of it. It's *lukpara* alright; I might just as well not think of those goods because they'll never be paid for."

Purchases at the commissaries and barges are in small amounts, regardless of whether the transactions involve cash or kind. The activity at Miller's shop one morning shortly after he had replenished his stock somewhat is illustrative. Cash sales included one-quarter bar of soap worth 25 centavos (U.S.$0.035); one-half bar of soap and 50 centavos worth of salt (U.S.$0.14); one bar of soap (U.S. $0.14); one yard of cotton cloth (U.S.$0.42); a bar of soap and a box of matches (U.S.$0.28).[8] Similar purchases were made using rice as the mode of payment: one bar of soap; three cigarettes and some salt; one bar of soap, one spool of thread, and two quinine pills. Credit was extended to one customer who bought one pair of work trousers, two and one-half yards of cotton cloth, a spool of thread, and a box of talcum powder.

Of equal significance to the Miskito is the psychological impact of an impoverished money economy. An ethic of poverty exists, which reflects a general feeling of deprivation and frustration regardless of the soundness of the subsistence economy. Almost any topic of conversation is introduced with the statement: "We are poor, we are miserable people; we have no money, we have no work, we have no food."

Some Miskito are more dependent upon the exchange economy than others, however, and for them cash, or its equivalent, is more of an essential for survival; conversely, lack of purchasing power makes them poorer in the subsistence as well as the capitalistic sense. Coastal Miskito with less easily cultivable land who thus have come to depend more consistently on purchasing power for subsistence foods fit this category. Within Asang, those families without a male head are often hard put to make ends meet because they cannot clear large enough plantations by themselves to meet their subsistence needs, and, in consequence, must earn the means to acquire staples. These are the people who are most anxious to hire out to others to help with plantation work in return for a share of produce. They are "poorer" in relation to those who hire them, who are "richer."

The terms "poorer" and "richer" are used here in preference to "poor" and "rich" in order to avoid any implications of social, political, or economic ranking based on relative wealth. Asang villagers do not choose their friends and associates on the basis of economic worth, nor do they accord differential social standing in terms of

8. The Miskito use the English term "shilling" to refer to a 25-centavo piece. Thus a customer will ask for "a shilling's worth of soap."

monetary resources. All are kinsmen, and are judged in terms of how well they follow the rules of mutual respect and obligations required of kinsmen. One who is "richer" does not carry more decision-making influence than one who is "poorer." The distinction here, as we have seen, is more between men and women. Economically, all are concerned, as families and individuals, with obtaining a share of the foreign items they require for a psychologically satisfying existence, and all aspire to acquire the same goods. That is, although there are individual differences in purchasing ability, there are no groups of persons who are distinguished one from the other by virtue of differential economic behavior, for example, purchasing more expensive rather than less expensive goods, or roofing their homes with corrugated iron rather than with thatch.

With respect to this latter point, corrugated iron roofs are seen as indicative not of high social position or influence, but of the ability to purchase foreign goods, i.e., to consume money. Since sheets of corrugated iron are expensive, not many have been able to accumulate the necessary funds, particularly since, as we have noted, long-term planning is not characteristic of the Miskito. Thus, even when cash was available during the banana boom, immediate consumption of this income through purchase of food and clothing was more common than accumulation for a roof. Only a few have been energetic enough to acquire iron roofs, and although others aspire, the process is slow. In more than one case expenses due to death, illness, or accident have consumed the funds which had been set aside.

"Richer" and "poorer" refer to individual and family differences in ability to balance the subsistence and the cash economies. Those who are successful in this two-way operation maintain a relatively more consistent and secure standard of living than those who lack sufficient involvement in one or the other. It is no longer possible for a Miskito to live a psychologically satisfying life without owning items of foreign manufacture. Yet sooner or later he will be impoverished if he relies entirely on purchased goods for food and other amenities, because of the fluctuations in the cash economy. At such times, he depends upon a cushion of self-sufficient subsistence techniques and activities until the cash economy strengthens again.

5

Political Integration

A POLITICAL SYSTEM can be seen as the relationship between three sets of variables: (1) laws or codes for behavior that (2) operate within and between social and territorial units or levels through (3) the mechanism of what we may call "maintenance agents" or "implementors." The exact nature of the system in any one case would be determined by the nature of the three variables. The political system operative among the people of Asang, for example, involves various types of laws, several levels of social and territorial units, and numerous implementors, all combined to form a single system. We can best begin a description and analysis of this system by identifying the types of laws, units, and implementors involved. This information is summarized in Table 4.

Introduction

To begin, three separate law codes may be distinguished: traditional Miskito custom, church regulations, and statutes of the Republic of Nicaragua. These codes operate within and between four levels of society: within Asang; between Asang and other Miskito villages; between the village and foreign mission organizations; between the village and the state. It is important to note that at the present time there is no interaction between the Miskito as a whole and the state.[1] Rather, each village interacts as an autonomous unit with the agents of the state.

Turning finally to the implements of the law systems, we again

1. The Miskito sometimes speak of themselves as forming a single "nation" in contrast to other peoples of other "nations." However, this unity is only conceptual, not corporate in any way. There is no group of individuals nor any single leader who represents all of Miskitodom to the outside world.

find three sets: traditional Miskito maintenance agents, church organization, and government agencies. These agents of law implementation are crucial for the operation of the entire political system, for it is through these channels that the several behavior codes and social levels are interwoven into a single network. This is possible only because certain implementors have dual areas of operation, that is, operate as agents for more than one law code and between several social levels. More specifically, traditional Miskito agents implement traditional Miskito customs, church regulations, and government laws and also operate on at least three of the four

TABLE 4

ELEMENTS OF MISKITO POLITICAL ORGANIZATION

Law Code	Sphere of Operation	Implementor
Traditional Miskito custom	Intravillage Intervillage	Traditional Miskito agents: Gossip Village headman Church organization
Church regulations	Intravillage Intervillage Village-foreign mission	Traditional Miskito agents: Gossip Church organization
National statutes	State-village	Traditional Miskito agents: Village headman Government agencies

social levels—intravillage, intervillage, and village to state. Similarly, church agents implement traditional Miskito customs as well as church regulations and operate within the village, between villages, and between village and mission organization. National agents, however, implement only government laws and operate only at the state to village level.

Tradition

The most important law and set of implementors is that arising from traditional, that is, pre-Christian Miskito custom. Most day-to-day activities are conducted at least in part within guidelines provided by traditional behavior rules. In addition, as we pointed out above, traditional implementors serve to connect all law codes and most, sometimes all, social levels, and thus provide the most important single cohesive feature in the entire political system.

The traditional behavior code centers upon the fulfillment of kinship obligations and thus functions not only within the village but also between villages. The main implementors are persons engaged in gossip. Gossip is defined here as the subjective and oral analysis of news. It is found wherever news is carried by word-of-mouth. In communities where oral communication provides the major means of information gossip likewise is of great significance.

In Asang, much time and energy is devoted to listening to and retelling, usually with a few additions, some story heard at the plantation, at the spring while washing dishes, or while visiting another village. Women seem more prone to gossip than men, although within their own circles men also indulge in considerable tale telling. As is well known, a major function of gossip lies in pressuring those who have deviated from accepted behavior until they mend their ways. In this way it maintains "the unity, morals and values of social groups" (Gluckman 1963:308). The end is achieved, however, by creating additional tensions and ill-feelings in that the defensiveness engendered by hearing what people are whispering can be relieved only by countergossip, which assures that the system will continue to operate.

Generally speaking, the people of Asang do not consider gossiping to be an admirable thing. The proper response to a probing question about a third party is simply to say you don't know (*no apu*). Gossip is judged to be proud, i.e., lacking in respect for others, which, incidentally, is usually the charge leveled at the person who is the subject of the gossip. Consequently, as several women settle themselves comfortably for a session, they inevitably begin their conversation by assuring each other that they themselves are not gossips, never tell lies, and don't carry damaging stories, but did you hear. . . .

The reassurances concerning truthfulness that gossipers use to open their conversations reveal that gossip is seen not just as a matter of talking about another's business, but also as containing a certain amount of untruth by definition. "The trouble with Asang," the anthropologist was repeatedly told, "is that people tell too many lies." In fact, one of the words heard most frequently as people converse is *kunin*, meaning "that is a lie, falsehood, deception." In reply, the speaker asserts, somewhat defensively, that his information is definitely not a lie. This feeling for the basic falsity of a story heard by gossip creates a face-saving way of escape for the person under discussion, since he can and does emphasize that the story is completely untrue, whether or not it actually is being totally irrelevant. However, much bitterness, anxiety, and self-righteous defensiveness is engendered in the process of protecting oneself, for to accuse others of slander in self-defense is to receive in reply the accusation of being "proud." Virtually everyone labors under feelings of potential shame and guilt about being considered bad or corrupt (*saura*) because of pride. "Why haven't you visited me lately, did you hear something bad about me?" was a frequent question put to the anthropologist by informants.

The best way to conduct a confidential conversation, villagers agree, is to go for a walk while the matter is discussed. Thus villagers often slip quietly away from the kitchen or porch as another person passes by for a short stroll and a few words with him. Similarly, the best way to avoid slanderous attacks is to avoid contact with those who have a reputation as gossips, or who are in a position to see or inquire unduly about the details of one's private life. In order to avoid being charged with spreading a story about something seen or overheard, many adults assert that they do not like to venture into the kitchen, i.e., private living area, of those who are not relatives. Because of the respect engendered by kinship ties, relatives are expected to be trustworthy and capable of holding confidences. Similarly, it is considered proper to instruct one's child to visit only with relatives, for the origin of many rumors and tales is attributed to undisciplined children's wanderings, where they can overhear "other peoples' business." No parent wants his children accused of this, since it implies not only that he is failing to properly socialize his children, but also that some adult, most likely he himself, is pumping the child for information.

Understandably enough, the anthropologist was also regarded with circumspection by some villagers, who, although they felt personally friendly towards her, were hesitant to chat for too long a period, or to answer questions that could lead to personal opinions about others or that inquired too deeply into their own lives. Similarly, those who did spend time with the investigator were often queried by other villagers as to the content of the conversations. Since the anthropologist lived in the lay pastor's home, people were particularly fearful that a confidential story would reach his ears, possibly leading to an investigation into their affairs. Thus it was incumbent upon both the lay pastor and the anthropologist to develop reputations for honesty and confidentiality, and to defend this reputation in the face of accusations to the contrary.

The system of gossip and countergossip has its own self-contained pattern of surges and resurges, peaks and subsidence. Occasionally, however, the charges and recriminations concern a point of such importance that a third party is needed either to settle the matter, or at least to reduce it to a size that can be handled again by the usual gossip circle. Damage to property, inheritance of property, and bodily injury are the areas where it is often most difficult for the persons involved to reach a decision among themselves.

The general principle behind the settlement of claims based on property damage and bodily injury is that the party responsible for the damage or injury should repair it or provide recompense, either by a cash payment for medical expenses, for example, or in kind equal to the value of the damaged property. Thus, when Lilian fell off the roof of the lay pastor's house, where she was helping to spread rice to dry, it was the responsibility of the lay pastor and his wife to see that she was properly tended until able to resume her normal activities. Consequently, she was put to bed and remained overnight with the lay pastor's family.

Another accident a short time later was not resolved as smoothly. Stedman's young son suffered a severe cut on his ankle while playing with a cousin. Stedman refused to seek medical aid because of the cost, saying that the responsibility lay with the other boy's father, Siverio. Had the accident occurred in the bush as his son helped him work he would bear the expense, he claimed. But this injury was the responsibility of another person. Hence he would not use his resources to do another's duty. Siverio, meanwhile, was not available for comment. The injured boy, unable to walk, sat about the house with a rag around his foot. The villagers speculated that each side would try to hold out as long as possible in hopes that the injury would eventually heal. And, in fact, after a few weeks the child was hobbling about, and the matter gradually died down.

Similar damages and settlement problems can result when a plantation is burned prior to planting. At these times, during dry season, a sudden shift of wind can send the fire out of control to damage another's field. If this should happen the individual whose fire got out of hand must compensate the owner of the damaged plantation in produce or cash equal to the loss.

According to informants, however, it is not uncommon for the individual responsible to attempt to avoid payment. "They will complain about the number of children waiting to be fed at home, and about their total poverty," one villager remarked, adding in a cynical aside that, far from being poverty stricken, the culprit probably had sixty quintals of rice and beans hidden in the rafters. This unwillingness to accept responsibility for damage is labeled arrogance and is deplored. In addition, it is considered foolish behavior to attempt to burn a field alone, since it is common knowledge that it is difficult for one person to control a brush fire. Rather, the prospective burner should notify the owners of the adjacent plantations of his plans to burn so that they may help him protect their fields, or arrange to burn the several plots at once. If he does so announce his intentions and damage occurs anyway, he will not have to provide full compensation. The losses are written off instead simply as bad luck.

Property damage in the context of stealing is widespread, and in line with what was stated above a thief, if caught, should pay for or return the stolen goods. Successful thievery, however, is based on the idea of not getting caught, in which case there is nothing that can be done. To listen to the day-to-day quarrels and complaints, one gathers that there are many successful thieves in the village.

Snatching chickens at night as they roost beneath the house, and then selling the fowl at another village or to the commissary barges is a frequent complaint, directed mainly at young men. The lay pastor's wife charged that unknown to her, children stole eggs and then sold them to her to prepare for the lay pastor and the anthropologist. "You sat down, the lay pastor gave thanks to God, and you ate," she despaired, shuddering at the hypocrisy even though it was unintentional.

Stealing is a major factor in intervillage relations also. People from neighboring villages are always considered potential thieves, unless they are kinsmen, and the general distrust of nonvillagers is largely predicated on the belief that one's money and portable property are not safe in their presence.

The third area of potential dispute is that of property inheritance. Traditionally all property including livestock, trees, and plantations, as well as personal effects, were either destroyed at the death of the owner or buried with him (Pim and Seemann 1869:307; Esquemeling 1893:253; Mierisch 1893:31; Conzemius 1932:155). This practice is no longer followed, possibly as a result of missionary influence.[2] As a result, there is property to be inherited today, but no easily discernible regulations to govern its division.

The first impression one receives when inquiring about inheritance is that the system is completely chaotic. Gradually, though, certain theoretically accepted trends emerge. When a man dies, his wife acquires his goods and land for the support of herself and his children. If the woman remarries, her children by her first marriage receive the property because her new husband should provide new goods for her. When the deceased is a woman, her husband acquires the property, and on his death their children acquire it. If the husband remarries, the children acquire the property and he must earn new goods for his new wife.

This is how the system is supposed to work. In actuality, the predominant behavior pattern is best defined as "grab and run." The distribution then is usually achieved by each person taking as much as he can wrangle. The largest areas of conflict occur between the spouse of the deceased and the latter's siblings, and between the deceased's children, especially if both parents have died. Quarrels often center on what we may call purchase rights versus gift rights. For example, *Dama* Mauricio bought his wife numerous *dikwas* (three-legged iron cooking pots) during the course of their marriage, and when she died he claimed the pots as his because he had bought them. His deceased wife's brother, however, argued that the *Dama* had given the *dikwas* to the deceased as outright gifts, thus relinquishing claim to them. Hence he (the brother) wished to take them. The outcome of the dispute was still in question when I left the village.

Children are often confronted with the alternatives of equal distribution of goods versus one child maintaining a kind of guardianship over the entire inheritance so as to keep the property intact. In the latter case saws, axes, sewing machines, guns, and dugouts may be borrowed as needed, but not claimed permanently by any one child. Items such as trees or livestock are more likely to be distributed permanently. In either case there is much room for argumentation. If the dispute becomes too bitter, one of the offended

2. "Our Christians bury their dead as we do, and do not destroy the property of the deceased. . ." (Ziock 1880:510).

parties may even break the contested items so that "everyone loses." In the case of land, the simplest method of laying claim is to plant bananas and plantains on the plot, and thus acquire it through usufruct.

Villagers feel that some of this rivalry could be avoided if the dying individual would specify his wishes regarding the distribution of his property. This practice is applauded, but there is not always time and certainly no guarantee that the deceased's wishes will be followed. Even if they are, the conditions of his request may irritate survivors. For example, at his death Maria's husband bequeathed his cow to Hermán's wife rather than to Maria because of Maria's unfaithfulness during their marriage. Even if the dying person indicates his preference for equal distribution, the problem of ascertaining portions of equal value can easily lead to quarrels, and usually does. It is, in the last analysis, every man for himself, although it is felt that the youngest child, or those who are still single, have a right to acquire more of the property since those who are married already own the necessary items for housekeeping. This is particularly true with respect to inheritance of the house itself, which is generally acquired by the child (either boy or girl) who has not yet married.

In problems of property inheritance, property damage, and bodily injury, the parties involved try to come to an agreement among themselves, but if a compromise cannot be reached a third party is contacted. The traditional arbiter of disputes is the village headman. Historical sources note that this individual was selected from among the oldest and most renowned villagers for his discretion and ability in settling grievances (Bell 1862:251; Hamilton 1904:4). Sometimes the duties of the headman were handled by the shaman (Conzemius 1932:101). In either case, each headman followed his own interpretations of traditional custom in handing down, or rather suggesting, decisions (Ziock 1882:312).

According to informants, the headman is responsible for the affairs which concern the village as a whole. A particularly good headman might also be approached for advice by strangers from other villages. For example, a conscientious headman will organize groups of men several times a year to cut and clear the weeds within the village confines, and see to it that there is always a supply of wood at hand for coffins. He might also instruct the village to aid any needy residents by requesting that the plantations of the sick or elderly be maintained through communal effort.

Added to these traditional duties are more recently acquired responsibilities toward the national government. Today the headman has become, in effect, the official channel between the village and the national government. Acting within this capacity, the headman is to maintain the general peace, and take anyone guilty of stealing or murder to the *commandante* at the nearest police station. He must also register village births, marriages, and deaths, inform the *commandante* if any suspicious strangers appear in the village, see to it that there is swift and proper burial, inspect slaughtered animals for signs of disease, and collect the slaughter tax required whenever a cow or pig is butchered. These taxes, 3 to 5 cordobas or about U.S.$0.50 for a pig, 10 cordobas or U.S.$1.45 for a cow, are often paid today in pounds of meat, rice, or beans and are retained by the headman as his salary, as are the fees for birth certificates and marriages. The Asang headman has been empowered to perform civil marriages since 1964 when, because of the size of the community, he was appointed a *Juez de Policia* within the official Nicaraguan political sphere.

The headman's effectiveness depends to a great extent upon his personal qualities. Traditionally if people were dissatisfied with the current headman he would be replaced by another. Today the position is filled by government appointment, and although the villagers have the right to petition for a change, such a request involves a lengthy process without certainty of success. This can lead to the situation which exists in Asang today where a headman is officially in residence, but villagers follow his requests in a half-hearted manner and only after much grumbling.

The Asang headman, who by his own admission is anxious to be relieved of his duties, does not enjoy good rapport with the village as a whole. He claims that he is too soft-hearted to be headman, and prefers to let people settle their own disputes. The villagers, in return, claim that they cannot obtain satisfactory arbitration from the headman, and would petition to replace him if they could find someone else who would take the job and would satisfy the Nicaraguan authorities. Several men were under consideration as potential replacements, but none wished to accept the nomination. Under the circumstances people tended to avoid contacting the headman if possible, and sought out the lay pastor instead when advice and arbitration were needed.

The Church

The role of the lay pastor as the third implementor (in addition to gossip and the headman) of traditional Miskito custom varies greatly from village to village, depending on the abilities of the headman and the strength of the church in the community. In Asang, the influence of the Moravian lay pastor is a reflection, at least in part, of the favorable conditions under which Moravianism was introduced to the village. Shortly after the establishment of the first houses in Asang about 1910, *Dama* Jesús George visited a Moravian mission station which had been set up at Sangsang, a few miles downriver. After vacillating for eight years, *Dama* George was baptized along with his relatives and invited the missionaries to visit Asang and organize a congregation and a school. A lay pastor was in residence by January, 1918 (Moravian Church 1890–1956: vol. 10, p. 349; 1903–1954:vol. 34, pp. 14–15).

Dama George's influence in this matter was greatly strengthened by the fact that he was renowned along the river for his wisdom in settling claims and disputes. By token of this ability, he was also headman of Asang. The fact that such an influential person espoused the new religion not only facilitated its establishment in Asang, but very likely helped to link Christianity and arbitration in the minds of the populace. From the point of view of the Moravian church, as we shall see below, involvement with secular matters was a long-standing tradition.

In view of this background it is not at all surprising to find that the lay pastor plays a major role in community affairs. In Asang at the time of this study he was, in fact, the preferred arbiter because of the discontent with the current headman's behavior. In contrast, the lay pastor was greatly respected.[3]

Within the normal course of activities there was close rapport between the headman and the Moravian lay pastor, even though the headman felt the lay pastor was rather arrogant, while the lay pastor considered the headman somewhat lacking in personal morality. Both held positions of importance—the headman as leader of the village and the lay pastor as leader of his congregation. Both were interested in maintaining a peaceful village—one because the na-

3. The Iglesia de Dios congregation was small and without prestige in the village at large. Hence its leadership was not consulted for juridical advice by the village in general.

tional government demanded it, the other because it was the Christian thing to do. Consequently, there were many times when headman and lay pastor cooperated. The lay pastor, for example, served as secretary for civil marriage ceremonies, and if the headman wished to make a public announcement he requested that the lay pastor read it in church. When Rinaldo was seriously injured in a bush accident the headman undertook the responsibility of sending him to the Moravian mission hospital downriver, and both the lay pastor and the headman signed the letter asking for credit for his bill. Again, when Asang petitioned the Moravian mission for a village medical clinic the headman signed the letter as official village representative, while a church elder, under the lay pastor's direction, signed for the congregation. Finally, the meeting held to discuss the clinic question was convened by the lay pastor not as a congregational meeting but as a village assembly and was attended by both Iglesia and Moravian families.

On the other hand, there was some tension between the two authority figures because the villagers preferred to have the lay pastor adjudicate quarrels rather than the headman. This did not bother the headman in one sense because he was anxious to be replaced, but on the other hand he was personally sensitive to the boycott. Matters came to a head on one occasion when the headman himself was involved in a dispute brought to the lay pastor's attention. The headman countered this blow to his position by refusing to attend church for several weeks.

The lay pastor is trained and given his assignment by the foreign missionaries. Among the Moravians, it is felt that in order to carry out his role of village-mission mediator most successfully, the lay pastor should not be a member of the congregation he serves. Therefore, he is usually not assigned to his home congregation where he may be tempted to favor relatives or friends, but enters another village as a presumably neutral "stranger." Within the congregation under his charge he can be an influence for cooperation, as is the present Asang lay pastor, or a source of much village discord, depending on how he perceives and handles his position.

The basic qualification for the position of lay pastor cannot be easily met by many Miskito although the requirement is one that lies at the foundation of proper traditional Miskito behavior, namely, the ability to show "respect," and not to be "proud." The lay pastor, ideally, is a man who is at the service of others. His own interests are secondary to the needs of his congregation and the requests of the foreign missionaries. The Miskito who is not "proud," who has "respect," also sees to it that his personal desires do not take precedence over the interests of the group. In actuality, though, the egalitarianism of Miskito society also forces people to assert their own interests and not to become subservient to others or to compromise easily. This individualism inevitably leads to a certain amount of "pride" which must be held in check constantly by gossip. The lay pastor cannot afford such single-minded "proud" behavior if he is to be successful. He must be willing instead to allow his congregation and the missionaries to direct the details of his life, to tell him where he will live, and to provide or refuse to provide him with subsistence. Thus, the individual who can become a good lay pastor is, in effect, an atypical Miskito.

However, to become a lay pastor is a desirable goal. In addition to a monthly salary paid by the church and contributions from the congregation, the position carries great prestige within Miskito society because it offers an excellent opportunity for a man to make his individualism visible by being in a position of authority. This authority, though, holds only as long as people will volunteer for activities and agree to abide by his decisions. Such voluntary acquiescence, in turn, can be obtained only if the congregation respects him; respect requires that he not be "proud."

The nature of the interaction between lay pastor and foreign missionary also is determined to a great extent by the type of behavior exhibited by the lay pastor. A "proud" lay pastor has difficulties with missionaries because he does not bother to carry out their requests just as he is usually in trouble with his congregation for the same reason. On the other hand, the humble lay pastor enjoys good relations with the mission board simply because he does abide by their wishes and is correspondingly popular within his congregation.

In addition to the lay pastor there is another aspect of Moravian church organization which is sometimes concerned with nonchurch matters—the Helper meeting. This assembly of congregational leaders (Helpers) is concerned theoretically only with those problems involving members of their congregation. However, since virtually the entire community of Asang, with the exception of four Church of God households, is at least nominally Moravian, the Helper meeting becomes, in effect, a vehicle for adjudicating disputes between almost anyone. Furthermore, since the Moravian

congregation of Asang includes some families from the neighboring
village of Yiasco, the Helper meeting can also operate on the intervillage level if necessary.

The effectiveness of the Helper meeting is based on the moral
obligation of the people involved to attend. If one of the parties in
a dispute does not appear the meeting cannot be held. The arbi-
trators in a Helper meeting can only suggest a course of action for
the quarreling parties. They, like the headman and lay pastor, have
no way to enforce a decision, and hence it is often difficult to fully
end a matter then and there. Excerpts from field notes describing a
Helper meeting show this clearly.

This evening the lay pastor announced that a Helper meeting
would be held. Accordingly, the church bell was rung and ten
Helpers (five men and five women) assembled in the church,
the men sitting to the left of the aisle and the women to the
right as usual. Three cases required discussion: G. versus L.;
O. versus M.; P.'s problem. Only the first and third issues were
handled since O. did not appear. M. came, though, as did L.
and G. P.'s presence was not required.

The lay pastor brought his chair down from the pulpit and
placed it in the aisle between the two groups of Helpers. The
building was lit by a single Coleman lamp, hung on the men's
side. The meeting opened with a prayer by the lay pastor who
then introduced the first problem.

He began the discussion by saying that G. and L. had talked
over the situation previously, but there was still trouble. He
then asked for both sides of the story. L. rose and spoke first.
The dispute concerned a claim by both parties to a particular
plantation. After L. had spoken a few minutes he sat down.
There was a moment's silence. Then the lay pastor asked for
G.'s version. G. spoke for a few minutes from his seat. L. in-
terrupted him, however, and they got into an argument. Each
denied having said what the other claimed he had said. Everyone else sat quietly until there was a lull in the quarrel. G.'s
wife then gave her opinion briefly at the lay pastor's invitation.
A Helper asked L. about a point, and tempers began to rise
again as both G. and L. began to talk simultaneously. Two
more Helpers (men) spoke up. One scolded both L. and G.
because they were church leaders and yet had this difficulty

between them. Finally the lay pastor said each was as much in the wrong as the other. Both were guilty of baiting the other, he maintained, and then appealed to Christian law as a reason for settling the dispute. He pointed out that both L. and G. were church workers, and were setting very poor examples for the rest of the congregation.

However, L. and G. began to argue again. The women Helpers started to talk among themselves. The lay pastor addressed everyone and charged G. and L. to try to get along. If one heard gossip about the other he was to come to the lay pastor before spreading more in return. L. and the lay pastor then began to argue.

Meanwhile, the lay pastor had spoken with G.'s wife and with M., presumably about their problem with O. He then announced that although there was another problem concerning O. versus M., all the parties had not attended the meeting so the issue could not be discussed.

The third problem involved the young widow P.'s illegitimate pregnancy. The lay pastor said he had heard a rumor about the situation and had sent a Helper to investigate and report, which the Helper did. All the Helpers then began a very noisy general discussion while the lay pastor waited vainly for quiet. Finally he took down the lantern and led the way to the door. The meeting was effectively ended by darkness.

The active interest taken by the Moravian church in attempting to settle such nonreligious questions as land ownership, for example, can be interpreted as an expression of the general Christian doctrine of living in peace with one another. But it is also in keeping with a traditional Moravian concern with secular affairs which is rooted in the fact that in its early days members of the church formed closed corporate communities to protect themselves from persecution and other evils of the world (see Appendix B). In this setting church leaders had to be concerned not only with spiritual matters, but also with mundane secular affairs of daily life. A statement by a church synod convened in Germany in 1849 succinctly summarizes this duality.

It is important to remember that the Brethren's Church, although a voluntary association of kindred souls, aiming to constitute a living congregation of Jesus, had its origin as a settlement. Thus, our community, from its very commencement, was necessarily not merely a spiritual, but, at the same time, an external and civil association, which, in the sequel, assumed also an ecclesiastical character (Moravian Church 1849:50).[4]

Thus the Asang Helper meeting, which also concerns itself with all aspects of daily life, can be seen as the local reflection of a long Moravian tradition.

In many respects, however, ideal Moravian living and "respectful" Miskito living require the same behavior patterns. Both emphasize egalitarianism, cooperation, and thoughtful consideration of others as kinsmen, to be treated with generosity and hospitality. Similarly, an individual may be criticized for un-Christian-like behavior because, for example, he has been "proud," shirked cooperative plantation labor, stolen, or told a lie—all misdemeanors which are equally serious offenses under Miskito custom. Consequently, it becomes virtually impossible for people to go about their daily activities without being aware of pressures to conform both to traditional Miskito custom and to Moravian requirements. As we shall see below, much of the success which Moravian missionary endeavors have enjoyed among the Miskito can be traced to the similarities and lack of serious conflict between traditional Miskito behavioral standards and those of the Church.

Although gossip, with its potential for disruption of the general peace is deplored by the church, it is very effective as an implementor of church regulations, just as the lay pastor and the Helper meetings serve to implement traditional Miskito customs. The strength of gossip in enforcing Christian behavior, and the high consciousness within Asang in general of what is proper Christian behavior reflects the fact that almost all of the adult population are either first- or second-generation Christians. As such they still view the world largely in terms of heathen versus Christian, and feel the need to defend their standing with the latter. Fear of an indictment of not acting "like a Christian" is particularly trenchant for those villagers, such as church elders or members of the choir, who are most active in church affairs, and who, as a result, are particularly conscious of their "Christianess."

4. See Gollin (1967) for a detailed account of the social, political, and economic interests of early Moravian communities.

A good example of the effectiveness to date of the Moravian church in the community is the ban on drinking within Asang. This remarkable sobriety makes the village quite atypical of Miskito communities in general. The ban has been in effect for approximately thirty years. According to informants rum was sold in Asang commissaries during the banana period and *wahmas* particularly were eager to buy it. Dismayed at the resultant disorder, the lay pastor resident at that time, backed by the older adults of the village, blocked further sale of alcoholic beverages in the community. The combined efforts of the headman, the lay pastor, and public opinion have served to fairly effectively maintain the ban to the present. The Asang stores do not stock intoxicating beverages today. Young men sometimes drink while visiting other villages, but say they are ashamed to do so in Asang.

In the course of my stay in the village only two young men were publicly observed to be intoxicated. The incident occurred one afternoon when the men staggered into the Moravian churchyard shortly after a service had concluded. The villagers, keeping a safe distance away, stared at their antics until friends steered the two men to the privacy of their homes. The lay pastor indignantly pointed out how the devil operates in those who are weak. Later on in the afternoon the wife of one culprit came to the lay pastor, who advised her to warn her husband that she would leave him if he repeated his performance. If he did drink again, the lay pastor admonished, she was in fact to leave him and not return.

The headman also took steps, lecturing the men and reporting the matter to the Nicaraguan *commandante* at Santa Izabel. The *commandante* wished to jail or fine the men, but the headman persuaded him to forego these punishments, pointing out that the men were poor. The young men were the subject of much gossip and were ostracized by their friends. They talked of going to the mines to escape further censure.[5]

The ban on drinking will probably remain operative at least until the first- and second-generation Christians have died. Whether the third generation will be as stringent in their demands remains to be

5. On one occasion a Nicaraguan schoolteacher from another village came to visit the Asang teachers. He was intoxicated when he arrived, and reeled off to one of the teacher's homes, to the great delight of the children who were enthralled by his behavior. The headman, hearing about the commotion, went to the house, ushered the man into the building, and closed the door to prevent the children from watching further.

seen. As long as depression conditions continue, the sheer lack of money to purchase rum may act as an inhibitor for those who do not feel morally obligated to abstain. When the economy improves, drinking may become more of a problem, particularly for the *wahmas*.

The State

The general tendency among the Miskito has been to avoid contact with non-Miskito state agents if at all possible; first, because it takes money to enlist state aid and, second, because the villagers feel that the result will be inconclusive and therefore a waste of time. Nicaraguan officials for their part consider assignment on the Miskito Coast to be virtual banishment and view the Miskito as considerably inferior to them socially. The desire to avoid contact is mutual. Therefore it is not surprising to find that most state-to-village and village-to-state business is channeled through the headman, and that the state generally keeps out of village affairs.

The major areas of government intervention are the maintenance of law and order by the establishment of police stations in several towns and villages along the river, and the appointments of Miskito headmen, answerable to the police *commandante*, in all villages; recording of births, marriages, and deaths for each village by the headman; provision for civil marriage ceremonies; maintenance of public schools staffed by Spanish-speaking Nicaraguans in most villages in order to teach Spanish and instill a feeling of being part of the state. No military service is required of the Miskito and there are no taxes on land or personal property although, as we have seen, small fees are required for the purchase of birth and marriage certificates and when pigs and cattle are slaughtered.[6] Periodically a medical doctor working under an Alliance for Progress program makes brief visits to those villages where police are stationed.

On one occasion the doctor stopped at Asang, and the nature of his reception is illustrative of the general relationship between the village and state. The visit came in response to long-standing complaints by the villagers that no medical services were provided for them. The matter had come to a head shortly before the doctor's visit by news that the Moravian church planned to build a clinic on the river, and Asang had submitted a request that it be located

6. Exemption from military duty and from personal taxation was provided by the terms of the Treaty of Managua (cf. Hooker 1945:57).

there. The doctor's mission was to explain to the villagers why the government had not been able to assist them.

His pending visit was announced in church on Sunday by the lay pastor at the headman's request, and on Tuesday the men of the village met with the doctor in the schoolhouse where the headman acted as interpreter. The doctor reviewed the state of the Alliance program in Nicaragua, noting that only one medical boat and one doctor had been assigned to the Río Coco. He pointed out that he made eight stops along the river, but, because he worked alone, he was unable to come to every village. Asang was one of those necessarily excluded.

At the end of the explanation the doctor prepared to leave. The headman stopped him, though, and asked the villagers if they had any questions or comments. They answered, rather forcefully, that they had none. After the doctor was on his way, the men shrugged their shoulders, remarking that they still didn't have any medical aid and, in addition, had lost a day's work.

Since 1952 the Nicaraguan government has provided schools and teachers for the area below the rapids under a program known as the "Projecto Piloto del Río Coco." In addition, there is an institute at Waspam where Miskito boys are trained as future teachers. Although the efforts of the government are commendable in theory, practice diverges from the announced ideal in large part due to the geographical and cultural isolation of the area from the Latin American world. It is hard to find teachers for the project, and those recruited usually remain for only a few years. Even these are not as effective as they might be, due to a lack of understanding of Miskito culture.

The school at Asang has classes from kindergarten through sixth grade. Although fifty-two children are officially enrolled in kindergarten, only about half are in attendance any single day. Thirty-four are registered for first grade, and daily attendance averages about twenty. Second grade has forty-five registered students, about half that number attending each day. From grade three through six, official registration is low, but attendance is better. Third grade has nineteen registered, most of whom attend regularly. Seven students are in the fourth grade, six boys and one girl; four are in the fifth grade, two boys and two girls; seven boys are in the sixth grade. Attendance for these three upper grades is also fairly regular.

In general, from the point of view of Asang, the institutions of the state are not very important factors in everyday life. There are no police stationed in the village. As we have seen, the school is very poorly attended, especially after the second grade level, and operates with almost no equipment. The four schoolteachers keep aloof from the rest of the community. Their occasional drinking makes them additionally undesirable. They generally do not speak Miskito. Even the two *maestros* who do know the language claim to be ignorant of it and prefer to speak Spanish. Miskito adults, on the other hand, never speak Spanish within the village except to the schoolteachers, and the children drop Spanish for Miskito each day the moment they leave school. Counting furnishes the only exception to this general rule. The Miskito system is based on units of twenty and becomes unwieldy after passing the number six. Consequently, either Spanish or English numbers are preferred.[7]

Nonetheless, Miskito parents have a high regard for education and want their children to learn to read and write, but in English and Miskito. They do not enforce attendance at "Spanish" schools, and spend much time criticizing the schoolteachers and their methods. Before government schools were built education was handled by the Moravian church with the lay pastor as teacher. Reading and writing of Miskito was taught in order that Miskito hymns could be written and the Bible translated and read. The villagers consider this system to have been very successful, and wish to return to it. There is no formal instruction in reading or writing Miskito at the present time, although young people may pick up a rudimentary reading ability from participation in church activities.

Through the efforts of the church most of the adults of Asang, both men and women, had some instruction in the skills of literacy when they were children. The women have largely forgotten them, singing hymns from memory today rather than by reading even if they own hymnals. Men put on a show of knowing at least how to read and write Miskito, although how functional this knowledge is it is hard to say.

At the present time, adolescents are probably the most literate group in the village, but their ability appears to be more oriented towards Spanish than Miskito. There is not much call for literate

7. In ordinary conversation large numbers tend to be avoided regardless of the language, and terms such as "many," "a lot," or "everyone" are used instead. This leads to seemingly blatant exaggerations and obvious falsehoods, but the terms are really generalized counters for situations involving large quantities.

skills anyway. What few letters an individual receives can be read by the lay pastor, if necessary, and he will also write letters upon request. The only constant sources of literature in the village are church news sheets, the Miskito Bible, and hymnals; but the contents of these last two are constant, and have largely been memorized. Spanish materials are almost nonexistent although the Moravian church is encouraging the use of Spanish in some services, and a few Spanish hymnals are available.

Peasants or Purchasers

When the political organization of Asang is viewed as a single unit the picture that emerges is that of a virtually autonomous village operating with its own more or less unique combination of traditional and church (specifically Moravian) regulations. It is a common saying in the village that "every town has its own laws," meaning that each village is likely to differ somewhat from all others in some particulars of its political life. In Asang, political affairs, as we have seen, involve a close rapport between Moravian church organization and traditional political channels. Actually church influence is unusually strong in this case and the village has a reputation for requiring very strict adherence to Christian principles. In contrast, other villages may have a reputation, in the eyes of Asang's residents, for dissension or laziness or drunkenness. Each village, in other words, has a more or less characteristic atmosphere with which people identify and are identified in return. That is to say, when a villager states that he is from Asang, he is referring not only to a geographical unit, but also to a political entity with a way of life considered unique.

This unity is also visible when the village officially interacts with the larger, non-Miskito society. Most contacts are effected between village and state or village and mission organization through specific individuals who act as official village representatives to the outside agency, and who are appointed for this purpose by those same agencies. Thus the headman interacts with the state and the lay pastor with the mission, while both cooperate to run the internal affairs of the village as smoothly as possible.

Furthermore, the nature of internal affairs reflects the nature of relations with these outside agencies. The mission is welcomed for the most part. Although there are times when relations between congregation and missionaries are strained, the overall position is one of acceptance of the church and the changes it introduces. This favorable attitude is illustrated in several ways.

First, to the best of their ability people will strive to make a financial contribution to church expenses, although it is important to note that this is completely voluntary, and, depending on the economic situation, people can and do decide to use this cash for other purposes. Thus in 1955, when the economy was more prosperous, the annual congregational fund-raising campaign at Harvest netted over C$2,000. In 1960 over C$1,000 was raised. In 1964, however, only C$636.40 was obtained. In like vein, although the annual pledge for the congregation is C$1,200, only C$900 was raised in 1963, C$600 in 1964, and C$700 in 1965.[8] Similarly, a typical Sunday service today, with approximately 300 in attendance, will yield about C$5.00 in the collection plate. Sunday school collections are about C$1.50–2.25, most of which is contributed by the shopkeeper, Miller.

Second, the position of lay pastor is highly prestigious, although, as was noted, often for reasons that have little to do with its religious significance. Finally, the power of gossip is used to force compliance with church regulations and Christian behavior.

The favorable attitude towards the church contrasts sharply with feelings towards the state. To put the matter briefly, people prefer to let it alone and wish to be left alone in return. For this reason the position of headman is not envied. Similarly, people grumble about the fees for birth and marriage certificates and complain about the slaughter tax, not because these payments constitute an economic burden, but because they represent the presence of the "Spanish." In like manner, when disputes or trouble occur every effort is made to settle the matter without resorting to state institutions.

To date the Miskito have managed to keep aloof from the state. There are at least two significant factors behind this. First, is the fact that the dominant mission group, the Moravian, does not represent the state religion. In fact, as Protestants they, too, prefer to avoid entanglements with Catholic Nicaragua. Consequently, involvement with this foreign religion has not inadvertently brought state involvement with it. Second, is the fact that although the Mi-

8. Harvest money is for the use of the Asang congregation alone. Annual pledges, on the other hand, are contributions to the Central Moravian Board for general church expenses on the Coast, including lay pastors' salaries.

skito live within the official boundaries of Nicaragua the state's power is exercised de jure rather than de facto. The state has been willing so far to let the Miskito alone. No annual taxation of any kind has been levied; there is almost no legislative interference with the Miskito village; and no military duty is required. Schools and police stations represent more of a show of power than its significant implementation. Mutual avoidance is mutually acceptable.

The absence of significant state controls and the political autonomy maintained by Asang as a result place this community and its inhabitants outside the category of peasantry. Peasants are subject "to the jural control of outsiders . . ." (Foster 1967a:6), to the "demands and sanctions of power-holders outside [their] social stratum . . ." (Wolf 1966:11). Specifically, they are subject to the political control of the preindustrial city, and of the agrarian state (Wolf 1966:3-4, 11-12; Foster 1967a:7). The purpose of this control is to obtain from peasantry the state's economic support. The outside power holder demands and obtains, through a claim on the peasants' time and labor, "funds of rent," in labor, produce, and/or money (Wolf 1966:3-4, 9). These rents make possible the life of the state, "supporting . . . the specialized classes of political and religious rulers and the other members of the educated elite" (Foster 1967a:6).

Consequently, peasants lack effective political control. "Peasant leadership is normally weak; it is truncated and ineffectual in meeting other than the most traditional and routine demands. In part this is because the more powerful extravillage leaders who hold vested interests in peasant communities cannot afford to let local leaders rise, since they would constitute a threat to their control" (Foster 1967a:8).

The people of Asang cannot be said to be subject to the state's jural control, to its demands and its sanctions, in the same manner as are peasants. Asang villagers do not contribute to the economic support of the state in any significant manner. Neither labor, time, nor produce is channeled toward the state on any regular basis. The fees paid for marriage and birth certificates and at the slaughter of an animal are minimal, both in financial amount and in frequency of occurrence for each family. Furthermore, these fees do not go beyond the village, but serve as salary for the village headman, who also maintains plantations. This arrangement, to be sure, is beneficial to the state, since it provides the village with a paid official through whom the state may communicate if necessary. But no further demands are placed upon the community. Should Asang and all other Miskito villages suddenly cease to exist, the state of Nicaragua would lose little.

It must be emphasized that the position of the Moravian church in the village should not be construed as a substitute for state controls. The mission exists there, as elsewhere on the Coast, at the suffrance of the villagers. Furthermore, the active part taken by the church in village affairs—the forum provided by the Helpers' meetings and the lay pastor's arbitrations—serve to strengthen, rather than to truncate village organization by providing a central point where village affairs can be discussed. The status of headman is not undercut by this arrangement; the hesitancy of the Asang villagers to deal with their present headman, and their preference for the lay pastor, reflects the personal qualities of the two leaders, and is not indicative of a declining role for the position of headman in village affairs. On the contrary, villagers would prefer to have a more effective headman.

Church collections and fund raising drives are also of a different order from the rents paid to the state by peasants. In a word, church collections are voluntary; state rents are involuntary. Those who do not wish to contribute to the church need not do so. If funds are low, as at the present, church payments fall accordingly, as we have seen. Furthermore, these payments do not help to support the church in the same way that rents paid to the state underwrite the state's activities. In fact, the situation is reversed. It is the goal of the Mission Board of the Moravian Church to make its mission provinces financially and, to a large degree, administratively independent of the home church. The Nicaraguan province is considered a Synodal province, meaning that part of its support is local, but much still comes from the home church abroad. The home church will continue to make up the deficit as long as necessary. Local funds do not help to support the home church as peasants' taxes help support the state.

No force other than verbal persuasion can be used on church members to continue or to increase their contributions if they do not wish to do so. In fact, it is entirely within the power of the village to have the church mission removed from the community if it wishes. It would simply be a matter of refusing to cooperate with the lay pastor, no longer providing for his needs, and stopping attendance and contributions to the church. Although the mission board would strongly lament such a move, it would not be able to stop it.

The ties which connect Asang and the Miskito to the wider world are not asymmetrical political holds by outside power holders. Rather, as was noted in chapter 1, the primary relationship is based on the balance of trade, a necessity to the Miskito because of their desire for items of foreign manufacture. Asang villagers are not peasants; they are, instead, purchasers.

6

The Role of the Missions

ACCORDING to the literature,[1] traditional Miskito ideology centered upon a wide number of evil spirits (*lasas*) which were held responsible for natural disasters and personal misfortunes, especially illness and death. These spirits were kept under control and the effects of their influence mitigated by shamans (*sukyas*). The shaman acted primarily as curer, diviner, and exorciser.

Traditional Ideology

Mueller (1932:49–53) describes several categories of these supernatural beings, beginning with *Won Aisa*, "Our Father," who was a rather vague and impersonal spirit not involved with human affairs. *Won Aisa* may have been a traditional deity, or perhaps was borrowed as a result of culture contact in the early seventeenth century (before the days of missionary activity) with Christians from the nearby island of Providence (chapter 1n15; Conzemius 1932: 132). More to be reckoned with, however, were the host of *lasas* who populated forests and streams and caused sickness, accidents, and deaths. Three particularly malevolent *lasas* controlled the air, land, and water, respectively. Drought and crop failures, drownings, river accidents, lack of fish, hurricanes, and heavy rain were their particular forte.

Minor *lasas* were not to be taken lightly, however. There were a

1. Almost all of the early accounts mention select aspects of traditional Miskito ideology. The most useful general descriptions are found in Roberts (1827), Young (1847), Bell (1862), Collinson (1870), and Esquemeling (1893). Moravian journals and accounts naturally abound in information. Concise reports also are found in Heath's notebooks (n.d.), Mueller (1932), and Grossman (1940). Finally, Conzemius (1932) provides considerable information, both observational and summarized from earlier literature.

number of these, including spirits of the deceased (*isingni*) and of various animals, as well as demons which caused illness and even death. Determination of which *lasa* was directly responsible for an illness and the routing of the spirit so as to effect a cure was the shaman's responsibility. These individuals were extremely shrewd and greatly respected for their abilities. Men usually held the position although elderly women practitioners were occasionally found.[2] Conzemius (1932:123, 124) gives a brief account of the processes of diagnosis and treatment practiced by *sukyas*.

> Through the use of narcotics, especially the excessive use of tobacco, the sukya throws himself in a condition of wild ecstasy, and goes into trances and hypnotic states. During such an abnormal condition he is supposed to be in relation with friendly spirits whom he had invoked previously, and who reveal to him the source of the illness and the mode of cure. . . . The cure proper consists in whistling over the sick person, blowing tobacco smoke over him, and massaging and sucking the afflicted body parts. The sukya purifies the drinking water, or any other beverage intended for the patient, by exposing it to the dew for some time, and then blowing into it with a bamboo rod or a tobacco pipe so as to produce bubbles. Painted sticks of hardwood are stuck in the ground around the bed of the sick person in order to keep evil spirits away. The sukya walks or dances around the sick bed, singing or muttering mysterious and incomprehensible words which are supposed to belong to the "spirit language." If a remedy does not seem to do any good, the sukya tries another, just as does his learned confrere in more civilized countries.

Sukyas received payment for their services in the form of goods such as guns, adzes, boats, or cows (Mueller 1932).

If the patient did not readily respond to treatment aimed at driving out an evil spirit, it was assumed either that he had not carried out the *sukya*'s instructions for his convalescence carefully, particularly in observing food restrictions, or, more likely, that the indi-

---

2. Shamans held equal status vis-à-vis each other with the exception of the *okuli*, who ranked above all others. Only one *okuli* lived at any one time. According to Conzemius (1932:142–44), the *okuli* was considered a special representative of the *lasas* controlling the air or thunder, and as such had control over the elements and could prophesy. The last true *okuli* died about 1895. His successor, while considered by many as *okuli*, was involved with the Moravian church, and was somewhat hesitant to accept full *okuli* status.

vidual had been poisoned. In the early decades of the twentieth century, peoples of the upper Río Coco believed that poisoning could occur in several ways. Native drugs or cyanide stolen from the mines might be directly administered in rum or coffee, often by a third person considered to be on friendly terms with the victim. More indirect poisonings were thought to be responsible for severe illness, specifically dysentery. The poison in this case was presumed buried in the ground where it ate through the bottle cork and entered the feet of those passing by, bringing illness and possibly death. Alternately, poison was thought to be wafted through the air to its victims. As protection against these dangers amulets were worn (Moravian Church 1890–1956:vol. 9, p. 417).

If poisoning was suspected, the shaman was called for, and, after a careful search, would find some mysterious looking objects buried in the ground, perhaps the skeleton of a toad or some fish bones, which he proclaimed to be the cause of the trouble. The villagers often then left the area for some other locality, at least for a season (Moravian Church 1890–1956:vol. 1, p. 90). Through his powers, particularly through dreams, the shaman would also identify a specific individual as the poisoner. The deceased's relatives then sought the poisoner's death in revenge for the death of their kinsman. No one was safe from such an accusation and, consequently, distrust and fear were widespread (Mueller 1932:53).

In addition to curing and divining poisons, shamans were consulted for help in finding a lost or stolen object, furnished remedies to cure bad luck or to increase a man's courage, provided love potions, and informed the hunter how to be sure of a good catch. *Sukyas* were also able to harm an individual's enemy by casting an evil spell over him, and were required to catch the spirit of a recently deceased person and take it to the cemetery in order to prevent its roaming about and annoying the living. There was a *sukya* in practically every large Miskito village:

> There are good and bad sukyas, who are sometimes at feud with each other. In his own village the sukya is generally said to be good, but in the neighboring settlement there is a bad one, whom he has to fight and send away the evil spirit which the latter dispatches in order to cause disease and death. The bad sukya will, for instance, send an animal or bird with poison to the neighboring village, but his confrere from the latter settlement sees it coming and sends it back. The animal goes

hither and thither, until finally the "stronger" of the two opponents wins (Conzemius 1932:141).

Group ceremonies were characterized by dancing and extensive drinking of intoxicating beverages, especially *mishla*. The ceremonies mentioned in the literature centered upon funeral rites, a commemorative ritual, the *sikro*, held about one year after the death of an individual, and annual celebrations in December.

Some of these traditional beliefs still exist, although missionaries have been active on the Coast for over one-hundred years. The first successful missionary endeavor began in 1849 when a Moravian mission station was established at Bluefields.[3] For the duration of the nineteenth century work was gradually and permanently extended north along the coast. At the turn of the twentieth century Moravian missionaries had reached the Río Coco and were beginning to work upriver (Moravian Church 1849–1887; 1890–1911; J. Hamilton 1901; 1904).[4]

During this period the Moravians were the only effective missionary group operating among the native coastal population. The Roman Catholic church was established in the area in 1894 when the region was incorporated into the Republic of Nicaragua. However, the Catholic mission served mainly Spanish-speaking Nicaraguans who gradually began moving into the area. Only in the last twenty-five years has work been extended to include the Miskito. Protestant denominations other than Moravian (Anglican, Baptist, Seventh-Day Adventist, Church of God, Jehovah's Witness) gradually appeared on the Coast, but for the most part restricted their work to the town populations (K. Hamilton 1939).[5] Of these, only the Church of God is found in Miskito villages today.

3. Efforts of Spanish missionaries during the colonial period were totally unsuccessful; see Floyd (1967) and Conzemius (1927b:269–76).

4. Until World War I the mission was administered by the mission board of the International Moravian Church located at Herrnhut, Germany. Consequently, a large majority of the missionaries were from Germany. There were also a number of West Indians, usually Jamaicans, assisting as ordained men and teachers (Borhek 1949:1–9). In the 1920's, however, the mission field was turned over to the American mission board, and shortly thereafter permanent work was begun in Honduras (Heath 1949).

5. Strictly speaking, the Anglican church was represented on the Coast prior to the advent of Moravian work. An Anglican catechist reportedly was resident in Bluefields, and worked with the English-speaking population of the town. However, the Moravians were the first to contact the native population (J. Hamilton 1901:129).

Christianity is still relatively new along the upper reaches of the Río Coco and its tributaries, and in some Honduranean areas. Asang stands about midway in terms of Christian influence, since the first missionaries visited the village about fifty years ago.

There are no shamans resident in Asang today, although everyone is familiar with the nature of their activities, either from having seen these practitioners operate in heathen times, or through hearing stories from people in those areas where shamans are still working. Shamans can be found openly practicing today in regions still relatively free of missionary influence. The Río Coco, however, where missionary activity is about half a century old, is relatively free of *sukyas,* and where they do exist they practice in secret.

At the present time the shaman performs mainly as a curer, operating under the assumption that an evil spirit has caused the illness. According to Asang informants, the shaman holds his power through connivance with Satan. Curing is achieved by first dreaming of the specific cause of the trouble, then singing and blowing on the affected area. Another category of native practitioner found today, the "spirit-healer," who may be a man or woman, is similar to the shaman in that he or she is also a curer. Unlike the *sukya,* however, certain Christian concepts are utilized in the spirit-healer's practice. Christian hymns may be sung, the sign of the cross made, and Christian supernaturals such as angels may be called upon to help. In the process of curing, the spirit-healer beats upon the patient's body and is himself seized with shaking through the presence of the spirit.

Although these practitioners are not presently found in Asang, certain of their beliefs remain. Dreams are taken quite seriously. Information concerning the proper herbs to use in case of illness is obtained by dreaming. Villagers also believe that it is possible to converse with one who has died or is absent by dreaming of him. The headman's wife smiled knowingly when the anthropologist arrived unannounced at the village late one afternoon after a brief absence. She had dreamt that I would appear, she said. Melisia remembered how she had dreamt that three men came to tell her that there would be a storm and that peoples' homes would be destroyed, but hers would survive; and so it was. There was a hurricane and villagers' houses, old and new, were blown apart. Three times the wind came, she recalled, but her house wasn't damaged. Recently, she said, she had been dreaming every night that the Moravian lay pastor would give her a piece of paper. She didn't know what the content would be, but was waiting expectantly.

Christianity also figured in Armando's father's ability to stop smoking. Eleven years ago, Armando recounted, he, his father (now deceased), his brother, and his brother's wife all tried to stop smoking at the suggestion of the Church of God pastor. All succeeded with the exception of the father. Then his father dreamt one night that the pastor stood before him with opened arms and demanded that he stop smoking. This time he succeeded.

Satan also uses dreams as vehicles for mischief, people claimed. It was not uncommon, they noted, for an individual to dream of traveling to a strange place, perhaps to the ocean, and then to wake up the next day feeling tired. That is the devil's work. Similarly dreams of sexual relations with animals or with strangers is the devil's mischief; he is assuming the shape of the animal or stranger.

The Christian concept of Satan and the indigenous belief in *lasas* are often equated today. Both words are used interchangeably in conversations, and both are considered to refer to real, animistic beings. In order to show their modernity, however, the people of Asang tend to joke about the *lasa*. At times villagers would warn the anthropologist with mock solemnity that a *lasa* would grab her if she went to the bush, or assumed amused amazement that she was able to cross a particular stream or travel through a section of bamboo unscathed. Yet this joking is tinged with uncertainty, as if one could never be too sure. This hesitancy is due to the fact that the Christian concept of Satan in which villagers do believe is equated with *lasa* today.

A similar ambivalence is shown towards the traditional belief in spirits which "owned" various natural phenomena, and which inhabited animals, trees, bushes, hills, or lagoons (cf. Conzemius 1932:128). Although people claim that as Christians they no longer believe in such spirits, nonetheless in actuality the idea is still expressed and a certain amount of credence given to it. Franciliano had recurrent dreams of a man with golden hair who repeatedly told him that for the last thirty years he has been guarding the gold in a particular stream for Franciliano and his brothers. Now the guardian is tired of his watch and wishes Franciliano to claim his property. According to Franciliano, the man is the owner of the gold. Although Franciliano was interested in the prospect of finding gold, he was somewhat concerned about the appearance of the "owner." "He prays and then falls asleep, but still dreams," his wife confided. "*Lasa alkisa*—the spirit has hold of him."

Forces of evil are thought to be particularly malevolent around Good Friday and Easter. Some villagers confessed they were really rather afraid to attend the Moravian Easter dawn service, which, furthermore, is held in the cemetery, a spirit-laden spot, because of the possibility of running into *lasas*. The general feeling is that Good Friday and Easter, and to a lesser extent the other major Christian holidays, are not just memorial days commemorating an event of church history, but are times when supernatural forces are liable to be literally encountered.

In addition to more or less formal beliefs in dreams, evil spirits, and owners of the landscape, the villagers put credence in strange stories and rumors that circulate from village to village about odd and inexplicable occurrences which, again, often involve the devil as an active agent. According to one story, a villager's brother, now living on the coast, once on Good Friday cut a large circle in the bush and at noon began a whooping call to north and south. Soon answering whoops came in reply, and a man—the devil—appeared. He offered to help the brother in any endeavor in return for the life of the Asang villager. Unfortunately, the brother loved that particular *moini*, and did not wish to comply, but had the devil requested someone else, the outcome might have been different.

Many beliefs also center around the power of the moon. To cut wood, to plant, to harvest, to gather during new moon is bad because the materials will not be usable. If beans are pulled, for example, they will be wormy; thatch cut then will only last two or three years instead of the expected seven or eight; if a tree is felled for lumber it will be sure to split. A lunar eclipse in the spring of 1965 was credited with damage to crops, causing them to become spindly and infested with insects. A villager who suffers from epilepsy is reported to have an increase in frequency of attacks during the time of the new moon.

A belief in the significance of various types of omens is also widespread. Dreams are one type of omen, and, as we have seen, are considered meaningful. Other signs give information on weather, provide forewarnings of death, and announce the imminent arrival of visitors. Almost any unusual event becomes an omen for something (cf. Conzemius 1932:132). Thus, to see a large fly buzzing nearby means that visitors will arrive; if horses or pigs are restless

it will rain; lightning over the cemetery means that someone some-
where is dying; benches being noisily knocked about in the church
during the night means a Christian will die.

Villagers' interpretations of the meaning of an omen or statements regarding the significance of the new moon were often followed by comments to the effect that such, at any rate, were the
meanings taught by their elders. The informant himself often
seemed unsure that the explanation was true, but offered it simply
as one possibility. Thus, although traditional beliefs are still widespread, a firm and absolute trust in their validity is often lacking.
There is, instead, an unmistakable element of uncertainty.

The Moravian Core

Traditional beliefs concerning the nature and power of the uni-
verse are given expression today only by individuals. Traditional
group ceremonies demonstrating social acceptance of beliefs are no
longer held. Death and seasonal holidays are all observed more or
less according to Christian regulations today. Yet a few of the oldest
residents of Asang remember, often with considerable pleasure,
some of the pre-Christian festivities associated with funerals and
the holiday period in December which they observed as children.
But the dances, drinking, and details associated with these ceremonies are no longer found. Instead, Moravian customs predominate
at periods of life crisis in Asang, and the seasonal holidays are those
of the Church.

Moravian activities, whether they be sacred or secular, are
marked by restraint and quiet dignity. Miskito Moravianism usually
follows this pattern, although there are occasions such as Christmas
when an atmosphere of holiday exuberance intrudes. Many other
Moravian traditions are also found in village religious activities.
There is a heavy emphasis on music in church services, for example,
and traditional Moravian ceremonies like the Easter morning sunrise service, the Christmas Eve candle service, the use of the multi-
pointed Moravian Star at Christmas, and the ritual of the weekly
Sunday services and Communion celebrations have all become features of normal Asang life.[6]

This assimilation of Moravian customs in Asang is likely due to
both the simultaneous growth of village and congregation, which

6. Readily available introductions to Moravian practices may be found in
Fries (1962) and Allen (1966). See also Appendix B.

has made almost everyone at least nominally a Moravian, and to the traditional interest of the Moravian church in all aspects of community life. Moravian services and traditions have become focal points for a feeling of unity within Asang that is communal as well as congregational in its overall effect.

The seating arrangement for church services illustrates one aspect of this unity. Consistent with early Moravian practice, men and boys sit on the left side of the center aisle, while women and girls are on the right.[7] Furthermore, the youngest children sit in the front pews with those just a bit older behind them, progressing in this way until the last benches are filled with elders.[8] This seating arrangement, based on divisions of age and sex which cut across and separate nuclear families and households in church, expresses the unity of the congregation just as similar divisions separate the village population outside of church into community-wide categories of adult men and women, *wahmas* and *tiaras,* and children. By employing identical society-wide categories in their organizational frameworks, church and village become one unit. Even more important, though, is the fact that the church seating arrangement provides visible evidence of these categories in a way that the village structure cannot, and thus emphasizes the unity of both to a greater extent than village structure alone could do.

Other areas of village unification through church activities have been mentioned before. The role of the Helpers and lay pastor in attempting to settle disputes provides a focal point in the political sphere. In addition, announcements of importance to both village and congregation are made in church, and public recognition is accorded those who have cooperated in fulfilling requests. For instance, several months after Rodolfo had returned to the village from the hospital where he had been undergoing treatment for injuries sustained in a bush accident, he was able to hobble to church occasionally. The first morning he appeared the lay pastor asked all those who had helped with the sawing and carrying of lumber to pay his expenses to rise. Later in the service this group sang a song for Rodolfo. The very existence of the building itself—the only fea-

7. Women wear a distinctive white head-kerchief whenever they attend any church gathering. This custom was introduced by the early missionaries to provide a visible distinction between heathens and baptized Christians (cf. Romig 1890:434).

8. See Gollin (1967), especially chapters 4 and 5, for a discussion of the separation of the sexes in early Moravian communities.

ture of Asang visible from points downriver—has come to identify the village by its simple physical presence. The church also provides recreational facilities through such activities as Young People's Association meetings, choir practice, and play and skit rehearsals. Finally, it is responsible for the rather self-righteous ideology of moral and upright behavior which, villagers feel, sets Asang as a geographical-political entity apart from and above all other communities.

It is features such as these rather than a burning desire to hear the word of God which make the Miskito feel that a village ought to have a church almost regardless of denomination. The success of the Moravian organization in particular may be due to the fact that its unusual history of communal living has pre-adapted it not only to be able to handle this wide range of sacred and secular village services effectively, but to see these roles as part of its duty as a church (see Appendix B). Whatever the reason, Moravianism is a popular denomination among the Miskito, who tend to settle for a Roman Catholic or Iglesia de Dios church only if the Moravians are unable to staff one.

The importance of the Moravian church within Asang is also illustrated by the manner in which daily work is adapted to the demands of the church during the various annual religious holidays, at times of death, and when the parson visits the village (about three times a year).

The calendar of annual holidays celebrated in Asang includes Christmas and New Year, Holy Week, Good Friday, Easter, and Harvest (Thanksgiving), all of which are held at the time of year traditional for them in Christian countries. Celebrations in December, however, date from premissionary times: "Christmas is universally observed all over the Miskito Shore, by both Indian, Zamboes and Kharibees; but for no other reason that I could ever learn, except that it was 'English fashion,' and happens at a time when it does not interfere with their fishing and other pursuits (Roberts 1827:270)."[9] These revelries centered around drinking *mishla*, dancing, and general relaxation (Moravian Church 1849–1887:vol. 19, pp. 315–16).

9. "Indian" here refers to natives considered to be unmixed with foreigners; "Zamboes" indicates natives with Negro ancestry imputed to them; "Kharibee" refers to Black Carib, most of whom lived in northern Honduras, although a few resided at Pearl Lagoon in eastern Nicaragua.

In Asang, Christmas and New Year remain the favorite holidays since they still correspond to the only period of the year when there is no plantation work. Days prior to the actual festivities are busily spent cleaning homes, scrubbing the church interior, cutting the weeds around the graves of deceased relatives, rehearsing church programs, slaughtering pigs, and sewing new clothes. The headman organizes the men of the village, Moravian and Iglesia alike, to cut the weeds and grasses that have grown up in the cleared but un-settled area at the rear of the village.

The evenings are given over to dancing the *aobaia* in the plaza-like area in front of the church. This is the only community dance performed in Asang, and one which is strictly limited to Christmas merrymaking. It is a circle dance with running and hopping steps performed in time to a rather monotonous chant sung by the dance leader and echoed by the dancers. Everyone, men and women, old and young, but especially the teenagers, indulge in the *aobaia,* and dance for hours. The *aobaia* is not a Moravian tradition, but, according to Conzemius (1932:115), was introduced by Creoles.

Christmas Eve and Christmas Day are spent mainly in church. In 1964 the traditional Moravian candlelight service was held on Christmas Eve in the now brightly decorated (with palm and coco-nut leaves and paper streamers) church. After church young boys and *wahmas* shot off quantities of dynamite caps as people as-sembled in the mission yard laughing and joking to await the dis-tribution of gifts by Santa Claus. All those who had previously con-tributed to a gift exchange fund organized by the church formed a circle while Santa, accompanied by two young men strumming guitars, distributed gifts from a wheelbarrow. Only about sixty par-ticipated in this gift exchange, a reflection of today's depressed economy. In more prosperous years, informants claimed, almost everyone participated. Gifts included pieces of cloth, plates, hair bands, soap, and talcum powder. Santa was masked and dressed in a bark-cloth suit to portray a whiskered old man, and his real iden-tity (the shopkeeper Miller) was to be hidden from the group. The lay pastor distributed used American Christmas cards.

A rather informal song and prayer service followed until mid-night, when Coleman lamps were hung on the mission porch to pro-vide some illumination for the *aobaia* enthusiasts in the yard and chatting spectators. Many of the adults and young children soon re-turned to their homes, but the lay pastor and the *tiaras* and *wahmas* noisily played a variety of circle games until two o'clock in the morning when they toured the village singing Christmas carols.

Surveying the quiet community during the caroling, the lay pastor expressed his gratification that no one was drinking. On the Sunday preceding Christmas he had urged from the pulpit that there be no carousing during the Christmas period, directing his comments particularly to the young men. Some of the *wahmas* always bragged a bit about how they would celebrate, he said afterwards, but usually nothing happened. In other villages, he pointed out, Christmas is a time for extensive drinking, a practice which, as we have noted, has roots in the premissionary past.

The main Christmas service was held the next morning to a packed church. Over 500 individuals, including visitors from neighboring Yiasco and Krasa, attended. This figure is almost double the normal attendance for weekly services. Children wore new clothes, and quite a few also wore shoes and socks, as did many women. Another service was held at noon, after which the tireless lay pastor organized the children for various foot races in the mission yard. In the evening, in the church, a group of young people presented a play dealing with the visit of the three kings to the Christ child, after which the exhausted village very quickly grew quiet.

As with Christmas, New Year activities also centered predominantly around the Moravian church. On New Year's Eve, in addition to the usual congregational services, the church elders held their annual meeting to discuss church affairs and promulgate new laws concerning church behavior for the coming year. This meeting is convened at the request of the elders and is not found in all communities. A number of topics dealing with the various duties required of church assistants (see below) were deliberated, and several recommendations made for the congregation at large. It was decided that the Helpers, both men and women, would no longer sit with the congregation, but would assemble on the raised choir platform which crosses the front of the church. The poor behavior of children during services was also discussed. The lay pastor announced that henceforth at the end of services the congregation would file out of the church row by row in an orderly manner, instead of crowding towards the door as they previously had done. These decisions were implemented immediately.

After the services a few young men stayed up all night listening to a radio, but rain prevented any more lively activities. A communal feast was held in the afternoon on New Year's Day. Each village family, regardless of religious affiliation, had been requested to make a contribution to help defray expenses. Although contributions were small, there was sufficient income to purchase a cow. The butchering and cooking of the animal was done by men of the congregation in an open-walled thatched shed at one side of the churchyard, which was built expressly for church-community feasts several years ago. The women tended the fires and prepared dishes of donated food. Each family in the community, together with a few visitors from Krasa and Yiasco received a share of food, and a general atmosphere of festivity prevailed, marred only by complaints about the current lack of cash which prohibited a more elaborate party.

During New Year's Day, games and plays were held in the churchyard under the direction of the Moravian lay pastor. The main play of the afternoon portrayed the types of doctors available on the Coast. Pantomimes of a shaman, a spirit-healer, a dentist, and a trained medical doctor were performed. Only the medical doctor was successful in curing his patient. Curiously enough, the cure was indicated by the doctor finding and removing a wooden animal from the patient's body. When queried later by the anthropologist, the lay pastor, who played the part of the doctor, was unable (or unwilling) to explain what significance the doll held.

Interestingly enough in view of the early raiding history of the Miskito, almost any play performance in Asang sooner or later will involve marching "armies" of boys and young men armed with imitation spears and lances rather than guns, and wearing gaily decorated cardboard helmets, breastplates, and bandoliers; their leader often carries a Nicaraguan flag. The regalia suggests a combination of Biblical warrior, as they are often portrayed on church leaflets, and Nicaraguan *guardia*; Conzemius also notes that reed and cotton armor and breastplates were used during the days of Miskito warfare (1932:73). On this particular New Year occasion, the story involved a king's soldiers who captured some cattle thieves. In punishment the thieves had their ears boxed by the king's women. The soldiers then pursued some maize thieves and were all killed in the resulting skirmish.

A New Year's Day highlight was the Dixie Man dance, which, like the *aobaia*, is celebrated only at this time (Fig. 27). Three young men were dressed to portray two men and a woman. They

Fig. 27. In bark-cloth shirts, palm fronds, and cardboard masks, "Dixie Man" dancers cavort to the music of a guitar and an empty cardboard box drum.

wore long coconut frond skirts and collars over bark-cloth shirts and coats of rubber sacking, or a dress. These three danced in time to the music provided by two guitars and a drum made from a cardboard box. Cardboard masks with the face outlined in black were worn, and each dancer carried a reed cane which he held in both hands much as in a vaudeville soft-shoe act. The costumes of the Asang performers appear to be similar in some respects to those worn by Miskito dancers observed by Young (1847:31) and also described by Heath (Moravian Church 1890–1956:vol. 9, p. 424) and by Conzemius, who saw them perform at a *sikro* or commemorative festival for the dead:

> The head and shoulder piece of the masquerade dress is made of a piece of tanned skin or the inner bark of certain trees; it is painted red and black. . . . Dry grass is used to simulate hair, while a crinolinelike fringe of palm leaves depends from the shoulder piece, so that nothing but the legs of the wearer are visible. The headpiece is surmounted by an upright bar of light wood with the likeness . . . of a certain animal or object (Conzemius 1932:162).

Conzemius (1932) also notes that these masked figures performed in groups of two or three. The *sikro*, it should be noted, is no longer performed.

Good Friday and Easter are celebrated in a more subdued atmosphere. On the one hand this is a busy agricultural period; on the other it is a solemn commemoration for Christians. The Asang observance begins on Palm Sunday and continues through Easter. Most of the emphasis is placed on church services which are long and numerous, and which again follow prepared Moravian texts. In spite of the amount of plantation work church attendance is good, partly because the lay pastor recounts sobering tales of the unnatural deaths that have occurred in other villages when individuals skipped church on Holy Thursday or Good Friday, partly because the text which recounts the Passion and death of Christ is written rather dramatically, and a good story is the most popular form of entertainment among the Miskito. Good Friday and Easter services again include a number of visitors from neighboring communities.

Good Friday is also felt to be a time when evil spirits are prone to be abroad, and, consequently, there is a certain amount of tension in the atmosphere. The only break from this solemnity is the "hanging of Judas" by the boys and young men on Easter Eve which takes the form of a prank. After everyone is asleep, the *wahmas* scour the village stealing any article, either from inside or outside houses, that is not firmly attached to the ground. At the same time, a crude figure is made of grass, dressed in trousers and jacket, and hung from a tree in a central part of town (Fig. 28). The "stolen" goods are piled beneath the figure.

Next morning (Easter day) as people return from the traditional Moravian sunrise service in the cemetery they stop beneath the Judas figure to reminisce about the good old days when a really good effigy was made. After several minutes of comment they sort out their pots, benches, chairs, and other belongings from the general pile and return home. In some villages a small fine is required by the Easter Eve "thieves" before the goods are returned to their owners, but Asang does not practice this.

The remaining annual church festival, Harvest, is held in November to raise money for congregational expenses. Families donate produce and livestock to the church, and commissary foods (sugar, flour, salt, lard) are baked into breads and biscuits by women of the congregation. This food is then auctioned off to the villagers. In former years, when cash was plentiful, Harvest activities lasted as long as three days, and as much as C$3,000 would be raised. Today, although the atmosphere again is light and festive, the depression has severely limited the amount of money that the auction can raise.[10]

The church is also a factor in Miskito life crisis rites. Some of

Fig. 28. A Judas effigy figure swings above "stolen" household goods in the chilly Easter dawn.

these, marriages and funerals, are situations in which the mission church has stepped in to play a role in activities that can exist outside the sphere of organized religion. Others, such as baptism and confirmation, are strictly oriented within the church and, along with church marriages, take place when the parson visits the congregation, usually three times a year.

The events surrounding death and burial in Asang provide the most overt evidence of village and congregational solidarity. All or-

10. In addition, informants felt that the congregation showed some hesitancy to contribute due to mismanagement of Harvest funds by a former lay pastor several years ago, which had somewhat dampened their enthusiasm for church collections.

dinary work ceases when a death occurs, and all adults regardless of church affiliation contribute in one way or another to the necessary business of preparing a coffin, holding the wake, and burying the deceased. The village headman as government representative is responsible for the secular problem of proper burial within an allotted time period, the lay pastor as sacred leader directs the funeral service, and the friends of the family make the actual preparations and console the mourning relatives.

For the most part, present-day activities at times of death are greatly influenced by Christianity. However, the oldest residents of Asang still remember heathen observances seen in their youth, when the dead were buried in a coffin prepared from a dugout canoe, and gifts of food and material items such as miniature tools and dishes were left at the graveyard for use by the spirit of the deceased (cf. M.W. 1732). While large amounts of *mishla* were being prepared, men went to the bush to carve balsa wood masks representing the deceased. The masks covered their wearers to the waist, and a skirt of leaves hung from the waist to the ground. So dressed, and accompanied by the carvers, the masqueraders emerged from the bush to the playing of deep-throated flutes. Swaying and dancing, they advanced towards the group of mourning relatives. The women began to wail, rocking back and forth from a sitting position. In an excess of grief, people sometimes tried to injure themselves with machete cuts, or attempted strangulation with a vine. Proceedings might last as long as a month. According to Conzemius (1932:153–64) the manufacture of masks and the period of mourning were not held at the time of death, but characterized the *sikro*, or commemorative festival for the dead held approximately one year after a death. Asang informants did not make this distinction.

Ceremonies such as these are not held today. The *sikro* is a thing of the past, as is the making of masks and drinking of *mishla*. However, food is still prepared for the mourners, and the dirge that is chanted by women today is no different from the pre-Christian lamentations recorded in the literature (cf. Conzemius 1932:154). In addition there is still a vague feeling for the *isingni*, or spirit of the dead. Traditionally, the *isingni* was thought to hover about the bed of the deceased after the body was buried. However, his presence was an annoyance to others in the household, causing an arm or a leg suddenly to twitch, for instance, and requiring food several times a day. To feed the *isingni*, hot meals were placed on the bed of the deceased until they became cold. The cooling indicated that the spirit had eaten his share. The cold remains were then consumed by the family. In order to put the spirit to rest a shaman was commissioned to drive the *isingni* to the cemetery. The *sukya* argued with the spirit, who would claim that it didn't want to leave its family, but after considerable effort the *isingni*, caught up in bedclothes, was taken to the burial ground and left there. According to some informants, the capture of the *isingni* ushered in the *sikro*. Today in Asang none of the ritual associated with the *isingni* remains, but the concept of a sort of soul which stays behind is still found, and is somewhat comforting to the bereaved. The comments made by the anthropologist's closest friend at the final departure of the investigator from the village are illustrative. Valerina was despondent over the impending departure, and as she helped with the packing she looked down at the anthropologist's bed and commented that although her friend was leaving, her *isingni* would still be there. Another informant corrected her, saying that in this case there would be no *isingni*, because the anthropologist was leaving the village alive, not dead.

According to informants, each village has its own traditions regarding details of funeral preparations today, and it is a point of pride among Asang residents that here the entire community becomes involved in the necessary activities. Other villages, they claim, do not show such solidarity, but leave the burden of the work to the bereaved relatives. The following description, abstracted from field notes, presents a picture of the activities and atmosphere surrounding death.

Gilberto's son, a young man of twenty, died of tuberculosis on Sunday morning. Immediately upon hearing the news, the lay pastor cancelled all the usual services for the rest of the day. A *wahma* was sent off to San Carlos to buy white cloth for a shroud and the church bell was tolled for several minutes. The lay pastor and the church elders went over to Gilberto's home and offered prayers, after silencing the women who had immediately begun to wail. Boards were brought to the front of the house and work on the coffin began there at once.

By 6 P.M. a calf, property of the deceased, was being slaughtered to provide food for the night's wake, and donations of food or money were requested from all village families. Wheelbarrows of produce soon began to arrive at the house. Funds

were also solicited to pay the headman the slaughter tax. It
rapidly grew dark, windy, and rainy—a suitable atmosphere
for the night's work. Next door at Edwina's home *tiaras* were
baking bread preparatory to feeding the workers. *Tiaras* and
wahmas told stories and joked as they worked at this or sat on
the porch. In the yard, Augusto placed one of the Coleman
lamps on his head to provide light for the men who were
building the coffin. Benches were brought out from neighboring
homes and placed in the yard in front of Gilberto's house, and
those men who were not working sat there and talked.

Inside the home, where a single poor lamp gave sputtering
light, the deceased, covered with a white cloth, lay on a cot
on a piece of bark cloth. His mother and sisters sat by the
side of the low bed, their faces to the wall, their heads covered
with cloths. They were wailing and sobbing. At the foot of the
bed and along the walls sat the *kukas* crouched on ancient
haunches, shoulders covered with cloths against the damp of
the night, heads draped with white cloths, each puffing on a
pipe. They sometimes talked together quietly and sort of
matter-of-factly, but often just sat.

Outside on one side of the yard several women were presiding
over iron pots filled with boiling meat, bananas, cassava, rice,
and beans. This food was to be served later in the night to the
watchers. The sparks from the fire under the pots, which sat on
two long logs, the light of the Coleman lamp, the wind, the
occasional rain, the sawing and hammering from the manufacture of the coffin, the thump-thump of the mortars where rice
was being hulled, and the wail of the bereaved combined to
create a strange and solemn scene.

The atmosphere gradually became less somber as those sitting
on porches or benches began to joke or tell stories to pass the
time. Gilberto sat on the porch of his home surrounded by
men. The men did not show marked signs of grief. Wailing is
the province of women only. By midnight the atmosphere had
become quite jovial, to the consternation of certain of the
women, with people laughing and talking around the fire, looking forward to food. Such lightheartedness was thought by
some to be disrespectful.

As time wore on the wailing gradually stopped and people

settled down for the night, many of the men going home as soon as the coffin was completed, but the women remaining. The next morning the wailing was resumed as the time approached for the funeral. Since the young man had not been confirmed, the lay pastor could not hold a funeral in the church. But the Moravian service was read at the graveyard while most of the village watched as the coffin, covered with white cloth and with a black cross on the top, was lowered into the ground and the grave filled. The villagers slowly left the disheveled graveyard which was full of broken crosses, pieces of rusty barbed wire intended to protect graves from animals, broken fences, weeds, and small mounds. At home Gilberto's family was finally left alone, the women still wailing slightly.

Given the variety of roles played by the Moravian church, it follows that the congregational leaders hold positions of considerable importance and prestige. The duties of the lay pastor have been discussed before, in the context of political arbitration. As was noted then, there is a gap between him and his congregation, first because he is not a native member of the congregation but comes to it from outside the village. As a consequence, he often has fewer years residence in any one village than even the men who reside there as affinals; yet he must assume a position of potential leadership. Second, he transmits the decision of the higher mission administration to the congregation and thus stands closer to the non-Miskito world. Finally, because he is a salaried employee of the church in addition to receiving support from his congregation, he is often fairly well off financially, or at least so it seems to the jealous eyes of the other Miskito men.

The lay pastor is also apt to be more highly educated than most of the other villagers. Preparation for the position requires three years attendance at the Moravian Bible Institute downriver at Bilwaskarma, which is primarily staffed by foreign missionaries. After completing his work there, the lay pastor is assigned to a congregation. However, he is still under the supervision of an ordained parson (generally a Creole or American) who manages the central station of which the lay pastor's village forms one of several outstations. For example, the Moravian congregation at Asang and its lay pastor are under the jurisdiction of the parson resident at San Carlos, a short distance downriver. In addition to Asang, this parson is re-

sponsible for six other villages on the river, all of which he periodically visits to conduct baptisms, confirmations, admission of new
adult members, marriages, and communion services. The lay pastors resident in these villages, although expected to offer instruction
classes in preparation for confirmation and communion, are unable
to conduct any of these services themselves since they are not ordained Moravian ministers.[11]

The lay pastor's rapport with his congregation is often heavily
dependent upon the nature of his wife's relationships with the other
village women. Women tend to be much more critical of newcomers
than are men, especially if the stranger is a woman. Thus when
there is strife between a lay pastor and his congregation, nine times
out of ten the women are involved.

The lay pastor's role of coordinator involves close cooperation between himself and the church elders and leaders. There are three
categories of leaders: Helpers, Church Committeemen, and Door
Marshals. Both men and women fill these positions, either by congregational approval (Helpers) or by appointment (Church Committee, Door Marshals) on the recommendation of the Helpers.
Note that the lay pastor is not responsible for the selection of in-
cumbents in the various positions. However, when policy is discussed, it is the men who make decisions; women attend the sessions, but rarely speak out. The number of Helpers, Church
Committeemen, and Door Marshals varies among congregations. In
Asang there are sixteen Helpers, eight men and eight women;
eleven Church Committeemen, seven men and four women; and
six Door Marshals, three men and three women.

Of these three positions, that of Helper is most important and
carries the most prestige. Once elected to the position, a Helper remains in office for life. When a vacancy occurs through death (or,
on rare occasion, through dismissal for misbehavior), the remaining
Helpers elect a replacement, subject to congregational approval.
The Helpers divide the families of the congregation among themselves, and each maintains vigilance over those in his or her charge.
Specifically, the families of the congregation are apportioned out

11. Shortly after I left Asang the lay pastor there was ordained as a minis-
ter of the Moravian church, thus joining the growing number of often very ex-
traordinary individuals who have become Miskito parsons. Asang is now a station with at least three outstations. The new parson's task will not be easy
since the individualistic Miskito are not used to permanent submission to one
of their own.

between eight pairs of Helpers, with one man and one woman responsible for the men and women, respectively, of the families in their joint charge. It is the duty of the Helpers to encourage those in their care to attend church and, if necessary, to serve as arbiters in family quarrels.

If the Helper cannot settle a problem satisfactorily, or if the dispute involves people from several Helper groups, a Helper meeting may be held in the church in order to arrive at a settlement. In order to perform this aspect of his work successfully the Helper's private life should theoretically be beyond reproach. He should be capable of holding confidences and should not give any indications of "pride." However, given the prevalence of gossip with all its aspects and implications, it follows that the foibles of Helpers are always a potential hindrance to a smoothly operating system.

Helpers should also be available for premarriage counseling, and are expected to conduct "speaking" sessions prior to each communion in which the potential communicant expresses his desire to commune and indicates that he is living in peace with his neighbors.[12] If he has had a quarrel with anyone he must settle the argument before he is given permission to commune. Since most individuals are more or less constantly at odds with someone, the simultaneous airing of all these grievances creates a particularly charged atmosphere during "speaking." It is not unusual for someone to abstain from communion rather than patch up an argument. In one case, two Helpers, a husband and wife, preferred to forego communion rather than to settle a dispute with another villager.

Finally, Helpers are in charge of church services when the lay pastor is away from the village; they also have the authority to formally request the transfer of the lay pastor to another village should that be necessary.

The work of the Church Committee revolves around the maintenance of the church building, the mission house, and surrounding grounds. The committee is also responsible for keeping the lay pastor supplied with food and firewood. The committee may fulfill this latter requirement in any way it wishes, either by supplying cash, by overseeing the preparation of plantations for the lay pastor, by requesting donations of wood and produce from the families of the congregation, or by any combination of these. In Asang, as we have

12. See Gollin (1967:86–87) for the significance of "speaking" in early Moravian life.

seen, plantations are maintained for the lay pastor's family. Firewood cutting sessions and donations of produce are also solicited from the congregation by the Church Committee. Six or eight families regularly send weekly contributions of food—perhaps a stem of bananas or several manioc roots—to the lay pastor's household. Others will contribute if specifically asked.

The success of this system depends greatly on the lay pastor's rapport with the congregation since the Church Committee depends on volunteer labor and/or produce in order to fulfill its obligation. Efficient compliance with the committee's requests indicates "respect" for the lay pastor, whereas lack of cooperation is taken as a reflection of trouble between congregation and lay pastor.[13] A small percentage of the lay pastor's income comes from first fruit contributions. Not everyone does this, but some men will send the first produce obtained from a brand new plantation to the lay pastor in the hope of receiving further blessing on their land through their generosity to God's representative.

Since the Asang lay pastor is greatly respected by his congregation, he does not have to worry much about receiving sufficient gifts of food and labor to provide for his family. In fact, even though not all families contribute regularly to the lay pastor's larder, the congregation as a whole is quite proud of their overall generosity towards him and his family, pointing out again that other congregations are not as thoughtful. The lay pastor, in turn, complains periodically that firewood is low or the food supply dwindling. In private, however, he concedes that the Asang congregation is exceptionally constant in their contributions, and provides adequately for him and his family.

The third level of church workers, the Door Marshals, are concerned with preparing the church for services and maintaining order during the service. Door Marshals are assigned in pairs by the lay pastor for tours of three months duty. The male Door Marshal is responsible for ringing the bell for services, preparing lamps, and seating visitors. His female counterpart removes obstreperous children during the service.

Just as Helpers, Church Committeemen, and Door Marshals hold

13. Size of congregation may be a further determining factor with respect to how well the lay pastor is fed. If the village is too small the drain on the individual families may be too great, while in Asang, if one family fails in its contribution one week, another will not.

posts of prestige and responsibility within the Moravian church, so all publicly declared members of the congregation stand in a similar status vis-à-vis other villagers. Strictly speaking, only those villagers who have publicly assumed church membership are considered Christians. These are the individuals who attend speaking sessions in preparation for communion. Not all may actually attend any particular communion service, but all are considered "accredited communicants" in the eyes of the Moravian church. When the church was first established in Asang, everyone became a member. Gradually, however, individuals have left the ranks of active membership. That is to say, they are no longer considered applicants for communion, although they may attend church, and many do so quite regularly. These noncommunicants include those who are in a period of instruction prior to assuming active membership, those who once were active members but who voluntarily left the communicant congregation, and those who were dropped or suspended by the church. Voluntary dropouts are still kept on the books as paying members, however, and are held responsible for paying their share of the annual pledge.

Presently approximately 250 persons, or almost half the village, are active Christians. Another 250 attend church but do not apply for communion. The remainder of the village, somewhat over 100 persons, includes baptized infants and those children and young people who, either because of age or lack of interest, have not entered a period of church instruction. In addition, there are the 27 members of the Iglesia de Dios congregation; 2 persons, a middle-aged man and an elderly widow, neither of whom is native to Asang, who are formally Roman Catholic and attend both Moravian and Iglesia services; and 2 women, one middle-aged and the other elderly, both of whom came originally from other villages, who are not affiliated with any denomination.

Because of the proselytizing pressure placed on them by communicant members, noncommunicant members and nonmembers often become quite defensive about their positions, and in retaliation are quick to criticize lapses in the behavior of Christians. In turn, Christian (communicant) members, somewhat self-righteous about their status as active church participants, defend themselves through gossip, which, because it is "proud" behavior, adds fuel for fresh attacks by noncommunicants. Consequently, there is a constant stream of talk between Christians and non-Christians. Active

church members, especially those in the most visible positions—
choir members, Helpers, Committeemen, Door Marshals—feel they
must be constantly on guard not to become targets for talk. Yet by
the very nature of the system it is virtually impossible for any individual to avoid being drawn into the gossip circle.

The Church of God

The foregoing discussion has been restricted to the activities of
the Moravian congregation since it is by far the largest and most influential church in Asang. However, a small congregation of the
Iglesia de Dios denomination is also found in the village, composed
of four household heads, the wives of three (the fourth is a Moravian) and their children—in all, twenty-seven persons—who have
broken with the Moravians. The beliefs and activities of this group
and the nature of their interaction with the Moravian congregation
forms another aspect of religion in Asang.[14]

To the best of my knowledge, the Church of God has been operating in Nicaragua for not more than fifteen years. In contrast to
the Moravians and Roman Catholics, the Iglesia de Dios congregations do not have a battery of foreign missionaries resident on the
Coast to serve as administrators, although foreigners occasionally
travel through as representatives of the official Church of God.

An Iglesia de Dios congregation has existed in Asang for ten
years. However, a separate church building was constructed only
four years ago. Prior to that services were held in members' homes.
The founders of the Asang congregation were originally members
in good standing of the Moravian church, until, through a series of
events, the several families went their own way.

A little more than a decade ago, informants related, a stranger
came to the village proselytizing for the Lutheran church. He
wished to take several young men to Guatemala ostensibly to train
for service as Lutherans. Three or four *wahmas* decided to go as a
lark, including a young man named Milton Collins. Before too long
all except Milton returned, saying they had gone broke, but Milton
traveled to El Salvador and was converted to the Iglesia faith.
When he returned to Asang he left the Moravian church and persuaded his two brothers to join him. Milton eventually became pastor of the Church of God congregation in Puerto Cabezas, but his

14. The third Christian church operating on the river, the Roman Catholic,
is not represented in Asang.

brothers, their wives (one a non-Asang woman, the other an Asang Moravian), and their children remained in Asang and formed the nucleus of the Iglesia congregation there.

Milton occasionally returned to Asang on visits, and on one occasion brought a bundle of used clothing obtained through the auspices of the Alliance for Progress. He distributed the clothing among his relatives, and also gave some to another family which was extremely poor. In gratitude, the head of the household, but not his wife, joined the Iglesia group. A bush accident was responsible for the fourth family's break with Moravianism. A member of the Bobb *kiamp* was struck by a falling tree and suffered a serious head injury while working for a rubber company. His behavior became somewhat disoriented and emotional as a result of the accident and, because he disrupted Moravian services, he was asked not to attend. He and his wife and children then joined the Iglesia congregation. These seven adults and their children, who range in age from a few years to the early twenties, comprise the Church of God membership in Asang today.

In terms of village-wide activities the members of the Iglesia de Dios congregation are as much a part of Asang as anyone else. The men of the congregation are expected to participate in the weed-cutting sessions organized by the headman, and do so. Similarly, when a meeting was convened in the Moravian church to discuss the matter of whether or not to request that the new Moravian medical clinic be built in Asang, the men of the Iglesia congregation were invited, and attended, since the clinic would benefit the entire village, regardless of its sponsorship. When the Moravian lay pastor organized sawing parties to prepare lumber for the new clinic, Church of God members took an active part.

However, in the realm of certain religious beliefs and ceremonies the Iglesia and Moravian congregations find little in common. Where Moravian services are dignified and restrained, Church of God worship is marked by loud singing and shouting, hand clapping, and speaking in tongues. Where Moravians tend to be pragmatic with a certain level-headed secularity in their beliefs and actions, Iglesia members preach emotionally against involvement with "the things of this world." Finally, the two groups disagree on details of ritual such as the proper rites for baptism and on some major theological points, especially regarding the importance of the Holy Spirit.

In Asang the two congregations coexist on a day-to-day basis, yet there is much tension between them. The Moravians regard the Church of God congregation as a group of fanatics, and find constant entertainment and much material for gossip in ridiculing and imitating their enthusiastic worship services. The Iglesia church is located close to the Moravian lay pastor's residence, and on evenings when Church of God services are in progress, Moravian leaders and friends of the lay pastor and his wife stop by to sit on the porch and porch steps where they listen to the outbreaks of song and prayer emanating from the closely shuttered church, and shake their heads over what they consider blasphemy. Occasionally shouts of "Amen" or "Hallelujah" can be heard in the service, with answering calls from other villagers whose homes, like that of the lay pastor, are near the church, and whose porches are also full of gossip about the Iglesia situation.

The Church of God families in return seek a refuge in "otherworldliness," and profess a desire to keep interaction with Moravians at a minimum. They argue that Moravianism, its beliefs and its activities, are "things of the earth," along with hunger, disease, lack of money, and hell. They, in turn, are concerned with the glory of God and heaven. The exuberant services are in keeping with the greatness of God and with their joy in their belief.

Most Church of God members live together at the south end of the village although one family is located close to the Iglesia church. Geographical isolation lessens the frequency of their contacts with the rest of Asang, and this, they feel, helps to reduce the potential for quarrels. "Our position is not understood by the others," one informant stated, "therefore it is best to live together peacefully as a group and avoid the rest."

The conflict in religious beliefs and church affiliation has placed some strain on those kinship ties which link Church of God members with Moravians. Generally speaking, members of the Iglesia congregation conduct as many of their daily affairs as possible within their group. Thus, meat for distribution to relatives is sent to congregational members first, many of whom are relatives, as we have seen, although some may be sent to Moravian kinsmen. Congregational families assist each other with weeding sessions, although here again a few non-Iglesia relatives may also participate. Moravian villagers also charge, somewhat cynically, that the only reason Church of God members assist with funerals is to assure assistance for themselves in return, since the duties and activities at the time of a death require extrahousehold help. When an Iglesia child died several years ago, the mother's brother, a Moravian, tolled the Moravian church bell (the Iglesia church does not have a bell). The Moravian congregational leaders, however, felt this was unseemly, and protested.

The major source of potential Moravian-Iglesia strife lies in those few families (two, currently) where husband and wife belong to different denominations. In one case, noted previously, the couple was already married when the husband joined the Iglesia congregation out of gratitude for their generosity. The second involves two young people, the daughter of an Iglesia family and the son of a Moravian household. Relatives and lay pastors of both faiths try to discourage such marriages, but if the couple insists, as this pair did, they are married.

Generally these marriages are as quiet as those where only one church is represented. On the other hand, special problems can arise. For example, there was considerable discussion as to which denomination would baptize the young couple's first-born child. The mother's father insisted that the Church of God perform the baptism; the child's father demanded a Moravian baptism, saying that he would sooner have the child remain unbaptized than be affiliated with the Church of God. The baptism was performed by the Moravian parson on his next visit. A potentially more serious conflict occurred when the usual tensions between Church of God and Moravian denominations were exacerbated by a period of revivalist services conducted by the Iglesia congregation for several months. The young couple were unavoidably caught up in the high feelings which developed between the two groups at this time, and for a while a separation seemed imminent. Fortunately the overall situation cooled before the marriage dissolved.

The difficulties began in November when a Spanish-speaking Nicaraguan woman appeared on the river, and spent several weeks holding a series of noisy revival services among Iglesia congregations in various villages. There was much loud singing, clapping of hands, stamping of feet, and frenzied speaking in tongues. The emotional fervor gained in intensity until it was rumored that the second coming of Christ was slated for February. In anticipation, the Iglesia families neglected to plant beans or to care for their plantations, preferring to spend the days in church. By March, when Christ hadn't arrived, the beans were belatedly planted and life gradually returned to normal. During this time the Asang Moravians were full of indignation at stories describing events in other villages and at the disruption of their own usually quiet community by numerous loud Iglesia services.[15] Yet except for occasional theological arguments between lay pastors and various members of the respective congregations, the conflict was expressed indirectly in heated gossip, and there was no overt confrontation between the two groups.

Group manifestation of impetuous emotion does not appear to be new in the history of missionary activity on the Coast. A description of modern Church of God prayer and worship services, particularly during the revival period, with their exuberant fundamentalist characteristics portrays equally well the brief period in Moravian church history in Nicaragua known as The Awakening (1881–96). Hutton describes conditions at that time, noting that people were subject to convulsions, sang and prayed loudly, sometimes had visions and dreams and spoke with tongues (1923:334–35). He remarks further that "at Yulu [a Miskito coastal community] people continued for years to be subject to physical convulsions" (Hutton 1923:338). Conzemius (1932:144) also describes "a new movement" which "appeared among the Christianized Miskito" around the turn of the century. "While engaged in fervent prayers, either in church or at home, certain people suddenly begin to act like mad; they shiver over the whole body, run and dance around, give out loud screams, and by other means seek to attract attention. They claim that at such periods they have no control over their actions, and that the latter are due to the presence of the Holy Ghost in themselves." If these examples are taken in conjunction with the pre-Christian ceremonies such as funerals and commemorative *sikro* rites with their heavy emphasis on intoxication and frenzied manifestations of grief, the successful introduction and maintenance of Moravian sobriety rather than Iglesia emotionalism would seem to be the more remarkable feature of Asang religion.

15. In several other Miskito villages along the river, which had larger Iglesia de Dios congregations, the disturbance reached such peaks that the Nicaraguan authorities threatened to forbid further Church of God sponsored activities in the Republic, and on at least one occasion, found it necessary to intervene in village services in order to prevent what was described as a potential child sacrifice.

Health and Ideology

Illness and its prevention or cure have always been closely associated with Miskito ideology, both in heathen and in Christian times. "Among the heathen Indians all cases of illness and death are ascribed to the influence of evil spirits" (Moravian Church 1903–1954:vol. 11, pp. 83–84). Consequently, sickness was dreaded and when it did occur a shaman had to be commissioned to effect a cure by exorcising the evil spirit (Bell 1862:251; Mueller 1932:50–51).

The people of Asang have an extreme fear of illness or *siknis*. *Siknis* is defined as anything not normal, from an infected insect bite to malarial fevers to a permanent crippled condition. This last state is considered particularly shameful and utmost care is taken to shield a deformity from public view for as long as possible. One woman in the village had a three-month-old baby born with club feet. One afternoon, while she and the anthropologist were chatting, she made a careful surveillance of the neighborhood and then uncovered the infant's feet in hopes that the anthropologist could suggest a remedy. She said that for two months no one knew about the deformity because she was careful to keep the child's feet covered. Finally, however, she showed her husband and her older daughters, and there was much sorrow in the family. The friends and relatives who had assisted her at the birth had agreed not to say anything to anyone, and vigorously denied any hints of gossip they heard. She had been treating the feet with various oils and thought she saw some improvement.

Conzemius reports a similar attitude, and further notes that "in former days deformed children were not allowed to grow up; they were either buried alive or left to starve" (Conzemius 1932:21; cf. Crowe 1850:246).

Whatever its manifestation, illness contains an aura of mystery, and while evil spirits per se are no longer considered to be responsible, the restlessness caused by a fever or any more drastic convulsions is still described as *lasa prukaia*, that is, "the evil spirit is attacking." Stories of the deaths of loved ones by poisoning are also still occasionally whispered about. Usually, though, illness is attributed either to God's will or to the vagaries of the weather—the air is too hot or too cold, the sun is too hot, the water is too cold. Yet both of these rationales are similar to that invoking evil spirits in that they, too, lie within the realm of the unknowable and uncontrollable. It is not surprising then that illness is still greatly feared.

In its efforts to halt reliance on shamans' abilities, the Moravian church has paralleled its program of spiritual ministration with a network of several hospitals, a tuberculosis sanitorium, and a number of clinics which now dot the coast. The Roman Catholic missions also dispense medication as part of their program. Finally, a few clinics and a roving doctor have been placed on the river as part of the Alliance for Progress.

Although the people of Asang have been appreciative of such efforts they have not really utilized these facilities fully. The expense of hospitalization and the distance to be traveled are the usual excuses given. Consequently, bush remedies or medical supplies left from a previous illness are tried first. Then, if the illness does not abate, clinics at ever greater distances from the village are visited one by one until the patient either recovers, dies, or reaches a hospital. The solution to this problem, according to the villagers, is to have a clinic in Asang. Their request was finally granted in 1965. Not only will the clinic provide medical supplies, but its presence will also help to reduce the fear and insecurity that accompany the onslaught of illness in the community. As of this writing, the clinic, permanently staffed by a trained Creole nurse, is in operation. The discussion below, however, refers to procedures used before a clinic was readily available.

When illness strikes suddenly, friends and relatives immediately flock to the bedroom of the sick, providing a generalized feeling of security at this time of great apprehension, and furnishing a range of specific ideas on proper procedure. There is an initial period of uncertainty about what to do filled with lamentations regarding the poor and helpless condition of the defenseless Miskito in this situation. Then pills are given, if available. Pills, and especially injections, are highly valued for their curing abilities, and are preferred to home or "Miskito" remedies.

If pills are unavailable or too expensive, or if they are ineffective, Miskito or bush remedies are applied. The people of Asang have an extensive knowledge of the properties of various herbs, roots, barks, and leaves. Medication is effected either by drinking a boiled infusion, or by rubbing the body with crushed leaves so that the medication can "penetrate the skin."[16] Several of these remedies have

16. The direct penetration of the skin by an injection may be what makes this form of modern treatment particularly meaningful to the Miskito.

some effect, as I can verify through direct experience, if only as pain killers. Combinations of bush remedies and pills, "grass tea" and sulfa tablets, for example, are also seen as highly effective.

Everyone has a rudimentary knowledge of bush medicines, but some individuals are more informed than others and are called in for consultation. They are by no means shamans, although like shamans they often obtain knowledge of plant uses by dreaming. Additional remedies may be obtained by exchanging "recipes" with individuals in other villages. In general, the people of Asang are proud of their knowledge of bush remedies, pointing out that without them the village would soon be empty. In their eyes the greater power of modern medicine does not entirely detract from the basic worth of their traditional remedies.

After an illness is treated with pills and/or bush remedies, if it is a serious case prayer is offered by the lay pastor, commending the final resolution to God. Members of the Iglesia faith subscribe only to healing by divine intervention as requested by prayer, and do not advocate pills, injections, or bush remedies. This difference constitutes another source of disagreement with the Moravians.

From the point of view of the outside observer, conditions of health in Asang are not too adverse when compared with health conditions often found among rural peoples in underdeveloped countries. A sufficient range of agricultural produce, domestic animals, fish, and game is available, and nutrition appears to be adequate. There is considerable infant mortality, but those children who survive rarely show signs of malnutrition. Adults are vigorous and, barring unusual accidents or disease, have a fairly good chance of reaching their fifties and sixties. Downriver, the coastal fringe, lacking fertile agricultural land, has a greater nutritional problem.

The major health hazards in the area are intestinal parasites, malaria, which debilitates though it does not cause many fatalities, and tuberculosis, which is responsible for many of the early deaths. Tuberculosis also presents the greatest problem in terms of treatment, for the Miskito dread the disease and are ashamed of it. Therefore, fearing the gossip of the village, families try to hide evidence of illness as long as possible, and especially avoid clinical medical care because of the possibility of publicity. Consequently, tuberculosis is widespread and, given conditions of household and kitchen sanitation and fairly crowded living arrangements, presents the greatest health problem.

Miskito-Moravian Compatibility

In attempting to summarize the significance of mission churches and Christianity for the people of Asang, it must first be emphasized that it is precisely because Miskito territory is not effectively controlled by the states within whose boundaries it is located that foreign mission churches have been able to operate so successfully. With regard to the missions themselves, the most successful of these endeavors (and the mission of major significance in Asang), the Moravian church, seems to owe its position to at least two factors: first, a similar basic organization underlies both Moravian and Miskito culture; and second, the level of religious organization of most interest to the foreign missionaries has not been the level of most significance to the Miskito themselves, although as a result of mission work it is becoming more important, but for secular reasons rather than sacred.

With regard, first of all, to the problem of basic organization, it is necessary to briefly summarize a few select aspects of Miskito and Moravian cultures in order to illuminate certain similarities. Traditional day-to-day Miskito life was channeled through a web of kinship ties which required, for smooth operation, that various kinship obligations be fulfilled. The Miskito express this behavior in terms of showing "respect" for others. Society was also egalitarian, egalitarianism balanced by a strong sense of personal individuality.

The Moravian church, as its original name *Unitas Fratrum* indicates, is conceived by its members to be a Unity of Brethren, stressing "the doctrine of Christian brotherhood" (Fries 1962:8; see Appendix B). This spiritual unity had at one time a secular counterpart in communal settlements where "brothers" and "sisters" in Christ endeavored to follow the requirements of Christian living while attending to the numerous mundane details of daily life. Along with an emphasis on unity, however, went a concern for the welfare of the individual. This is expressed at length in the Results of the Synod meetings for 1848, particularly with reference to foreign missions (Moravian Church 1849:125–37).

Turning to one mission field in particular, the Miskito Coast (first contacted by the Moravians in 1849), it is obvious how an interest in the individual members of society would be met with ready understanding by the native inhabitants. Yet the missionaries' approach was not only to convert individuals, but also to create a unity of Christian kinsmen, of "brothers" and "sisters" who would show "respect" for each other by mutual abidance by the rules of Christian behavior. The extension of the Miskito kinship terms *moini* and *lakra* to include Christian (i.e., Moravian) "brothers" and "sisters" has been noted before, and can be seen, in a sense, as symbolic of the number of similarities between Miskito and Moravians in their mutual emphasis on "kinship" organized society. Moreover, the Moravians, by virtue of their own traditional experience in combining sacred and secular interests into a single pattern for daily living, were able to understand the all-pervasive nature of Miskito beliefs and, in attempting to replace those beliefs with their own, felt similarly obligated to intervene also in secular affairs.

The results of this intervention in Asang have been noted above. Aspects of marriage have been changed, drinking severely curtailed, and traditional ceremonies halted. Church organization has been added to village political organization and village solidarity has benefited greatly as a result; new prestigious statuses of lay pastor, Helper, Church Committeeman, and Door Marshal have been added to Miskito society. That such changes were accepted not only by Asang villagers, but by many other Miskito communities as well may be due to the fact that there was a common understanding between Moravians and Miskito regarding certain basic organizational tenets of society which the missionaries did not try to change.

Ironically enough the church has not succeeded as well in changing the nature of Miskito ideology itself. On the positive side, the shaman has been replaced by the lay pastor, although in some areas shamans can still be found. Throughout the Coast hundreds of villagers attend weekly Sunday services, look forward to the annual religious festivals, willingly pay their pledges if they have the cash, are active in church affairs, and consider themselves to be earnest and God-fearing Christians. Yet, in many ways Miskito Christianity still retains aspects of pre-Christian beliefs, or at best is an imperfect rendering of Christian concepts. The organization of the church is strong, but on the individual level progress has been more halting. The explanation might again be sought in the basic organizational principles underlying Moravian and Miskito society, although now the emphasis is more on points of difference than on areas of similarity between the two cultures.

Religion to the Moravians was strongly bound up with communal organization: the settlement of Brethren was organized basically for religious observances. The Miskito, on the other hand, did not emphasize the group aspects of ideology as much as the individual. Individual shamans were the only practitioners, and, except for group ceremonies concerning the dead, shamans dealt solely with individual spirits as these attacked individual persons. Moravian missionaries, as would be expected, stressed the formation of an organized group, a church, as basic to the furtherance of their belief system. Since secular interests were by definition also intertwined with such a group in Moravian life, the mission churches were unavoidably oriented towards secular as well as sacred activities. The Miskito, with their individual emphasis on religion, had little in the way of organization to oppose the new church system, and therefore could accept the congregational structure relatively easily, but not for the sacred aspects as much as for the secular. Consequently, the village church has become a social and political center, but still lags as a spiritual center. The missionaries have succeeded in their attempts to bring heathen Miskito into the Christian fold, although they have fallen somewhat short in their efforts to convert them to true believers.

Finally, we may ask why the Moravians were accepted in the first place. Why were the Miskito tolerant of and disposed to listen to these missionaries at all? Two answers come to mind. First, the Moravians were not Spanish, and therefore were not automatically rejected. Second, missionary activity was not the first form of contact with the West which Miskito culture had experienced. Two hundred years of successful dealing with buccaneers and traders preceded the onset of missionization. These beneficial contacts no doubt predisposed the Miskito to at least investigate the possible advantages of dealing with the newcomers. Having obtained an initial foothold, the missionaries, by virtue of their own cultural tradition, were then gradually able to pursue their ends without serious opposition.

7

Views of the Outside World

THE ATTITUDES held by the people of Asang concerning the nature of the world and their position in it reflect on yet another plane the interaction between the indigenous Miskito and various agents of the Western world which has influenced to a greater or lesser extent virtually all aspects of Miskito life for over three hundred years. Yet the Miskito themselves do not recognize such an extensive time depth, taking instead as their historical base line the beginning of missionary work. Everything prior to this period is considered heathen by definition and therefore best forgotten. Consequently, there is no firm recollection by the villagers of Asang of the events and activities of the *patitara*, as this early period is called in Miskito. A few individuals may refer briefly to a former period of warfare, and some mention with uncertainty stories attributed to their grandparents regarding an early expansion of armed coastal Miskito up the river, displacing the timid Sumu. However, these reminiscences are vague.

The World Defined

History and proper living are said to begin with Christianity, that is, about 1910 for Asang. The villagers delight in contrasting the "modern" conveniences introduced by missionaries with the "dirty" pattern of life in heathen days. Homes with walls, windows, and floors raised on pilings have replaced open-walled huts which stood directly on the earth; the cooking fire is placed on the *kubus* (clay cooking platform) now, instead of being built between three logs; individual utensils have replaced the communal pot and leaf plates from which people ate with fingers or wooden spoons; the "unclean" habit of masticating manioc for *mishla* was stopped, and polygyny

217

forbidden; Western suits of clothing, either purchased or sewed from manufactured cloth are worn now instead of locally woven cotton or bark-cloth loincloths for men and cotton waist wraps for women. Informants chuckled as they remembered the early opposition to wearing trousers in this warm climate.

For Asang villagers today to refer in detail to events of the nineteenth century or earlier would require reference not only to pre-Christian days but also to deceased relatives. Such references are frowned upon, with the result that the significant genealogical depth of Miskito society does not exceed three or four generations, and includes only the living. A shallow historical view, therefore, is also a function of Miskito social organization. In the case of Asang, the coincidental correspondence between the shallow historical depth required by social custom, which reaches back only to approximately the turn of the century, and the introduction of Christianity shortly thereafter may further account for the emphasis currently given to the role of the church in identifying the starting point of significant time.

On the synchronic level, world view is heavily conditioned by the fact that the Miskito are well aware of the existence of other cultures or "nations," as they call them, in the world. The location, size, and geographical features of various foreign lands are always good topics for conversation. Men particularly are interested in learning about other countries. Perhaps because of their wider experiences (most of the adult men of Asang had travelled in their youth both for pleasure and for work opportunities), they are more knowledgeable of other countries than are women, whose opportunities for travel are few.

It is a favorite recreation for men and boys in the evenings or on Sunday afternoons to sit comfortably on a front porch chatting about other countries. On a typical afternoon, when five or six were sitting on the lay pastor's porch, César asked the anthropologist if there were any hills in the "States," as the United States is commonly called. He thought it might be flat. He knew, he said, that there was a road from Managua to Guatemala, and one through Mexico to the States, but, he queried, could one travel to England by road? Augusto pointed out that England was an island, and asked, somewhat sarcastically, how one could travel to an island by car. Cuba, Corn Island (a small key off the Miskito coast), and Belize (British Honduras) were also islands, he said. (Augusto apparently included

Belize as an island because it is most readily reached from the Miskito Coast by water.) Cuba, although an island, had hills on it, he noted, which just goes to show the diversity God used in creating land. The population of Cuba, he continued knowingly, was seven million inhabitants, which "fact" gave the others considerable food for thought. After a moment's silence Edmond discussed how frightening it was to travel in airplanes when the weather was rough. The lay pastor noted that sea travel was the same.

The presence of churches of foreign denomination in the village also keeps thoughts of other peoples and cultures in villagers' minds. American missionaries periodically visit the community, and on church holidays such as Christmas and Easter the lay pastor emphasizes in his sermon that "the whole earth" (*tasba aiska*) is happy and celebrating with the community of Asang. Places of Biblical significance, for example, Bethlehem and Jerusalem, are also discussed by the villagers at such times.

Information regarding the nature of the outside world also enters Asang by radio, although what is heard is often misunderstood because of language barriers, and by word of mouth or rumor. Verbal communication takes the form of story-telling, in which it is legitimate to embellish and rearrange details to obtain effect, so that the truth of the statement may yield to the achievement of a good tale. Consequently, as a bit of news is repeated and changed it quickly becomes distorted. It is not unusual for several versions of the same general theme to reach the village through various media, thus generating an atmosphere of uncertainty and an inclination to disbelief. This in turn creates the general feeling that the nature of the outside world and its events is unreliable.

Concrete evidence for the unpredictability of the non-Miskito world is afforded by such events as the sudden loss of Honduranean land as a by-product of the Nicaraguan-Honduranean border settlement, and the cyclical, boom-and-bust nature of the market economy over which the villagers also have no control. In these cases the unreliable outside world has struck directly at the economic base of the village by limiting agricultural land and by regulating the availability of cash. Consequently, the villagers have developed feelings of personal insecurity which are expressed in a number of ways.

Positive Approaches to Culture Contact

One avenue toward amelioration of stress caused by strange or undesirable conditions lies in seeking a better understanding of the situation. Presumably because the history of contact with the West has not been severely disruptive, the Miskito try to bridge cultural gaps initially by what we may label attempts to become "modern." In addition to an open academic interest in other countries, modernity takes the form of adding select aspects of Western civilization to more traditional Miskito customs. Examples of attempts to feel psychologically a part of modern times can be seen in the extent to which foreign words and names have been added to the Miskito vocabulary; the desire for pills and injections; the emphasis given to becoming a Christian which, in addition to secular community benefits, allows individual identification with all other Christians in the world; and a lively interest in transistor radios (owned by only a few villagers), particularly in those programs which feature Protestant hymns. Although the villagers cannot understand the English words, the melodies are identical to those they themselves use in church. To hear these tunes coming over a radio from a distant country, the "Voice of the Andes" from Quito, Ecuador, for example, creates a definite feeling of identification with the larger world.

The historical literature offers additional evidence of this proclivity towards keeping in touch with new developments and suggests that this mode of adaptation to culture contact is by no means recent. For example, de Kalb remarks that "The Mosquito Indians are quick to learn. They are ready imitators. They aspire to emulate the types which enjoy the favor and respect of the majority" (1893:270–71). Roberts notes the disappointment among Miskito leaders when, at one point, English merchandise became scarce and they were unable to "dress themselves and live 'right English gentleman fashion'" (1827:131–32).

Missionaries indicate that young people in particular imitated foreigners in food, clothing, and leisure activities. Along these lines, and in a lighter vein, a missionary traveling the Río Coco in the early 1920's noted that Sumu children on the Río Waspuk (a tributary of the Río Coco) were singing "London Bridge is Falling Down," while children in Asang knew a garbled version of the nursery rhyme "Bingo" (Moravian Church 1890–1956:vol. 11, pp. 367–

68). On a moonlit night during the anthropologist's stay, playful Asang youngsters performed a version of "London Bridge," singing to the familiar tune seemingly nonsense syllables which, onlookers asserted, were meant to be English words.

Sometimes, however, acceptance of modern things and attempts to be modern lead to renewed fears and anxieties because the Miskito do not fully understand the nature of the modern world. That is, they approach the outside from a background of their own logic and experiences, and attempt to fit the piecemeal information they receive into a meaningful whole; yet because their understanding is limited, the coherent whole they form differs from the actual situation. When, in the evening, the villagers speak of modern war, of work at the mines, of the political situation in Nicaragua and Honduras, the things that are emphasized are different from those a Westerner would discuss.

For example, at the time of this study the news was heavy with the increasing military involvement of the United States in Vietnam. However, reports of fighting in the Far East were interpreted by the people of Asang to mean that the war would very likely soon affect them, because once they too experienced conflict on their river in which the United States was involved (the Sandino Affair), and if it happened once it could happen again. People talked incessantly about keeping an eye out for airplanes and awaiting an attack. Yet beneath the tension was a feeling that it was a mark of importance and recognition to have war on the river, or, in other words, if warfare were part of the modern world, the Miskito should be involved also.

It is important to note, though, that emulation of the modern world is not indiscriminate. Of the two major outside spheres of influence which affect the Miskito, the Hispanic and the Anglo-American, it is the latter which is usually imitated, while the former is generally rejected. To judge from historical evidence this has been the case since the days of the buccaneers. At the present time enthusiasm for Americans and their culture is predicated on the attitude that it is the Americans who are concerned with the welfare of the Miskito, replacing the earlier British in this respect. Americans have owned and operated the various lumbering, mining, and banana enterprises that have offered the Miskito jobs and cash, villagers explain, and it is Americans who serve as missionaries, and who are responsible for gifts of used clothing and food distributions.

Most of these distributions go to coastal villagers, Asang residents ruefully note, "but at least the Americans care." Specifically, villagers emphasize, these programs reflect the personal concern of the United States' President for the well-being of the Miskito nation. Similarly, "when an American missionary passes you on the street he stops to shake hands and inquire how things are going."

In contrast, Spanish-speaking Nicaraguans are distrusted because unlike Americans, villagers claim, the "Spanish" are interested only in taking advantage of them. The loss of Honduranean land is attributed to Spanish dealings, and the anthropologist was charged by more than one villager to report this matter to the President of the United States so that it could be remedied. The price differential between selling and buying rice and beans is also blamed on the "smartness," i.e., underhanded cunning, of the Spanish. "If a Miskito boy grows up with a Spanish boy, the Spanish boy will call him 'amigo,' and then knife him. Spanish are 'smart' that way," so *Dama* Silvester denounced the Nicaraguans, to the accompaniment of exclamations of complete agreement from the other men sitting on the porch with him one afternoon. "The Nicaraguan president gives much money to the Spanish schoolteachers, who drink it all," Winston noted, "but he doesn't give any to poor people like us." *Dama* Mauricio asked the anthropologist whether she had heard Nicaraguans in the capital or elsewhere say that the Miskito have tails (she had not). "The Spanish say that," he noted, pointing out that obviously it was false. Other villagers returned the compliment by saying that the Spanish ate buzzards.

The degradation which the villagers feel in their relations with the Hispanic world is somewhat counterbalanced by their own feelings of superiority over the shy and defensive Sumu. The residents of Asang ridicule the strange customs and language of these people, seeing them as definitely inferior to their own. The Sumu are also considered guilty of the grave charge of lack of hospitality to strangers: "They close their doors when visitors come." It is claimed that they eat spoiled food—food that has been kept for a week or so until it sours or molds. One informant said the Sumu were not as intelligent as Miskito. "They don't have deep thoughts; they have smaller minds."

The villagers also feel that Río Coco Miskito are superior to coastal and Honduranean Miskito. These latter Miskito groups are criticized for speaking a somewhat different, and therefore "bad," form of Miskito, and for thinking in their own turn that the Río Coco population speaks an improper dialect. Furthermore, according to the villagers, the way of life *en toto* of the Río Coco Miskito represents proper, "pure," Miskito culture, while the other two divisions are "mixed" with elements of Creole and Spanish customs, since there are more Creole and Spanish peoples living in these areas.

In contrast to the stereotypes of good or bad, superior or inferior behavior accorded to Americans, Spanish, and Sumu, the villagers had no general attitudinal category for Creole peoples. This may be attributed to the fact that unlike Spanish and Americans, whose homelands are elsewhere, Creoles, like the Miskito, are permanent residents of the Coast. Sumu also are local residents, but because they live in the most isolated regions of the country, they are less readily met with and thus more easily stereotyped. The Creole population, however, is found in more readily accessible towns and villages, and persons are known individually to the villagers rather than as representatives of a foreign group. Thus, there are good and bad Creole persons, but no general categorization of Creoles as a group. Mr. Miller, the shopkeeper, was considered a sober, serious, respectful, Christian member of the community; the owner of one of the barges was well thought of and generally respected; however, the Moravian parson, also a Creole, under whose charge the village fell, was intensely disliked and considered extremely proud. Among other things, he was cited as refusing to give free rides to Miskito in his motorized dugout when he was traveling.

One of the gauges used by the villagers in deciding the merits of non-Miskito individuals and categories of foreigners is the level of generosity they exhibit. When a Miskito meets a non-Miskito, especially a Creole or American, he employs an ethic of poverty in an attempt to extract goods or cash from the stranger. He spins a sad tale of economic poverty and lack of cash, poor clothing, and ill health without benefit of medication in order to obtain a handout.

To view this interaction as simply begging would constitute an oversimplification. Rather, it may be better understood as an extension of the traditional Miskito concept of respect. As we have seen, in Miskito culture one of the basic rules governing behavior requires that one show concern for a kinsman's welfare. Concern or respect may take various forms, one of which involves gift giving. It is also permissible to request a needed item, perhaps several plantains or a manioc root, from a relative who is duty-bound to provide it as a gift.

The Miskito tend to view Americans, particularly, as high level relatives interested in the fate of their Miskito kinsmen, an attitude nourished by missionary paternalism and international aid programs. From this point of view it is permissible for the Miskito to expect assistance from Americans, and equally proper for them to request it if it is not forthcoming. For the foreigner to refuse to honor the request brands him as "proud" in Miskito eyes. Thus, the wife of one American Moravian parson was well thought of by the lay pastor's wife because she gave handouts of food and clothes. The wife of another, however, was "proud" because she often refused. "Even though the bread is right there on the table she says she doesn't have any."

In return, many of the missionaries deplore aid programs because of the demanding, acquisitive attitude they feel such programs encourage among the Miskito. The reaction of a Creole businessman, who owns a shop in San Carlos, when faced with a similar situation was to be equally demanding in return. A Miskito customer wished to purchase C$5.50 of cloth, but had only C$5 in cash. The man then reminded the shopkeeper that he had helped him moor his dugout on the previous day, but had not been reimbursed for this service; the extra 50 centavos worth of cloth thus was due him for this service. The shopkeeper, loath to lose a sale, reluctantly agreed, but then stipulated that henceforth the customer would not get any more free rides to Sunday afternoon baseball games in neighboring communities. The customer tried to return the cloth at that point, but the shopkeeper held firm to the bargain. "If they get hard with you, you get hard with them," he said afterwards.

The theme of hardship employed by the Miskito is also heard in another context with yet another connotation. The poverty ethic fits well the Protestant creed of the inherent worthlessness of man, and, consequently, the same plaintive address is a constant theme in Miskito prayers. Instead of being manipulative in purpose, however, the religious usage constitutes an expression of fatalism. In this context, the Miskito describe themselves as poverty-stricken and worthless humans living in a frustrating, hard-to-understand world in which there is no better way to handle things than to put them in God's hands and wait. This feeling is not only expressed in formal prayers, but also is often heard in daily conversation: "*Dia daukaia; help apu; pruaia baman*—what's to be done; there is no help; we can only die."

Yet at the same time such an attitude can also pave the way toward doing something concrete about the situation in the sense that Christianity is also modernity, and a properly humble Christian attitude gains the respect and support both of other Christian Miskito and of the missionaries who represent one aspect of the modern world. In this way the ends of the mission groups are also met when, in the face of such events as land loss, economic depression, or war scares, the Miskito turn to the church as a rallying point for group identification, morale building, and security.

The sermon preached by the Moravian parson on one of his visits was directed to this point. He spoke, with some exaggeration, of how the United States and Russia can build bombs capable of killing "300 million" people in one minute; that there are machines that can plant hundreds of acres of crops in a day, while the Miskito labors with ax and machete; that a trip downriver by traditional dugout takes four days while a plane can make the journey in "minutes"; that the Miskito can saw one log a day if they use eight men, while other peoples use machines that can saw one hundred logs a day. In such a world, he thundered, the only strength left to the Miskito is faith in God.

Defensive Reactions toward the Outside World

The church is not the only support available to the Miskito during troubled times. Another reaction evidenced by Asang villagers to the frustrations of modern living is the strong spirit of village pride and unity. This identification and loyalty quickly develop into an attitude of defensive superiority whenever the villagers feel challenged by the non-Asang world.

Most of this aloofness is also based on a religious foundation, and revolves around the theme that Asang is most definitely a Christian village. As we have seen, the Moravian congregation in particular emphasizes its superiority with regard to other congregations in such terms as willingness to cooperate in church activities and to care well for the lay pastor. The regulation against drinking and the successful maintenance of this rule provide additional points of pride for all of Asang, but also create a certain amount of defensiveness in that Asang villagers feel that others will find their village dull and therefore boycott it. This in fact is at least partially true.

Defensiveness is expressed as pride, however, by pointing out that only Asang can maintain such rigid standards of behavior because only Asang operates with a spirit of *kupya kumi,* literally "one heart," or, in other words, singleness and unity of purpose. Full co-operation in funeral preparations, hospitality for visitors, the manner in which women tie their headcloths, even whether or not girls wear lipstick and makeup (Asang girls usually do not) are all seen as factors separating Asang from other communities.

One of the results of this somewhat self-righteous attitude is the suspicion automatically cast on anyone who is not from Asang. Village young people express their increasing tendency toward village endogamy in terms of being afraid to marry a "stranger" because you can't be sure what type of individual he or she may be. Yet fellow villagers and even kinsmen are not completely exempt from the general suspiciousness which is another characteristic of Miskito world view. Although Asang residents and relatives are considered to be more trustworthy than strangers, only a fool would trust another individual completely. Probably there is at least some justification for this attitude. When, for example, Asang's unity is under discussion the claim is made that Asang people do not steal. At other times, though, considerable gossip can be overheard regarding intravillage thefts.

The type of defensive mechanism expressed at a particular time or with reference to a particular event depends to some extent on whether people view the threat as potentially harmful for the group or for an individual. A villager usually views situations from both points of view. Within the normal course of Miskito life ego's individuality is expressed when he is addressed by a nickname which is uniquely his, or by his "first" name which theoretically also is held by no one else in the community. On the other hand, he may be addressed by a kin term, by his *kiamp* or surname, or by a teknonymic reference, all of which contain the implication that he receives his identity through relationships with others. By the same token, the egalitarian nature of Miskito society signifies that no one is better than anyone else, and to put on airs is to invite criticism for "proud" behavior, while, on the other hand, "egalitarian" can also be interpreted to mean that each individual is as good as anyone else, and therefore will not willingly be subservient.

The dichotomy appears at the level of defense mechanisms when ego suspiciously views all other individuals, including people of his own village, as being potentially untrustworthy, while in the next sentence he defends the morality and honesty of Asang as a unit vis-à-vis all other villages. Still again, he enters into independent business contracts with foreigners while at the same time viewing himself as representative and defender of that vague entity, the Miskito "nation."

8

Summary and Conclusions

TWO APPROACHES to the study of the Miskito have been used in the preceding chapters. The focal point of the analysis rests on data obtained from the village study of Asang. Yet this material becomes meaningful only when placed in the wider perspective of developments on the Miskito Coast, both past and present. Therefore, pertinent ethnohistorical background has been provided wherever feasible.

In Retrospect

Culture contact and interaction with Western society is particularly significant for an understanding of Miskito culture since there is good reason to believe that the existence of the Miskito as an identifiable ethnic group with a distinctive way of life is a direct result of trade with the West. In fact, it is virtually impossible to descuss any aspect of Miskito life without recourse to the history of culture contact on the Coast.

The pressure and new directives generated by adaptation to Western ways have been neither seriously disruptive nor unbearable. In fact, judging from Asang, the Miskito have been able to cope successfully with the outside world, maintaining a pride in their customs and traditions and evidencing a positive curiosity towards the non-Miskito world.

The reasons behind this positive reaction to culture contact lie both in the nature of that contact and in the structure of Miskito society. Of fundamental importance is the fact that until 1960 the Miskito were in complete control of all their land. This territory was obtained during the early decades of culture contact as a result of the advantages which firearms gave the Miskito over their unarmed indigenous neighbors. In addition to, and partly as a result of, successful maintenance of land, the traditional Miskito subsistence economy has never been permanently disrupted. Whatever the vicissitudes of culture contact, there has generally been enough to eat.

Successful Miskito control of their land results from the fact that the east coast of Nicaragua and Honduras is a frontier territory characterized by traders, missionaries, and short-lived boom-and-bust commercial enterprises, rather than by pioneer agriculturalists. In other words, this region has never been part of the effective national territory of any state. Although various foreign powers have exploited natural resources, either by trading with the native inhabitants or by hiring them for wages, they have not established many permanent settlements. It is also important to note that the foreign nations involved in commercial dealings with the Coast were never those states within whose theoretical boundaries the coastal territory is located. Britain and the United States have been the major Western powers with operations in the area; Nicaragua and Honduras have intervened only recently. Consequently, although the region is geographically closer by far to Hispanic areas of Central America than to the English-speaking countries, its inhabitants feel culturally closer to Northern Europe and North America than to Western Nicaragua and Honduras.

Even though land holdings have remained intact, it does not follow automatically that Miskito culture itself resisted reorientations through contact. In fact, many changes have occurred since seventeenth-century buccaneers wrote the first reports of local customs. Yet it appears that until the latter part of the nineteenth century, culture change was characterized more by the addition of new items to the basic Miskito inventory than by large-scale replacement of indigenous customs and traditions. A strong sense of Miskito cultural identity was maintained such that new items could be added without threatening the old order.

Addition, rather than replacement, and maintenance of an ethic of "Miskitoness" seems predicated upon the nature of traditional Miskito family organization. The salient features here are, first, uxorilocal postnuptial residence, and second, a division of labor such that while women were responsible for the more sedentary agricultural pursuits, men were concerned with hunting and fishing.

With regard to the latter point, it was possible for Miskito men to fit trade contacts with the West into their basic hunting and fishing pattern with no serious difficulty. As hunters and especially fishermen, men were used to spending considerable periods of time away from home. Consequently, to travel with the buccaneers as provisioners, or to spend time collecting forest products for traders did not require new patterns of mobility. Furthermore, hunting and fishing apparently were not full-time occupations, so that collecting trips could be geared to the hunting and fishing timetable without detracting greatly from them. Finally, all this could be done without affecting women's agricultural work.

Agriculture required that women be more sedentary than men. While men were free to come and go, to visit trading posts or to go to the bush, women were more restricted to the confines of the village. Hence, women did not come into contact with foreigners as much as men did, and as a result became the more conservative element of Miskito society. Men, on the other hand, had much more firsthand contact with the West.

Women's conservatism seems to have played an important role in maintaining a stable, definitely Miskito, cultural core, that is, in maintaining Miskito cultural identity. In addition to relative lack of direct contact, villages approximated a matrilocal settlement pattern, so that a nucleus of related women, mothers and daughters, formed the permanent element. Regardless of their husbands' wanderings, these women formed a stable consanguineal core in and of themselves. Therefore, all children born to Miskito women (who were not adverse to marrying or at least mating with non-Miskito men if the opportunity arose) grew up in a village where the Miskito language was spoken, and where traditional Miskito customs, many of them based on the duties and obligations of kinship, were taught and practiced by a close knit and cooperative group of related women. Whatever the nature of later contact with agents of change, and this applies especially to boys, there was a solid background of "Miskitoness" already firmly established. This organizational pattern is an important reason why Miskito culture still remains viable today.

Beginning with the second half of the nineteenth century and continuing up to the present time, the nature of culture contact changed somewhat, necessitating a readaptation on the part of the Miskito. This readaptation involved more widespread changes not only in the economic realm, but also in ideology and, secondarily, in social organization. Throughout the course of this second adaptation, however, the conservative core of related women remained fairly well intact. The basic familial division of labor was maintained, allowing men to deal with commercial ventures while women's work remained basic to subsistence. In turn this division has provided a continuing traditional cultural cushion to balance the vagaries of Western demands.

The second adaptation arose in response to missionaries and a cyclical boom-and-bust economic pattern. The history of missionary activity on the Miskito Coast as a whole is largely synonymous with the activities of the Moravian mission, although presently the Moravians are not the only group operating in the region. Generally, missionary activity has been successful, both from the point of view of the mission and the contacted Miskito. The church has come to provide a much needed focal point for village unity in Asang, and furnishes sociopolitical as well as ideological services for the village. Traditional Miskito religious practices have been largely replaced by Christian ritual, and proper everyday behavior theoretically requires adherence to Christian morals as well as to traditional Miskito patterns. The transfer of Christian ethics has been slower, but although traditional ideology can still be found, most of Asang is at least nominally Christian in creed as well as in ritual.

Part of the success of Christianity may be due to the fact that it has come to provide ideological compensation for the insecurity brought about by the fluctuations of a boom-and-bust economy. Seventeenth-, eighteenth-, and nineteenth-century trade patterns appear to have been fairly constant activities compared with the cyclical nature of commercial enterprises from the late 1890's to the present. Corresponding fluctuations can be seen in Miskito reactions to the economic situation. During times of economic boom when jobs and cash were readily available, buying of commissary items, especially foodstuffs such as sugar, salt, flour, and lard as well as Western clothing and cloth, increased while subsistence activities were somewhat neglected. Church dues were paid in full and lavishly generous community feasts were held at holidays such as New Year. These festivities consumed in abundance a wide variety of native and "foreign" (that is, made with commissary ingredients) foods, and many domestic animals were slaughtered. Friends and relatives from miles around were welcomed. Even ordinary day-to-day life was characterized by much intervillage visiting, and a general feeling of satisfaction and security was in the air.

When economic boom was replaced by bust, the picture changed radically. This was the situation prevalent during the study of Asang, and the village showed the effects of economic depression. Food came predominantly from traditional subsistence activities while the commissaries were practically empty of stock with not much effort made to replenish it. The use of cash to purchase goods was rare since cash was practically nonexistent. Rather, rice and beans provided substitutes in kind, although the market for them was low and their buying power correspondingly limited. Church contributions had fallen off greatly, and festivities were almost entirely out of the question. In addition, people were not psychologically in the mood for lightheartedness. Intervillage contacts were reduced, and a general pall of isolation hung over Asang.

Possibly the boom-and-bust cycles, which have been operating for perhaps sixty or seventy years, have been responsible for changes in social organization which are recent enough historically so that village elders could remember the old patterns. Specifically, village autonomy is gradually replacing those aspects of the kinship system which had served to connect the region into a single social web. Instead of intervillage, uxorilocal postnuptial residence, village endogamy is becoming more and more prevalent, while within the community marital residence is increasingly virilocal and neolocal. People explain their hesitancy to marry outside the village in terms of distrust of strangers, and it may be that increasing economic insecurity is the basis for this fear. Concurrently, the traditional bifurcate-merging system of kinship terminology has lost its cross-parallel cousin distinctions, while first ascendant generation terms are becoming increasingly descriptive.

Yet there is no doubt that the villagers of Asang are maintaining their identity as Miskito. Kinship obligations within the village are still strongly emphasized and are in the hands of the women, still the conservative element. The Miskito language is the everyday tongue, and provides a traditional cognitive frame of reference. Women still spend most of their time socializing children and tending to traditional subsistence agriculture. However, men have also recently turned to agriculture to provide a money crop. In short, it seems that while boom-and-bust market conditions may be beginning to effect more radical changes in Miskito life, the basic pattern still remains fairly well intact.

In fact, the very recurrence of economic cycles, which has at times led to insecurity, restricted sociability, and economic depression is perhaps also responsible for the maintenance of the Miskito subsistence economy and, by extension, a certain amount of self-sufficiency which permits cultural identity to continue. The periodic return to depression conditions after more or less short-lived booms has meant that the Miskito have had to continue to fall back on their traditional economic practices to tide them over depression periods. The relative frequency with which boom-and-bust have followed each other in the last sixty or seventy years has meant that there has not been an extended period of time such that an entire generation would be divorced from subsistence activities long enough to begin to forget relevant techniques. The division of labor between men and women makes this even more unlikely. As long as women remain relatively village-bound and are concerned primarily with agriculture, the subsistence cushion will in all likelihood remain.

A few other predictions may be ventured with regard to future pressures for change and the possible line of adaptation that Asang and the Miskito in general may take. It seems inevitable that the arm of the Nicaraguan government will gradually make itself felt on the Coast. That is, the effective national territories of the state will gradually be extended to its Caribbean shore. The process has already begun, although progress to date is almost negligible. The power of the state so far is in symbolic evidence, but is not yet a significant factor in terms of major interference with Miskito life. There is a long-standing mutual dislike between the Miskito and Spanish-speaking peoples of Nicaragua such that cultural assimilation appears to be far in the future. Yet the imposition of state authority in terms of meaningful political control and/or some degree of economic incorporation of the Miskito peoples into the state organization may not be so far ahead.

Theoretical Significance

How the Miskito will react to these pressures is hard to predict. If present trends continue, however, there will probably be a shift from a kin-based society to strictly territorially defined villages. The role of the church in providing a center for village-based activities will probably remain of crucial importance just as common membership in a particular religious denomination is likely to provide the major form of intervillage sodalities. Defensiveness will perhaps become more characteristic of Miskito society as state control replaces traditional customs, personal taxes are levied, and perhaps military duty is required. In other words, Miskito society will become increasingly "peasantized."

The obvious implication in the preceding statement is that presently the Miskito are not peasants. Yet, after 300 years of involvement with the Western world they can hardly be considered tribal or aboriginal. In fact, the very origins of the Miskito as a society with a separate and identifiable culture pattern is due to this contact. Under these conditions, many anthropologists would consider the Miskito an example of peasant society—that common anthropological catchall for rural peoples today. As with peasants, the Miskito are part of a larger, nonprimitive world; they, too, have formed ties with a wider society. But, as we have argued in the introduction to this study, it is not simply the development of wider ties, but the *nature* of the ties that becomes the crucial point.

Current overviews of the nature of peasant societies stress the fact that peasants, generally seen as rural cultivators, traditionally have been tied to agrarian states which demand the production of surpluses from them to support the nonagricultural segment of the state hierarchy. It is the production of these rents, this surplus of labor, produce, or money extracted by the power holders of the state which becomes the distinguishing criteria of peasant society.

If we apply these guidelines to the Miskito, we encounter difficulties. As we have seen, the Miskito are indeed part of a larger society, and have been for centuries, but of what society and in what way? They are officially citizens of the Republic of Nicaragua, and are certainly rural, but this part of Central America is significant specifically because it is not integrated with the effective national territory, either economically, socially, politically, or ideologically. Nicaraguan authority is de jure rather than de facto. The few fees levied on the people of Asang represent more a show of potential state control than actual authority. These few taxes do not constitute much of a burden for the villagers, and are negligible in their contribution to the state's support. The Miskito do control their own land and they are cultivators, although hunting, fishing, and wage labor also are major factors in the economy. Since wage labor is important, it is obvious that although the Miskito are not contributing members of Nicaraguan society, they are considerably involved with the Western world. The point is, however, that the character of this involvement is different from that described in the traditional concepts of peasantry.

As with peasantry, Miskito interaction with a wider society involves the production of goods and services for this society. The crucial point, however, revolves around the source of motivation for this production. The peasant is motivated to produce a surplus above and beyond that amount needed by his own family or household because he is subject to a superior outside power holder who requires payment of some sort of rent from him. It is this pull from above, which is a feature of the political organization of the wider society of which the peasant is a part, that produces the contrast between peasantry and the adaptation illustrated by the Miskito.

The interaction between Miskito society and the wider world is characterized not by an asymmetrical flow of payments to central authorities, but by the economics of trade. Local products or labor are exchanged in a more symmetrical fashion for desired foreign material goods. The motivation to enter this system comes not directly from an outside "demand," as far as the natives are concerned, but from within Miskito culture in the sense that foreign items—salt, flour, clothing, tools—have become essentials for daily life, and hence raw materials, produce, and labor will be "volunteered" to obtain them.

This is not to say that peasants do not trade, or that foreign items are not viewed as cultural necessities. The point is that peasants also have another demand placed upon their production—that of providing rents to the state—which "purchasers" do not encounter. Purchasers, as we shall call the Miskito and any other such cultures, do not have to contend with someone who, because of his higher political position, has a superior claim on their labor or produce. Of course the introduction of foreign goods came from the wider society's desire for local products, and in this sense the forces which placed the once self-sufficient culture into a wider economy also came from outside. But once the foreign items became necessary for daily life, they were sought by the natives of their own accord. Note also that purchasers need not be viewed only as agriculturalists, as peasants often are, but can practice agriculture, fishing, and hunting, collect wild products, and/or engage in wage labor to fulfill their role in the wider economy.

The difference between these two systems can be stated in any number of ways. Because of the asymmetrical nature of their ties with the outside world, peasants, from their point of view, are dependent upon the wishes of their overlords. Whatever the amount produced by the peasant, a certain amount *must* be forfeited to the state. Native purchasers, on the other hand, contribute the amount they choose to collect or raise. The phenomenon of the unreliable native laborer who works only when he wishes and for as long as he wishes to the constant frustration of his European employers is often found in the literature. These workers will labor only long enough to earn the items they and their families need at the moment. Then they quit, only to turn up two weeks or six months later for another period of work, perhaps brief, perhaps lengthy.

The same situation holds where forest products are traded. When there is no more money for salt and sugar, or if a new axe is needed, a man might betake himself to the bush to cut chicle, or join a lumber crew. The extent to which foreign items are needed governs the extent to which trade or labor occurs (assuming that trade or work opportunities are consistently available).

I propose, then, that the Miskito do not fit the conceptual framework of what constitutes peasantry, but are instead an example of a purchase society. The fundamental difference between peasant and purchaser is based on the presence or absence, respectively, of effective state political control, particularly as it affects the means of production and especially the distribution of finished products. Consequently, adaptations to the wider world may be expected to differ significantly between peasant and purchase societies. Additional cross-cultural analysis of this point should prove extremely interesting and fruitful.

APPENDIX A

Household Composition, 1964–65

Forty-nine households were composed of a single nuclear family. An additional thirteen households, however, included a nuclear family and various other relatives. The composition of these households was as follows: (1) a married daughter and her husband who alternate between their parents' homes; (2) two adult, single daughters, one of whom was mentally retarded; (3) a widowed daughter with her two small children; (4) the wife's deceased sister's child; (5) the husband's deserted sister and her five young children, who later established their own household; (6) the husband's father and one granddaughter; (7) the wife's two adolescent sisters, whose mother was deceased; (8) the wife's five younger siblings whose parents were deceased; (9) a retarded adult son; (10) the wife's sister, who was ill; (11) the husband's deserted sister and her four small children; (12) the wife's father, a widower, and her adolescent sister; a sister with two small children, whose husband was working at the mines; the four young children of a deceased sister, whose father remarried; (13) the husband's three children by another woman.

Ten households contained two nuclear families, the second in all cases newlyweds, while an additional three households contained two nuclear families along with other relatives. In two of these three cases, the second nuclear family was a newlywed couple, one of which, a married daughter and her husband, rotated between their parents' homes. In the second case, a sister of the household head and her children also lived in the same household. In the third household lived a sister and her child, in addition to two married brothers and their spouses and children.

Two households in the village contained three nuclear families.

In one case there were two sets of married children, one a middle-aged son, the other a newly married daughter, with their spouses and the son's two small children, in addition to the parental family. The other household included the widowed mother of the household head, in addition to the wife and five children of the household head, the wife's newlywed brother and his spouse, and a newlywed son and his spouse and infant daughter.

Thirteen households did not contain a nuclear family, but were composed of single individuals or various dyads: (1) a deserted mother and her children—there were three such households in the village; (2) a widower and his two adolescent children; (3) a widower and two adolescent children, together with an estranged daughter and her five young children; (4) a widow and her children—there were three such households in the community; (5) an unwed mother and her two small children; (6) a widow with her deserted daughter and her four small children; (7) a widow, together with her aged father, her deserted daughter, and the daughter's three small children; (8) two households, each containing an elderly widow living alone.

APPENDIX B

"In Essentials Unity"

A Brief Survey of the Moravian Church

The formal designation of the Moravian church is "Unitas Fratrum" or "Unity of the Brethren." However, the term "Moravian" is often used in English-speaking countries and refers to the place of origin of many of the early members of the church (Gollin 1967: 1n). The first congregation and traditional focus of the Moravian church was the community of Herrnhut, established in 1722 on the estate of a Saxon Count, Nicholas von Zinzendorf, in what is today East Germany. However, the roots of the order are found in the various Protestant groups which composed that socioreligious movement called the Czech Reformation.

The Czech Reformation antidated the better known German Reformation by one hundred years. John Hus, whose death instigated the Hussite Wars and the rise of Protestantism in Bohemia and Moravia (later to become provinces of Czechoslovakia), was killed in 1415; Martin Luther did not publish his ninety-five theses until 1517 (Brock 1957:11). The most enthusiastic supporters of the Czech movement were the peasantry, joined by the lower strata of town populations. In addition, many of the nobility, eager to obtain the wealth of the Roman Catholic church which was in possession of at least one-third of the total area of Bohemia at the time, aided the reformation (Brock 1957:22).

The doctrine to which these reformers subscribed was concerned with the nature of moral and ethical conduct rather than with points of theology. (For a detailed and scholarly account of the Czech Reformation in general the reader is referred to Brock 1957.) There was a strong emphasis on utopianism which, by offering protection from an immoral world, would strive to realize the maximum moral potentiality of human beings. The framework or guide for morally upright behavior was to be provided by Christianity as it was taught by Christ and the Apostles. The Bible and the life of Jesus rather than declarations of the Romish pope and clergy were taken to be the supreme directives for life. Any connection between church and state was opposed. Oath-taking, government work, and courts of law were all to be avoided. In order to express these beliefs in actual practice, separate communities of believers were established.

Within the context of the existing society such an ideology inevitably became a gospel of revolt and protest against the existing social and political order. Consequently, from the latter half of the fifteenth century on, the Protestants of Bohemia and Moravia were subjected to a number of persecutions. Those members of the nobility who were Protestants provided havens for persecuted Brethren on their estates as long as they, too, were able to preserve their freedom, but many were finally driven from the country. After 1630 only a few reformers remained in Bohemia and Moravia.

In 1722 a handful of the surviving Protestants left Moravia for sanctuary on the estate of Count Zinzendorf. The settlement they established, Herrnhut, became the focus of the renewed Moravian church.

Life in Herrnhut during the eighteenth and first half of the nineteenth centuries contrasted greatly with that of neighboring communities. (Gillian Gollin presents a detailed picture in her informative account.) The unifying ties of a utopian religious outlook provided a framework within which particular forms of social, economic, and political life emerged. However, in spite of their inward, community-oriented approach, the Moravians did not become completely shut off from the secular world around them. There was a heavy emphasis on missionary activity (see below) which forced the Moravians to learn to cope with the non-Moravian world in order to further their own goals.

The Bible was still the source of all religious truths. In addition, a certain amount of emotionalism crept into religious practices. Feeling, rather than thought, was stressed; religious experience was valued above dogma and doctrinal stands. Particular emphasis was laid on glorifying the sufferings and death of Christ as the road to God. Finally, religion was considered a "social experience in which the faithful were bound together in a community of brotherly love but at the same time separated from the rest of mankind, who did not adhere to their beliefs, and who, therefore, were not to be numbered among God's chosen people" (Gollin 1967:15).

Moravianism was also greatly concerned with the elaboration of religious ethics, with particular reference to the importance of work. Diligence, frugality, punctuality, and attention to detail were virtues essential to the Christian way of life since they permitted an individual to work to the best of his ability. Work was necessary since, although it did not guarantee salvation, it was requisite to the maintenance of a state of grace. In another vein, the social character of religious experience provided a powerful ethical basis for cooperation as a group. Individuals were taught to subordinate their own interests to the demands of the community, and generally did.

Religious rituals were numerous and served to integrate all aspects of community life. In addition to strictly ideological events, rituals were held at the start and completion of many economic activities. These celebrations were generally of the type known as "love feasts." Derived from the ancient Christian *Agapae,* the service was intended to signify the unity of all in Christ and consisted of hymn singing or liturgical chanting while a simple meal of coffee and bread was consumed. Ritual penetrated political life mainly through the use of the lot (see below), and provided the glue for the social cohesion of the community. The all-pervasiveness of religious ritual declined somewhat during the nineteenth century, but still was highly important to both individual and village life.

De facto power in the community was held for many years by the count on whose lands the village was situated. In his official capacity as overseer, he also represented Herrnhut's interests to the outside world. However, much authority also resided in a group of elders selected from the common people of the village. It was they who granted permission for immigrants to join the community, for villagers to leave, for changes in occupation, even for marriages. Yet the elders had no force other than moral sanctions by which to enforce obedience to their directives. Persistent lawbreakers were eventually referred to the local court of a neighboring village. As the community grew, other political bodies—the Helpers Conference, Judiciary Council, Trades Conference, to name but a few— were formed to handle the increasing legislative and judicial needs of the village. Much administrative authority also fell within the domain of the bishops (the principle of Apostolic succession was upheld by the Czech Brethren and carried over by the Moravians) and Church Synods.

As each new board, conference, and/or council was established the count assumed a position of authority within it, and named others of the nobility to advise him. Even after his death in 1760 the aristocracy continued to hold the reins of power, while in place of his one-man rule the Elders Conference became equally dictatorial. The majority of the populace had little say in the government of the community.

To some extent the demands of those in power could be checked by use of the lot. By this mechanism God, the highest elder, was expected to render final verdict on matters of communal significance. For example, the lot was used to decide whether to accept newcomers and to give final permission for baptism, communion, and even marriage. The filling of occupational positions, election to all major political offices, selection of missionaries and of ministers were also determined by the lot as were decisions regarding the establishment of new missionary outposts or the abandonment of old ones, the buying of new land, the erection of a new building, the borrowing of money, or the type of punishment given an offender.

Although the lot was regarded as a means of establishing God's will with regard to a matter, in practice there was much flexibility in its use which often permitted earthly rulers to have their way. The wording of questions to be determined by the lot, the number of ballots used, and the interpretation of answers were all areas where human judgment was necessary and human power could intervene. On the other hand, by providing for divine guidance on points which could be unpopular, the lot served to reduce criticism with its potential for disrupting the social order. Use of the lot was particularly fancied by the count and was used with much greater frequency during his lifetime. After his death its use gradually declined until the Synod of 1889 erased altogether the use of the lot as an element of communal decision making.

Like most utopian communities, the Moravians were faced with a problem posed by the existence of the family: participation in the family detracts from total participation in community affairs. Hence a family surrogate was formed in an attempt to subordinate familial ties and maximize the individual's loyalty to and participation in the goals of the community.

To achieve this end the community was rigidly stratified according to age, sex, and marital status. Groups known as "choirs" were formed: the Single Brethren's choir, the Single Sister's choir, the Children's choir, the Married People's choir, and the Widows' and Widowers' choirs. The primary function of the choirs was to deepen the participants' religious life. To this end members of each choir lived together in a common house if at all possible. Gradually, however, economic and social roles were also assumed. The provisioning of clothing and food became the responsibility of each choir, and home industries were developed in each. As a result, the choirs developed into more or less self-contained economic units.

Unfortunately, the strict separation of the sexes affected efficiency to a considerable extent and primary attention to religious goals often clashed with the realities of economic life as individuals spent more time in devotions than in carrying out the necessary tasks. Consequently, donations from the aristocracy more than once helped the choirs over serious financial straits. There was a problem of occupations, also, for the trade learned as a child or in a single person's choir might not be useful in the married people's choir.

Socialization and much day-to-day social control also became the work of the choirs. Children were handed over to the nursery at an early age. After being taught the proper rules of conduct and the necessary skills for a trade, they were initiated into the single choirs to carry out their work. The choirs functioned adequately in their socialization roles until population increase jeopardized the intimate nature of the groups, weakening social controls. As a result of this and related problems, the choirs were gradually stripped of their social responsibilities during the late eighteenth century. Segregation of the sexes was also relaxed and the number of choirs reduced while those remaining came to be based on voluntary membership.

Economically the Moravians regarded Christ as sole owner of man's possessions with the choirs and community as administrators of the wealth. However, communal ownership and sharing were never strongly ascribed to, and the worldly goods of the members technically never appropriated. Some attempts at communistic practices were made, but with limited success.

In terms of occupations, skilled craftsmen dominated with a topping of aristocracy. However, missionary labors took precedence as a preferred line of work, and prevented the formation of a completely closed society through constant forced exposure to secular life. Due to the presence of state churches in nearly all the countries of Europe, Moravians were prohibited from establishing large European congregations. A number of centers based on the style of Herrnhut were established, but membership remained small. In spite of numerical insignificance, however, Moravian influence was considerable.

One reason for the wider interest in Moravians lay in their commitment to education. The establishment and maintenance of schools were an integral part of Moravian life both at Herrnhut, in Europe, and in the more distant mission fields. Indeed, a respect for education can be traced as far back as the days of the Bohemian Brethren. The organization and maintenance of numerous boarding schools in Europe during the eighteenth and nineteenth centuries put many non-Moravians into contact with the church.

The diaspora provided another channel through which Moravians extended their influence in Europe far beyond church membership. The term refers to the procedure whereby pairs of Moravians traveled throughout Europe with the intent simply to organize societies for Bible study and religious services. These societies were not considered official Moravian congregations and great efforts were made to avoid encroachment upon the prerogatives of the state churches to which the members of the society often belonged. The need to send ministers to carry out the work of the diaspora also helped to ease the persistent problem of unemployment at Herrnhut, a factor which quite likely helped to maintain the uniqueness of the settlement by reducing pressures that would lead to change (see Gollin 1967:154–55).

Informal societies were established in England and Ireland as well as on the continent. The Moravians attempted to establish in England a number of settlements modeled after Herrnhut with church, school, and choir homes, but only two succeeded. With the development of the Industrial Revolution, however, self-sufficiency based on home trades became impossible, and all attempts to continue these communities were abandoned.

While work was carried on in Europe, colonies were being established in North America. An initial attempt to settle in Georgia failed, but the second effort, in Pennsylvania, succeeded. In 1741 the village of Bethlehem was established and the Moravian congregation there became the mother church of the Moravians in America. Bethlehem was modeled closely on the Herrnhut settlement, but because of the frontier conditions it faced in the New World, was forced to modify and adapt some of the more characteristic aspects of Herrnhut life. Thus, for example, agriculture rather than crafts formed the economic base, the choir system ended earlier than in Germany, the use of the lot was never as important, and the government of the settlement rested more heavily with the common people than with an aristocracy. However, the community was ideologically committed to the Moravian way of life just as strongly as were the Herrnhutters, and the sale of land to non-Moravians was prohibited up to 1844 (Gollin 1967:211).

Other settlements, including numerous educational institutions, sprang up around Bethlehem and Winston-Salem, North Carolina, the second major Moravian community in North America, established in 1766. Here again the church, school, sisters' house, brothers' house, and other standard Moravian features were built. Like Bethlehem, Winston-Salem quickly became a home church in its own right, partly as a result of communication difficulties with Herrnhut, partly because of the extensive missionary work carried out among the Indians of the Atlantic seaboard. Like the European diaspora, relatively few permanent congregations were established among the Indians, but many missionaries traveled widely among the eastern tribes of Georgia, Pennsylvania, Ohio, New York, and Michigan.

The mission fields served by the Moravian church soon reached far beyond the Indians at the back door. Much of the overseas work was handled by the German province until World War I curtailed activities. England and the American provinces then assumed a major portion of the work. Even before the war, though, the extent of Herrnhut's missionary endeavors would seem to have been entirely beyond the limited resources of this community of 600–800 (Hamilton 1900:66, 115). In fact, considerable money and personnel became available through the contributions of the diaspora societies. In the field, missionaries often operated purely secular business enterprises as a further means of financing their churches.

In addition to business, Moravian missionaries invariably organized schools for their congregations, thus providing what was often the only educational channel open to the people they contacted. On the other side of the educational process quite a few missionaries became distinguished scholars in their own right as they studied local customs and particularly language.

Another area of missionary work strongly endorsed by the Moravians lay in the realm of medical care. It is not unlikely that the presence of medical help and school facilities inclined the unconverted to listen to the more strictly religious teachings of the missionaries.

Finally, it is interesting to note that Moravian missions almost without exception were established among the isolated and dispossessed peoples of the earth. Many of these areas still rank among the most backward stretches of the world, indicating that during the eighteenth and nineteenth centuries they were even more remote.

To work in the most ignored reaches would seem to follow logically from at least two points of view. First, at home Moravians were a minority group taking constant care not to tangle with the interests of the larger, established state churches and probably wishing to avoid their emissaries abroad as well. Second, the follies and temptations of the European world were less likely to be found in these backwoods areas, thus providing, as in Herrnhut, an atmosphere of freedom from distracting worldly pleasures in order to advance religious experience.

The initial impetus to establish missions in a particular area often came through Moravian contacts with Dutch, English, and Danish sympathizers. Merchants or plantation owners, for example, might petition for Moravian missionaries to visit their territory overseas. Consequently, many Moravian missions are located in regions which were once colonial territories of England, Holland, or Denmark.

The following are the areas where Moravian missions are found at the present; with the exception of Honduras (which, however, was really an extension of the Nicaraguan field), all were established in the eighteenth or nineteenth centuries. The West Indies (ten islands including Jamaica): ministering originally to African slaves, later to the freed Negro population. British and Dutch Guiana: working among Creoles, bush Negroes, Javanese and other East Indians, interior American Indians. Nicaragua and Honduras: emphasis on West Indian Negroes, Miskito, Rama, and a few Sumu Indians. California: work among mission Indians. Alaska and Labrador: working with Eskimos. A successful mission to Greenland has been turned over to the state church of Denmark. South Africa: original efforts among Hottentots; now working with Cape Colored and Kaffir. Tanzania: emphasis on maintenance of a leper colony. W. Tibet: medical work predominates. Jordan: maintenance of a leper colony.

Not all mission attempts were successful. Work in Lapland, Guinea, Algiers, Ceylon, Persia, Egypt, the Nicobar Islands, and southeast Australia (and the Cape York Peninsula) was abandoned due to local political turmoil, excessive expenditure of money or lives with no results, or the prior existence of another Christian church in the area.

At present, responsibility for the mission fields is divided between the three church provinces—America, England, and Germany. However, these three are united under a common constitution and profess the same basic beliefs. The foundation for the principles and disciplines to which all Moravian congregations subscribe is found in the Brotherly Agreement, first composed and formally ascribed to by the Herrnhut congregation in 1727. By using the Agreement and the *Book of Order of the Moravian Church in America, Northern Province* as guides, the continuity of the present church with the early Herrnhut Brethren and the Bohemian Protestants becomes apparent in a number of ways; differences are seen too.

To indicate the "living fellowship of the individual members of the church with their Head and with each other" the designations "Brethren" and "Sisters" are still maintained among members. Christ is the Head of the church, while the Old and New Testaments remain the surest guide for life. That which the Scriptures do not reveal is not to be determined by other means. Hence, it is not surprising to find that "the all too common practice of substituting culture, natural evolution, human methods and philosophies in the place of Christ the Saviour" is deplored and condemned (Moravian Church 1954: no. 899, p. 2,c).

The nature of the ritual remains at the heart of public worship. All services are characterized by great simplicity and dignity. Love feasts are recommended particularly for festive occasions such as the celebration of Holy Communion. In all services personal feel- ing (but, it must be emphasized, not undue emotion) is strongly stressed and often heightened by careful use of light and sound; dramatic use of music is often featured. Christmas and Easter services are particularly striking, the latter being conducted at sunrise in the congregational cemetary with the aid of brass bands if at all possible (Allen 1966:81–83).

Faith is also revealed through good works, and in the Continental province the work of the diaspora continues. Schools remain important, particularly for mission work, and education on all levels is carefully fostered.

In regard to worldly pleasures and amusements, while giving no directions in detail, we declare most emphatically that worldly-mindedness and vanity, as well as the love of gain and pleasure, are not to be regarded with indifference and must never obtain entrance among us. These things do not harmonize with the true spirit of the Church of Christ, but exert an injurious influence, turning its members away from that noble simplicity, which must continue to remain its fundamental characteristic (Moravian Church 1954:no. 900, p. 2).

The Book of Order goes on to provide directives with regard to behavior with even graver consequences than worldly enjoyments: "more harmful in its consequences than the love of pleasure is intemperance in the use of strong drink . . . the Moravian Church, therefore, gives its most hearty support to all proper measures for the suppression of intemperance, and of the manufacture and sale of intoxicants" (Moravian Church 1954:no. 901, p. 1; no. 901, p. 2). The strong lure which the advertising of the use of tobacco presents to young people is opposed, and ministers urged not to smoke for the sake of example. Particular care is to be taken that on Sunday all unnecessary travel and labor be avoided and recreations be of a suitable nature.

Although the harmful and dissolute side of life is avoided as much as possible, the church is still open and strives to maintain its openness in many ways. In the area of religion, the Moravian church in America is a member of the larger National Council of Churches of Christ in the United States of America and of the World Council of Churches. The right to receive Communion is extended to members of all Christian churches.

Obedience to the state's demands is required and oaths may be taken "but swearing lightly, without the constraint of the state, is not allowed among us" (Moravian Church 1954:no. 967, p. 3). Great effort is to be made, however, to avoid presenting the state with the problems that may arise between Brethren in daily life:

When any one has just cause of complaint against his brother, he ought not to make it a subject of conversation with others, but should first speak with the brother himself in a friendly manner, and then if necessary both should endeavor, through the mediation of the pastor or of some other member of the congregation, to settle their differences amicably; but to go to law with one another before a magistrate, we will avoid, unless the case be of such nature as to make a legal decision indispensable (Moravian Church 1954:no. 1022, p. 19).

In the course of day-to-day activities order, diligence, thrift, and trustworthiness are essential, and, significant for an understanding of the mechanisms behind the survival of the church, "a diligent and capable tradesman, *who knows how to adapt himself to the times,* and also relies on the blessing of the Lord, still finds his daily bread among us" (Moravian Church 1954:no. 970, p. 3; my emphasis).

With respect to social organization, the home and family are charged with the careful raising of children. As far as the community is concerned:

The congregations of the Moravian Church are very different in their outward form, according to their origin, location, age, and development . . . a number especially in Germany, are Moravian settlements on the model of Herrnhut. The majority, especially of the British and American congregations, are town and country congregations (Moravian Church 1954:no. 802).

With respect to local congregational organization, particularly as it concerns the traditional choirs:

The division of a congregation into choirs or classes according to age, sex and station in life, is a practical help to the life of the Church. . . . In the older congregations there are still choir or class houses, meetings and festivals. In Great Britain and America they are not frequent. Other methods have come into use which seem more suitable. Prayer Unions, Sunday-schools, Young People's Societies . . . and other similar organizations for social intercourse and Christian work, irrespective of age and sex, have superseded the older forms (Moravian Church 1954:no. 979, p. 2).

Some Moravian congregations, particularly the older ones, maintain choirlike distinctions in the organization of the church cemetary. Married women and widows are buried in one area, married men and widowers in another, single men and boys in a third, single women and girls in a fourth. "The idea is that those who were most closely associated in life . . . will want to be together in repose" (Fries 1962:48).

In sum, to an outside observer the character of the church would still seem to be one of basically uncomplicated dogma oriented towards attainment of a Christ-like existence by following a strictly disciplined life. In order to pursue these high goals, a certain amount of contact and compromise with the surrounding secular world is permitted. This adaptability has no doubt been of major importance in preserving the life of the church. The Moravians themselves seem to recognize the importance of this duality and express it aptly and succinctly in the church motto:

> *In Essentials Unity*
> *In Non-essentials Liberty*
> *In All Things Charity*

(ALLEN 1966:6)

Bibliography

Adams, Richard N. "Cultural Components of Central America." *American Anthropologist* 58(1956): 881–907.

————. *Cultural Surveys of Panama-Nicaragua-Guatemala-El Salvador-Honduras.* Pan American Sanitary Bureau Scientific Publication No. 33. N.P. 1957.

Allen, Walser H. *Who are the Moravians?* Bethlehem, Pa., 1966.

Altschul, Francisco. "Informe presentado al señor Presidente de la República Dr. Miguel Paz Baraona, acerca de La *Mosquitia* Hondureña." *Revista del Archivo y Biblioteca Nacionales de Honduras* 6(1928): 280–82, 298–301, 379–82.

Anonymous. "Report on the Mosquito Territory." In *The Kemble Papers,* vol. 2: *1780–1781.* Collections of the New York Historical Society for the year 1884, pp. 419–31. New York, 1885.

Augelli, John P. "The Rimland-Mainland Concept of Culture Areas in Middle America." *Annals of the Association of American Geographers* 52(1962): 119–29.

Bancroft, Hubert H. *The Works of Hubert Howe Bancroft: The Native Races.* Vol. 1: *Wild Tribes.* San Francisco, 1883.

————. *The Works of Hubert Howe Bancroft: History of Central America.* Vol. 2: *1530–1800.* San Francisco, 1886.

————. *The Works of Hubert Howe Bancroft: History of Central America.* Vol. 3: *1801–1887.* San Francisco, 1887.

Bard, Samuel A. *Waikna: Adventures on the Mosquito Shore.* New York, 1855.

Beals, Carleton. "With Sandino in Nicaragua." *The Nation* 126(1928): 204–5, 260–61, 288–89, 314–17, 340–41, 404–6.

————. *Banana Gold.* Philadelphia: J. B. Lippincott Co., 1932.

Bell, Charles N. "Remarks on the Mosquito Territory, its Climate, People, Production, Etc." *Journal of the Royal Geographical Society* 32(1862): 242–68.

————. *Tangweera: Life and Adventures among Gentle Savages.* London, 1899.

Belt, Thomas. *The Naturalist in Nicaragua.* London, 1874.

Borhek, Mary V. *Watchmen on the Walls.* Bethlehem, Pa., 1949.

Bowman, Isaiah. *The Pioneer Fringe.* American Geographical Society Special Publication No. 13. New York: American Geographical Society, 1931.

Brinton, Daniel G. "Vocabularies from the Musquito Coast." *Proceedings of the American Philosophical Society* 29(1891): 1–4.

Brock, Peter. *The Political and Social Doctrines of the Unity of Czech Brethren in the Fifteenth and Early Sixteenth Centuries.* Slavistic Printings and

Reprintings, edited by C. van Schooneveld, Vol. 11. The Hague: Mouton & Co., 1957.

Brown, Vera Lee. "Anglo-Spanish Relations in America." *Hispanic American Historical Review* 5(1922): 329–483.

———. "Contraband Trade: A Factor in the Decline of Spain's Empire in America." *Hispanic American Historical Review* 8(1928): 178–89.

Burney, James. *History of the Buccaneers of America.* London, 1816.

Butland, Gilbert J. *Latin America, a Regional Geography.* London: Longmans, Green and Co., Ltd., 1960.

Callejas, S. "The Development of Eastern Nicaragua." *U.S. Consular Report* 50(1896): 523–24.

Carr, Archie. *High Jungles and Low.* Gainesville: University of Florida Press, 1953.

———. *The Windward Road.* New York: Alfred A. Knopf, 1956.

———. *So Excellent a Fishe.* Garden City, N.J.: Natural History Press, 1967.

Chamberlain, Robert S. *The Conquest and Colonization of Honduras 1502–1550.* Washington, D.C.: Carnegie Institution of Washington, 1953.

Chapman, Anne M. "An Historical Analysis of the Tropical Forest Tribes of the Southern Border of Mesoamerica." Ph.D. dissertation, Columbia University, 1958.

Christelow, Allan. "Contraband Trade between Jamaica and the Spanish Main, and the Free Port Act of 1766." *Hispanic American Historical Review* 22(1942): 309–43.

Coghill, J. P. *Economic and Commercial Conditions in Honduras.* London: Her Majesty's Stationery Office, 1954.

Collinson, John. "The Indians of the Mosquito Territory." *Memoirs Read Before the Anthropological Society of London 1867–8–9* 3(1870): 148–56.

Conklin, Harold C. *Hanunóo Agriculture.* FAO Forestry Development Paper No. 12. Rome: Food and Agriculture Organization of the United Nations, 1957.

Conzemius, Eduard. "Die Rama-Indianer von Nicaragua." *Zeitschrift für Ethnologie* 59(1927[a]): 291–362.

———. "Los Indios Payas de Honduras." *Journal de la Société des Américanistes de Paris* 19(1927[b]): 245–302.

———. "Notes on the Mosquito and Sumu Languages of Eastern Nicaragua and Honduras." *International Journal of American Linguistics* 5(1929): 57–115.

———. *Ethnographical Survey of the Miskito and Sumu Indians of Honduras and Nicaragua.* Bureau of American Ethnology Bulletin No. 106. Washington, D.C.: U.S. Government Printing Office, 1932.

———. "Les tribus Indiennes de la côte des Mosquitos." *Anthropos* 33(1938): 910–43.

Coon, Carleton S., ed. *A Reader in General Anthropology.* New York: Holt, 1948.

Costa Rica. *Costa Rica-Panama Arbitration.* Documents Annexed to the Argument of Costa Rica. Washington, D.C.: Gibson Brothers, 1913.

Cotheal, Alexander I. "A Grammatical Sketch of the Languages Spoken by the Indians of the Mosquito Shore." *Transactions of the American Ethnological Society* 2(1848): 235–64.

Crowe, Frederick. *The Gospel in Central America.* London, 1850.

Dampier, William. *A New Voyage Round the World.* 5th ed. Vol. 1. London, 1703.

Danneberger, Adolph A. *The Atlantic Coast of Nicaragua, Central America: Its*

Political, Economic and Religious Conditions. Transactions of the Moravian Historical Society No. 14, pts. 5 and 6, pp. 325–40. Bethlehem, Pa., 1951.

De Kalb, Courtenay. "Nicaragua: Studies on the Mosquito Shore in 1892." *Journal of the American Geographical Society* 25(1893): 236–83.

De Las Casas, Bartolomé. *An Account of the First Voyage and Discoveries Made by the Spaniards in America.* London, 1699.

De Lussan, Raveneau. *Raveneau de Lussan, Buccaneer of the Spanish Main and Early French Filibuster of the Pacific; a Translation into English of his Journal of a Voyage into the South Seas in 1684 and the Following Years with the Filibusters.* Translated and edited by M. E. Wilbur. Cleveland: Arthur H. Clark Co., 1930.

Dole, Gertrude E. "The Development of Patterns of Kinship Nomenclature." Ph.D. dissertation, University of Michigan, 1957.

Edwards, Bryan. "Some Account of the British Settlements on the Musquito Shore." In *The History, Civil and Commercial of the British West Indies,* 5th ed., Vol. 5, pp. 202–14. London, 1819.

Esquemeling, John. *The Buccaneers of America.* Edited by H. Powell. London, 1893.

Evans, Hubert. *Economic and Commercial Conditions in Nicaragua.* London: Her Majesty's Stationery Office, 1954.

Farrington, W. D. "The Language of the Mosquito Shore." *Journal of the American Geographical Society of New York* 24(1892): 559–64.

Floyd, Troy S. *The Anglo-Spanish Struggle for Mosquitia.* Albuquerque: University of New Mexico Press, 1967.

Forbes, Jack D. "Frontiers in American History and the Role of the Frontier Historian." *Ethnohistory* 15(1968): 203–35.

Foster, George M. "Introduction: What is a Peasant?" In *Peasant Society, a Reader,* edited by J. M. Potter, M. N. Diaz, and G. M. Foster, pp. 2–14. Boston: Little, Brown and Co., 1967[a].

————. *Tzintzuntzan.* Boston: Little, Brown and Co., 1967[b].

Fried, Morton H. "Land Tenure, Geography and Ecology in the Contact of Cultures." *American Journal of Economics and Sociology* 11(1952): 391–412.

Fries, Adelaide L. *Customs and Practices of the Moravian Church.* Rev. ed. Winston-Salem, N.C.: Board of Christian Education and Evangelism, 1962.

Fries, Adelaide L., and Pfohl, J. Kenneth. *The Moravian Church Yesterday and Today.* Raleigh, N.C.: Edwards and Broughton Co., 1926.

Gillin, John. "Mestizo America." In *Most of the World,* edited by R. Linton, pp. 159–211. New York: Columbia University Press, 1949.

Gluckman, Max. "Gossip and Scandal." *Current Anthropology* 4(1963): 307–16.

Gollin, Gillian Lindt. *Moravians in Two Worlds.* New York: Columbia University Press, 1967.

Great Britain Foreign Office. *Correspondence Respecting the Mosquito Territory.* London, 1848.

Greenberg, Joseph H. "The General Classification of Central and South American Languages." In *Men and Cultures,* edited by A. F. C. Wallace, pp. 791–94. Philadelphia: University of Pennsylvania Press, 1960.

Grossman, Guido. *Nikaragua, Land und Leute.* Herrnhut, 1940.

Halpern, Joel M., and Brode, John. "Peasant Society: Economic Changes and Revolutionary Transformation." In *Biennial Review of Anthropology 1967,* edited by B. J. Siegel and A. R. Beals, pp. 46–139. Stanford: Stanford University Press, 1967.

Hamilton, J. Taylor. *A History of the Church Known as the Moravian Church or the Unitas Fratrum or the Unity of the Brethren during the Eighteenth and Nineteenth Centuries.* Bethlehem, Pa.: Times Publishing Co., 1900.

————. *A History of the Missions of the Moravian Church During the Eighteenth and Nineteenth Centuries.* Bethlehem, Pa.: Times Publishing Company, 1901.

————. *Central and South America.* The Missions of the Moravian Church among the Heathen No. 3. Bethlehem, Pa.: Society of the United Brethren for Propagating the Gospel among the Heathen, 1904.

————. "Extracts from the Diary of the Rev. Guido Grossmann." *Periodical Accounts Relating to the Missions of the Church of the United Brethren Established among the Heathen, Second Century* 6(1905): 354–63, 728.

————. "Latest Missionary Intelligence from Nicaragua." *Moravian Missions* 18(1920): 19.

Hamilton, Kenneth G. *Meet Nicaragua.* Bethlehem, Pa.: Comenius Press, 1939.

Harrower, David E. "Rama, Mosquito and Sumu of Nicaragua." *Indian Notes and Monographs.* Vol. 2, pp. 44–48. New York: Museum of the American Indian, Heye Foundation, 1925.

Heath, George R. "Notes on Miskuto Grammar and on Other Indian Languages of Eastern Nicaragua." *American Anthropologist* 15(1913): 48–62.

————. "Bocay." *Moravian Missions* 14(1916[a]): 3–6.

————. "By-paths in Honduras." *Moravian Missions* 14(1916[b]): 172–73.

————. *Grammar of the Miskito Language.* Herrnhut, Saxony: F. Lindenbein, 1927.

————. "Beginnings in Honduras." *The Moravian* 94, no. 23 (1949): 1–2.

————. "Miskito Glossary with Ethnographic Commentary." *International Journal of American Linguistics* 16(1950): 20–34.

————. Unpublished manuscripts, n.d.

Heath, George R., and Marx, Werner G. *Diccionario Miskito-Español, Español-Miskito.* Tegucigalpa D.C., Honduras: Papelería e Imprenta Calderon S. de R.L., 1961.

Helbig, Karl M. *Die Landschaften von Nordost-Honduras.* Hamburg: Hermann Haack, 1959.

Helm, June. "Patterns of Allocation among the Arctic Drainage Dene." In *Essays in Economic Anthropology,* edited by J. Helm, pp. 33–45. Proceedings of the 1965 Annual Spring Meeting of the American Ethnological Society. Seattle: University of Washington Press, 1965.

Helms, Mary W. "Matrilocality and the Maintenance of Ethnic Identity: The Miskito of Eastern Nicaragua and Honduras," in press.

————. "The Cultural Ecology of a Colonial Tribe." *Ethnology* 8(1969[a]): 76–84.

————. "Culture Contact and the Languages of the Miskito Coast." Unpublished manuscript, 1969[b].

————. "The Purchase Society: Adaptation to Economic Frontiers." *Anthropological Quarterly* 42(1969[c]): 325–42.

Helps, Arthur. *The Spanish Conquest in America.* Vol. 1. New York: John Lane, 1900.

Hodgson, Robert. "Some Account of the Mosquito Territory." In *Waikna; or, Adventures on the Mosquito Shore,* edited by S. A. Bard, pp. 354–59. Facsimile of the 1855 edition. Gainesville: University of Florida Press, 1965.

Holmes, John. *Historical Sketches of the Missions of the United Brethren for Propagating the Gospel Among the Heathen.* Dublin, 1818.

Honduras. *Review of Commercial Conditions.* London: His Majesty's Stationery Office, 1948.

Hooker, Roberto Montgomery. *La reincorporación de la Mosquitia desde el punto de vista del derecho internacional y patrio.* Leon, Nicaragua, 1945.

Hutton, J. E. *A Short History of the Moravian Church.* London, 1895.

————. *A History of Moravian Missions.* London: Moravian Publication Office, 1923.

Ireland, Gordon. *Boundaries, Possessions, and Conflicts in Central and North America and the Caribbean.* Cambridge: Harvard University Press, 1941.

Irias, Don Juan Francisco. "Río Wanks and the Mosco Indians." *Transactions of the American Ethnological Society* 3(1853): 161–68.

————. In *The States of Central America.* Edited by E. G. Squier, pp. 400–404. New York, 1858.

Izikowitz, Karl G. *Lamet: Hill Peasants in French Indochina.* Ethnologiska Studier No. 17. Göteborg, Sweden, 1951.

Johnson, Frederick. "The Linguistic Map of Mexico and Central America." In *The Maya and Their Neighbors,* pp. 88–114. New York: Appleton-Century Co., 1940.

————. "Central American Cultures." In *Handbook of South American Indians,* Vol. 4: *The Circum-Caribbean Tribes,* edited by J. H. Steward. Bureau of American Ethnology Bulletin No. 143, pp. 43–67. Washington, D.C.: U.S. Government Printing Office, 1948.

Johnson, Wayne E. "The Honduranean-Nicaraguan Boundary Dispute 1957–1963: The Peaceful Settlement of an International Conflict." *Dissertation Abstracts* 25(1965): 4802.

Juarros, Don Domingo. *A Statistical and Commercial History of the Kingdom of Guatemala in Spanish America.* London, 1823.

Karnes, Thomas L. *The Failure of Union: Central America 1824–1960.* Chapel Hill: University of North Carolina Press, 1961.

Keenagh, Peter. *Mosquito Coast.* New York: Houghton Mifflin Co., 1938.

Kepner, Charles D., Jr. *Social Aspects of the Banana Industry.* New York: Columbia University Press, 1936.

Kepner, Charles D., Jr., and Soothill, Jay H. *The Banana Empire.* New York: Vanguard Press, 1935.

Kidder, Alfred V., II. "South American Penetrations in Middle America." In *The Maya and Their Neighbors,* pp. 441–59. New York: Appleton-Century Co., 1940.

Kirchhoff, Paul. "The Caribbean Lowland Tribes: The Mosquito, Sumu, Paya and Jicaque." In *Handbook of South American Indians,* Vol. 4: *The Circum-Caribbean Tribes,* edited by J. H. Steward. Bureau of American Ethnology Bulletin No. 143, pp. 219–29. Washington, D.C.: U.S. Government Printing Office, 1948.

————. "Mesoamerica: Its Geographic Limits, Ethnic Composition, and Cultural Characteristics." In *Heritage of Conquest,* edited by S. Tax, pp. 17–30. Glencoe, Ill.: Free Press, 1952.

Kirkpatrick, Frederick A. *The Spanish Conquistadors.* 2d ed. London: A. and C. Black, 1946.

Kroeber, Alfred L. *Anthropology.* Rev. ed. New York: Harcourt, Brace and Co., 1948.

————. *Cultural and Natural Areas of Native North America.* Berkeley and Los Angeles: University of California Press, 1963.

Leacock, Eleanore. *The Montagnais "Hunting Territory" and the Fur Trade.* American Anthropological Association Memoir 78. American Anthropological Association, 1954.

Lehman, Frederick K. *The Structure of Chin Society.* Illinois Studies in Anthropology No. 3. Urbana, Illinois: University of Illinois Press, 1963.

Lehmann, Walter. "Ergebnisse einer Forschungsreise in Mittelamerika und México 1907–1909." *Zeitschrift für Ethnologie* 42(1910): 687–749.

————. *Zentral-Amerika*, vol. 1: *Die Sprachen Zentral-Amerikas in ihren beziehungen zueinander sowie zu Süd-Amerika und Mexiko.* Berlin: Dietrich Reimer, 1920.

Lothrop, Samuel K. *Pottery of Costa Rica and Nicaragua.* Vol. 1. New York: Museum of the American Indian, Heye Foundation, 1926.

Lucas, Charles P. *A Historical Geography of the British Colonies.* Vol. 2. Oxford: Clarendon Press, 1905.

Lundberg, J. E. "From Br. J. E. Lundberg." *Periodical Accounts Relating to the Missions of the Church of the United Brethren, Established among the Heathen* 23(1858): 113.

Macaulay, Neill. *The Sandino Affair.* Chicago: Quadrangle Books, 1967.

Martin, A. "Handel und Kreditwesen der Moskito-Indianer." *Globus* 65 (1894): 100–101.

Mason, J. Alden. "The Native Languages of Middle America." In *The Maya and Their Neighbors,* pp. 52–87. Salt Lake City: University of Utah Press, 1962.

Matson, G. Albin, and Swanson, Jane. "Distribution of Hereditary Blood Antigens among Indians in Middle America: V in Nicaragua." *American Journal of Physical Anthropology* 21(1963): 545–59.

May, Stacy, and Plaza, Galo. "The United Fruit Company in Latin America." *United States Business Performance Abroad.* Vol. 7. Washington, D.C.: National Planning Association, 1958.

McQuown, Norman A. "The Indigenous Languages of Latin America." *American Anthropologist* 57(1955): 501–70.

Mierisch, Bruno. "Eine Reise nach den Goldgebieten im Osten von Nicaragua." *Petermanns Mitteilungen* 39(1893): 25–39.

Minneman, Paul G. "The Banana Circles the Globe." *Agriculture in the Americas* 2(1942): 123–26.

Mintz, Sidney W., and Wolf, Eric R. "An Analysis of Ritual Co-Parenthood (Compadrazgo)." *Southwestern Journal of Anthropology* 6(1950): 341–68.

Moravian Church. *Results of the Synod of the Protestant Church of the United Brethren, or Unitas Fratrum: Held at Herrnhut in the Year 1848.* London, 1849.

————. *Periodical Accounts Relating to the Missions of the Church of the United Brethren, Established among the Heathen,* Vols. 19–34. London, 1849–1887.

————. *Regulativ des Missions-Departements betreffend das Verhältnis der Missionare zur Missions-Diakonie.* N.p., 1881.

————. *Periodical Accounts Relating to the Foreign Missions of the Church of the United Brethren, Second Century,* Vols. 1–17. London, 1890–1956.

————. *Rules and Regulations of the Moskito Mission Province, in Connection with Chapter X of the Results of the General Synod of the Brethren's Unity, 1897.* Herrnhut, 1898.

————. *Moravian Missions.* Vols. 1–52. London, Moravian Mission Agency, 1903–1954.

————. *The Book of Order of the Nicaraguan Mission.* N.p., 1928.

————. *The Book of Order of the Moravian Church in America, Northern Province.* 4th ed. Bethlehem, Pa.: Times Publishing Co., 1954.

Mueller, Karl A. *Among Creoles, Miskitos and Sumos: Eastern Nicaragua and its Moravian Missions.* Bethlehem, Pa.: Comenius Press, 1932.

Munro, Dana G. *The Five Republics of Central America*. New York: Oxford University Press, 1918.

Murdock, George P. "South American Culture Areas." *Southwestern Journal of Anthropology* 7(1951): 415–36.

Murphy, Robert F., and Steward, Julian H. "Tappers and Trappers: Parallel Process in Acculturation." *Economic Development and Cultural Change* 4(1956): 335–55.

Nash, Manning. *Primitive and Peasant Economic Systems*. San Francisco, Calif.: Chandler Publishing Co., 1966.

Naylor, Robert A. "The British in Central America Prior to the Clayton-Bulwer Treaty of 1850." *Hispanic American Historical Review* 40(1960): 361–82.

Newton, Arthur P. *The Colonizing Activities of the English Puritans*. New Haven: Yale University Press, 1914.

Nicaragua. *Documents Relating to the Affairs in Bluefields, Republic of Nicaragua in 1894*. Published by authority of the government of Nicaragua. Washington, D.C., 1895.

Nicol, John M. "Northeast Nicaragua." *Geographical Journal* 11(1898): 658–60.

Nogales, Rafael De. *The Looting of Nicaragua*. New York: McBride and Co., 1928.

Parsons, James J. "English-Speaking Settlements of the Western Caribbean." *Yearbook of the Association of Pacific Coast Geographers* 16(1954): 3–16.

————. "Gold Mining in the Nicaragua Rain Forest." *Yearbook of the Association of Pacific Coast Geographers* 17(1955[a]): 49–55.

————. "The Miskito Pine Savanna of Nicaragua and Honduras." *Annals of the Association of American Geographers* 45(1955[b]): 36–63.

————. *San Andrés and Providencia*. Publications in Geography Vol. 12. Berkeley: University of California Press, 1956.

Pataky, László. *Nicaragua desconocida*. Managua, D.N., Nicaragua, 1956.

Peralta, Manuel M. De, ed. *Costa Rica y Costa de Mosquitos*. Paris, 1898.

Pijoan, Michel. "The Miskito Indians." *América Indígena* 4(1944): 255–83.

————. *The Health and Customs of the Miskito Indians of Northern Nicaragua: Interrelationships in a Medical Program*. Ediciones del Instituto Indigenista Interamericano. Mexico, D.F., 1946.

————. "An Introduction to a Medical Program among the Miskito Indians of Nicaragua." In *A William Cameron Townsend en el vigesimoquinto aniversario del Instituto Linguistico de Verano*, pp. 327–46. Mexico, 1961.

Pim, Bedford, and Seemann, Berthold. *Dottings on the Roadside, in Panama, Nicaragua and Mosquito*. London, 1869.

Porta Costas, Don Antonio. "Relación del Reconocimiento Geométrico y Político de la Costa de Mosquitos." In *Relaciones Históricas y Geográficas de América Central*, pp. 257–86. Madrid, 1908.

Potter, Jack M., Diaz, May N., and Foster, George M., eds. *Peasant Society: A Reader*. Boston: Little, Brown and Co., 1967.

Redfield, Robert. *Peasant Society and Culture*. Chicago: University of Chicago Press, 1956.

Roberts, Orlando W. *Narrative of Voyages and Excursions on the East Coast and in the Interior of Central America*. Edinburgh, 1827.

Robertson, James A. "Some Notes on the Transfer by Spain of Plants and Animals to its Colonies Overseas." *James Sprunt Historical Studies* 19,2 (1927): 7–21.

Romig, Br. "Official visitation by Br. Romig." *Periodical Accounts Relating to the Foreign Missions of the Church of the United Brethren, Second Century* 1(1890): 200–442.

Roys, Ralph L. *Indian Background of Colonial Yucatan.* Carnegie Institution Publication No. 548. Washington, D.C.: Carnegie Institution of Washington, 1943.

Sahlins, Marshall D. *Tribesmen.* Englewood Cliffs, N.J.: Prentice-Hall, Inc., 1968.

Sapper, Karl. "Reise auf dem Río Coco (nördliches Nicaragua)." *Globus* 78 (1900): 249–52, 271–76.

————. "Beitrage zur Ethnographie der südlichen Mittelamerika." *Petermanns Mitteilungen* 47(1901): 25–40.

Sauer, Carl O. "Cultivated Plants of South and Central America." In *Handbook of South American Indians*, Vol. 6: *Physical Anthropology, Linguistics and Cultural Geography of South American Indians*, edited by J. H. Steward. Bureau of American Ethnology Bulletin No. 143, pp. 487–543. Washington, D.C.: U.S. Government Printing Office, 1950.

————. *Agricultural Origins and Dispersals.* New York: American Geographical Society, 1952.

Schneider, David M., and Gough, Kathleen, eds. *Matrilineal Kinship.* Berkeley: University of California Press, 1961.

Schneider, H. G. *Kaisa! Nach Schriftlichen und Mündlichen Mitteilungen Missionar Siebörger's.* Stuttgart, 1890.

Schultze, Adolf. "Moskitoküste in Nicaragua." In *Die Mission der Brüdergemeine in Missionsstunde*, Heft 5. Herrnhut: G. Burkhard, 1905.

Service, Elman R. *Primitive Social Organization.* New York: Random House, 1962.

Siebörger, W. "From Br. W. Sieörger." *Periodical Accounts Relating to the Missions of the Church of the United Brethren, Established Among the Heathen* 22(1881): 254.

Solien de Gonzalez, Nancie L. "Family Organization in Five Types of Migratory Wage Labor." *American Anthropologist* 63(1961): 1264–80.

Spicer, Edward H., ed. *Perspectives in American Indian Culture Change.* Chicago: University of Chicago Press, 1961.

Spinden, Herbert J. "The Chorotegan Culture Area." *Congrès International des Américanistes, Compte-Rendu de la 21st session* 2(1925): 529–45.

Squier, Ephraim G. *Nicaragua.* London, 1852.

————. *The States of Central America.* New York, 1858.

————. *Honduras.* London, 1870.

Stanger, Francis M. "National Origins in Central America." *Hispanic American Historical Review* 12(1932): 18–45.

Steinberg, S. H., ed. *The Statesman's Yearbook.* New York: St. Martin's Press, 1965.

Steward, Julian H. "The Circum-Caribbean Tribes: An Introduction." In *Handbook of South American Indians*, Vol. 4: *The Circum-Caribbean Tribes*, edited by J. H. Steward. Bureau of American Ethnology Bulletin No. 143, pp. 1–41. Washington, D.C.: U.S. Government Printing Office, 1948.

Steward, Julian H., and Faron, Louis C. *Native Peoples of South America.* New York: McGraw-Hill Book Co., Inc., 1959.

Stone, Doris. "Urgent Tasks of Research Concerning the Culture and Languages of Central American Indian Tribes." *Proceedings, 34th International Congress of Americanists, 1960*, pp. 43–47. Vienna: F. Berger, 1962.

————. "Synthesis of Lower Central American Ethnohistory." In *Handbook of Middle American Indians*, Vol. 4: *Archaeological Frontiers and External Connections*, edited by R. Wauchope, pp. 209–33. Austin: University of Texas Press, 1966.

Stout, Peter F. *Nicaragua: Past, Present and Future.* Philadelphia, 1859.

Swadesh, Morris. "Afinidades de las lenguas amerindias." *Proceedings, 34th International Congress of Americanists, 1960,* pp. 729–38. Vienna: F. Berger, 1962.

Tamayo, Jorge L., and West, Robert C. "The Hydrography of Middle America." In *Handbook of Middle American Indians,* Vol. 1: *Natural Environment and Early Cultures,* edited by R. Wauchope, pp. 84–121. Austin: University of Texas Press, 1964.

Taylor, B. W. *Estudios ecológicos para el aprovechamiento de la tierra en Nicaragua.* República de Nicaragua: Ministerio de Economía, Instituto de Fomento Nacional y Organización de las Naciones Unidas para la Agricultura y Alimentación, 1959.

Thaeler, A. David, Jr., Arnold, John, and Alving, Alf S. "A Clinical Study of Primaquine in the Treatment of Malaria among the Miskito Indians of Nicaragua." *American Journal of Tropical Medicine and Hygiene* 2(1953): 989-99.

Thomas, Cyrus, and Swanton, John R. *Indian Languages of Mexico and Central America, and their Geographical Distribution.* Bureau of American Ethnology Bulletin No. 44. Washington, D.C.: U.S. Government Printing Office, 1911.

Thompson, Augustus C. *Moravian Missions.* New York, 1890.

Tosi, Joseph A., Jr., and Voertman, Robert F. "Some Environmental Factors in the Economic Development of the Tropics." *Economic Geography* 40 (1964): 189–205.

Travis, Ira D. *British Rule in Central America.* Michigan Political Science Association Publication No. 5. Ann Arbor, Mich., 1895.

Union Panamericana, Departamento de Asuntos Sociales. "Conclusiones y recomendaciones del primer grupo nacional de trabajo sobre: Formación de personal para el desarrollo de la comunidad re 'Programas Planificados Projecto Piloto del Río Coco.' " Mimeographed, n.d.

United States Department of State. *Documents Relative to Central American Affairs.* Washington, D.C., 1856.

Valle, Alfonso. "Interpretación de nombres geográficos indígenas de Nicaragua." Nicaragua: Talleres Gráficos Perez, 1944.

VanStone, James W. *The Changing Culture of the Snowdrift Chipewyan.* National Museum of Canada Bulletin No. 209. Ottawa: Queen's Printer, 1965.

Von Hagan, V. Wolfgang. "The Mosquito Coast of Honduras and its Inhabitants." *Geographical Review* 30(1940): 208–59.

———. "The Jicaque (Torrupan) Indians of Honduras." *Indian Notes and Monographs.* Vol. 53, pp. 1–98. New York: Museum of the American Indian, Heye Foundation, 1943.

W., M. "The Mosquito Indian and His Golden River." In *A Collection of Voyages and Travels,* Vol. 6, edited by A. Churchill, pp. 285–98. London, 1732.

Wafer, Lionel. *A New Voyage and Description of the Isthmus of America.* Edited by L. E. Elliott Joyce. Oxford: Hakluyt Society, 1934.

Wagley, Charles. *Amazon Town.* New York: Alfred A. Knopf, 1964.

Wagley, Charles, and Harris, Marvin. "A Typology of Latin American Subcultures." *American Anthropologist* 57(1955): 428–51.

Wells, William V. *Exploration and Adventures in Honduras.* New York, 1857.

West, Robert C. "The Mining Economy of Honduras during the Colonial Period." *Actas del XXXIII Congreso Internacional de Americanistas* 2 (1959): 767–77.

Wickham, Henry A. "Notes of a Journey Among the Woolwa and Miskito Indians." *Proceedings of the Royal Geographical Society* 13(1869): 58–63.

————. *A Journey among the Woolwa or Soumoo Indians of Central America. Rough Notes of a Journey through the Wilderness*, pt. 2. London, 1872.

————. "Notes on the Soumoo or Woolwa Indians of Blewfields River, Mosquito Territory." *Journal of the Anthropological Institute of Great Britain and Ireland* 24(1895): 198–208.

Williams, Mary W. *Anglo-American Isthmian Diplomacy 1815–1915.* Washington: American Historical Association, 1916.

Wilson, Charles M. *Empire in Green and Gold.* New York: Henry Holt and Co., 1947.

Wolf, Eric R. "Types of Latin American Peasantry: A Preliminary Discussion." *American Anthropologist* 57(1955): 452–69.

————. *Peasants.* Englewood Cliffs, N.J.: Prentice-Hall, Inc., 1966.

Young, Thomas. *Narrative of a Residence on the Mosquito Shore with an Account of Truxillo, and the Adjacent Islands of Bonacca and Roaton.* London, 1847.

Zelinsky, Wilbur. "Population Growth in Central America and the West Indies: Prospects and Problems." *Mineral Industries,* Vol. 35, no. 6. 1966.

Ziock, H. "From Br. H. Ziock." *Periodical Accounts Relating to the Missions of the Church of the United Brethren, Established among the Heathen* 31 (1880): 509–12.

————. "From Br. H. Ziock." *Periodical Accounts Relating to the Missions of the Church of the United Brethren, Established among the Heathen* 32(1882): 312.

————. *Dictionary of the English and Miskito Languages.* Herrnhut, 1894.

Index

Acculturated natives: Miskito viewed as, 3

Acculturation. *See* Culture contact

Adoption: maternal relatives and, 97–98

Affines: village identity and, 53, 54–55; kinship terms used by, 102; joking behavior and, 103; avoidance behavior between, 103, 104; cooperation between, 104

Agriculture: riverine and seacoast, 30; flooding, 38–39, 124; household gardens, 48, 145–46; cooperation in, 104; beans, 128–33; rice, 134–38; root crops, 141–42; bananas and plantains, 143–44; maize, 144–45; miscellaneous crops, 145; crops damaged by moon, 188. *See also* Labor exchange

Alliance for Progress: Río Coco medical program, 41, 175

Americans: economic activities on Miskito Coast, 27–28, 34, 112, 114. *See also* Anglo-Americans; Foreigners; United States

Amulets: as protection against poisoning, 184

Anglo-Americans: Miskito preference for 2, 221–22, 224

Annatto: uses of, 119

Arbitration: headman and, 165, 166; lay pastor and, 167, 170–71; Helpers and, 169–71, 203

Asang: theoretical significance of, 3–9, 179–81, 234–36; location of, 10, 45; size, 45; physical appearance of, 46–52; as political unit, 53–54,

56; as social unit, 54–55, 56; as economic groups, 55–56; as religious groups, 55, 56; reputation of inhabitants, 57; disunity in, 203; organization trends, 233

Auasbila, Río Coco, 33, 43

Avocado, 145

Avoidance behavior, 103, 104

Balsa, 120. *See also* Silk cotton

Bamboo: uses of, 36, 49, 51–52, 120

Bananas: commercial production of, 13, 27–28, 42, 112–14; as traditional food staple, 15, 143; utilization of, 50, 142–44; varieties of, 143; storage techniques, 144. *See also* Land, agricultural utilization of

Baptism, 95–96

Barges. *See* Commissary barges

Bark cloth, 49, 52, 119, 137

Baseball: between villages, 85

Basketry, 50–51, 121

Bawihka: linguistic group, 18

Beans: origin of cultivation by Miskito, 128; varieties of, 128; planting and harvest procedures, 128–32; yield, 133; second planting, 133; as exchange item, 133, 155; allocation as food and cash, 133, 135, 139–41. *See also* Land, agricultural utilization of

Belize, British Honduras: Miskito men employed at, 23

Betrothal: early age for girls, 25

Beverages: soured, 142; fermented, 142–43; *wabul*, 144; maize, 144–45

Bilwaskarma: Moravian hospital at, 41